Our Lady of La Vang

Our Lady of La Vang

History and Theology of a Vietnamese Devotion

Mary Kim Anh Thi Tran

Foreword by John C. Cavadini

◆PICKWICK *Publications* · Eugene, Oregon

OUR LADY OF LA VANG
History and Theology of a Vietnamese Devotion

Copyright © 2024 Mary Kim Anh Thi Tran. All rights reserved. Except for brief quotations in critical publications or reviews, no part of this book may be reproduced in any manner without prior written permission from the publisher. Write: Permissions, Wipf and Stock Publishers, 199 W. 8th Ave., Suite 3, Eugene, OR 97401.

Pickwick Publications
An Imprint of Wipf and Stock Publishers
199 W. 8th Ave., Suite 3
Eugene, OR 97401

www.wipfandstock.com

PAPERBACK ISBN: 979-8-3852-1969-8
HARDCOVER ISBN: 979-8-3852-1970-4
EBOOK ISBN: 979-8-3852-1971-1

Cataloguing-in-Publication data:

Names: Tran, Mary Kim Anh Thi, author.

Title: Our lady of La Vang : history and theology of a Vietnamese devotion / Mary Kim Anh Thi.

Description: Eugene, OR : Pickwick Publications, 2024 | Includes bibliographical references.

Identifiers: ISBN 979-8-3852-1969-8 (paperback) | ISBN 979-8-3852-1970-4 (hardcover) | ISBN 979-8-3852-1971-1 (ebook)

Subjects: LCSH: subject | subject | subject | subject

Classification: CALL NUMBER 2024 (paperback) | CALL NUMBER (ebook)

VERSION NUMBER 10/24/24

For You, the People of God.

Contents

Foreword by John C. Cavadini | ix
Acknowledgements | xv
Abbreviations | xix

Introduction | 1

1   The Story of the Apparitions of Our Lady of La Vang | 6
2   The History of the Devotion to Our Lady of La Vang | 56
3   The History of Devotion to Our Lady of La Vang Continues | 100
4   Our Lady of La Vang: The Ecclesial Mother | 146
5   Vietnamese Theologians and Commentators on Our Lady of La Vang | 180

Conclusion | 210

Appendix: Timeline of the Church in Vietnam and of Our Lady of La Vang | 215
Bibliography | 223

Foreword

THE READER ABOUT TO open this book will be amply rewarded by its contents. For the story it tells is a love story. It is the story of the intimately tender love of the Blessed Virgin Mary for the people of Vietnam, whom she adopted as her own children under the title of Our Lady of La Vang. It is also the story of the loving devotion offered back to her in response. It is a story by turns piercingly beautiful and grimly harrowing yet at all points inspiring. The beauty and the suffering related in this story are inextricably intertwined. Doesn't this apply to all true love stories? Scripture itself tells us that "love is stronger than death" (Song of Songs 8.6). If there ever were a story that bears out the truth of this Scripture, it is this one.

As it has been remembered and treasured and passed down through the generations, this story begins in 1798 when the Blessed Virgin Mary appeared to a group of lay villagers who had fled into the jungle to escape a wave of persecution. The area to which they had fled indirectly demonstrates the atrocity of the persecution from which they had fled, for it was itself filled with dangers ranging from wild beasts to lack of food. These villagers were saying the Rosary together when Mary appeared to them, holding the infant Jesus. The presence of the infant Jesus is a unique feature of this apparition which, as Sr. Kim explains, was intended as a gesture of affection and of solidarity appealing to the cultural sensibilities of the villagers. They could recognize her instantly as the Mother of God, whose intercession they had been seeking in each "Hail Mary" of the Rosary.

In her apparition, Mary, as Sr. Kim relates, did not ask for anything that echoed any other known Marian apparition, no matter how noble the things requested may have been, such as prayers for the conversion of sinners, requests to build a church or chapel, instructions for how to make a medal, and the like. Mary came simply to comfort her children, offering her assistance, promising them her accompaniment in their struggles both present and future, and speaking words of healing. She came to strengthen them in a time of persecution, another unique feature of this personal gesture of intervention by Mary, who appeared precisely as Mother and offered herself to the villagers, all of them layfolk, as their maternal protector and intercessor. The sweetness of this encounter persisted in the devotion it inspired in these villagers and in those who treasured the story in their hearts through decade after decade of continuous persecution, much of it almost unimaginably savage. But love did, in fact, prove stronger than death.

By appearing with the baby Jesus, that is, as *Theotokos* or Mother of God, Mary enfolded the villagers, or rather highlighted their already having-been-enfolded, into a larger love story, the Gospel itself, the story of the Word made flesh, of God's bending down to redeem humanity, by his sojourning with us, from the desolation of sin and death. He sowed the seeds of compassion and love into the midst of our affliction, seeds which would grow to take over the whole of our sad story as they took root and grew, turning it into a new story of the victory of love and of life, a story we could not have initiated or enacted for ourselves, but one into which we were welcomed and enfolded. "Mother of God" as a title for Mary, sums up the whole love story of the Gospel, as John of Damascus once said, because the title indicates how God the Word bent down to us, all the way down, to the point of entering human life as vulnerable and helpless as any of us, completely dependent on our mothers. Mary's apparition "inculturated" this larger story. Through her offer of maternal love to these adoptive brothers and sisters of her uniquely beloved Son, the villagers and the Vietnamese devout to whom they passed on the story were able to experience the love story of the Gospel as a love story at once universal and as uniquely and personally offered to them in a tender and intimate relationship to the *Theotokos*. It is "under *her* protection," or "*praesidium*," that the faithful had been "flying" for refuge, invoking her help under this title since at least as early as the third century.

The story that Sr. Kim tells is thus a story of inculturation. But it is one that is so penetrating and so sensitive that it expands and revises our very understanding of inculturation itself. Generally speaking, "inculturation" is understood as a decisively contemporary concern. Conventionally, it has been contrasted with the past, construed as the spread of the Gospel outside the Western world as though it were essentially a Western story, marked by European devotional titles and devotional images with a theology expressed in irreducibly Western categories. As this conventional narrative goes, it has only been recently proposed that for the Faith to be truly appropriated by non-Western or non-European peoples, these older forms must be changed so that the devotional images, liturgical gestures and theological categories or language are thoroughly anchored in the culture of the people. Of course, these are unquestionably appropriate aspirations, yet they can operate from a vastly oversimplified and even superficial understanding of the past.

It is precisely this, and much more, that Sr. Kim shows us as she unfolds the story of devotion to Our Lady of La Vang. From the start it was a personalized and localized relationship between the Mother of God and the Vietnamese lay faithful, soon accompanied by their clergy, both indigenous and foreign, who were also subject to the same atrocious persecutions. Shortly after the apparition, in other words, shortly after the intimately personalized – we could say "inculturated" – enfolding into the love story of the Gospel it represented, devotion to Mary developed under the title of Our Lady Help of Christians. This title was of old related to the title "*Theotokos*," but more to the point, it was at this time undoubtedly imported from nineteenth century French piety as well as from the sensibilities of the beleaguered Pius VII. Other European devotional titles, related to this one, such as Our Lady of Grace and Our Lady of Victory, were attracted into the devotion, along with corresponding liturgical imagery.

But what Sr. Kim shows us is that to regard these Western markers as indications of a constitutively European devotional life simply transplanted into a foreign culture and living there as an alien growth, does not adequately convey the reality. Namely, that these very titles became, as they were, inculturated as they were used to express and cultivate a relationship of loving devotion that was irreducibly personal and unquestionably local.

The persecutions of Christians in Vietnam persisted, almost continuously, for nearly a century. But the devotion of the faithful was equally persistent. Devotion to Our Lady, who had given herself to them personally as Mother at La Vang, enabled these Christians, most of them uneducated and without social standing, to bear heroic witness to the one, holy, Catholic and apostolic faith and to hand it on, as a treasured love, to the next generation. Persisting in devotion they contoured the Faith to their own heroic witness, inflecting it with their continuing response to the Mother of God who had singled them out for her protection and accompaniment. When the persecutions were mitigated, towards the end of the nineteenth century, this devotion burst forth in very public forms, in pilgrimages, liturgies and building projects, all of them invented by the genius of a specifically Vietnamese Catholicism that had been forged through decades of solidarity in faithfulness.

The Mariology that emerged was not primarily a Mariology of Mary's unique privileges as Mother of God, though these were admired and certainly not denied. We do not find a Marian "maximalism" emerging from this devotion, but we do not find a Marian "minimalism" either. Sr. Kim shows us that what emerges is an integrating theology associated with a title that comes into its own only with *Lumen Gentium* and subsequent papal reception and promotion, especially under Pope Francis, namely "Mary, Mother of the Church." It is as though the Vietnamese Catholics had, through their "personalized" or "inculturated" relationship to the Mother of God, developed the sensibilities and sensitivities which were later aptly captured in this very title.

As the post-Conciliar period went on, the bishops of the Vietnamese dioceses most closely associated with the devotion to Our Lady of La Vang, and then, following suit, the newly established Catholic Bishops' Conference of Vietnam, began to promote devotion to our Lady of La Vang under various titles featuring her as Mother of the Church in Vietnam, and, indeed, by extension, Mother of the whole Vietnamese people. We know that the Church is the Bride of Christ, and therefore her presence in the world is the sacrament of the presence of the spousal love of Christ. The world without the Church in it is therefore not the same world, so to speak, as the world with the Church in it. The world with the Beloved Spouse of the Lord in it is a world that is as a whole God's Beloved, that very "world" which "God so loved that He gave His Only-Begotten Son" (Jn. 3.16). Just so, the nation without the Church and so *a priori* without the personalized presence of Mary, Mother of the Church, is a different nation, so to speak, than the one with her present. The latter is a nation in whose midst the Motherhood of Mary, as Our Lady of La Vang, is personally present in the midst of the faithful, and, through them, personally extended to the whole nation.

Sr. Kim explains that this deep level of inculturation occurs not simply as a result of late twentieth century innovations, but rather in the living faith of the Vietnamese people over decades of devotion through hardship after hardship. She shows how, through the use of titles such as "Our Lady Help of Christians," the uniquely Vietnamese relationship with Our Lady "localizes" the European title, filling it with uniquely Vietnamese sensibility, feeling and insight. At the same time, the title serves to "universalize" the irreducibly local devotion. It enables the universal Church to receive and experience the uniquely Vietnamese devotion as an expression, interpretation and performance of the one, true, Catholic and apostolic faith. It thus gives that very faith a new life and vitality for everyone, stemming from the hearts of a people localized in time and space, possessed of their own cultural profile and temperament, but united by Baptism and the Eucharist to the whole universal Church.

The same is true with the title Mother of the Church. This is a title that is "universal," that belongs to the whole Church, and yet the faith and devotion of the Vietnamese Church to Our Lady of La Vang enabled them to recognize her as Mother of the Church in Vietnam and at the same time enables the universal Church to recognize her as Mother of the Church universal, the Body and Spouse of her most glorious Head, the one People of God.

Sr. Kim ultimately helps us understand how the late twentieth century joyful appropriation of Vietnamese cultural forms in which to receive, interpret and present the devotion to Our Lady of La Vang, is not a revolution of inculturation just newly initiated in the contemporary Church, but rather a natural expression of the inculturation that had already taken root in the apparition of the *Theotokos* herself and in her presence, as Our Lady of La Vang, in the loving memory and tradition of her children. Sr. Kim invites us, her readers, into this story, both those of her readers who are privileged to live in Vietnam and participate in the annual and national pilgrimages, those Vietnamese faithful living in diaspora, and all of us in whose hearts the Mother of God, Mother of the Church, has come to dwell. As Our Lady of La Vang, she offers both consolation and challenge to all who would live up to the faith and courage demonstrated by those villagers who, so long ago, fled to her protection. All of us owe to Sr. Kim a great debt of gratitude for the labor of love which, with the publication of this book, she now brings to completion.

John C. Cavadini, University of Notre Dame

Acknowledgments

IT TAKES A VILLAGE to write a dissertation, now a book. It is undeniable that this work involves divine and human help. I give thanks to God for entrusting me with the task of writing about Our Lady of La Vang, the story of the Mother of God, Mother of the Church in Vietnam. I hope I have done justice to Her basic history and theology in this book. Thank you, Our Lady of La Vang, for protecting and helping me through many ups and downs.

First, I would like to express my deepest gratitude to my dissertation director and committee. This work was only made possible by Dr. John C. Cavadini, who taught me how to search for sources, examine them, and organize them into this work. He has inspired and enriched the course of my scholarship and the path of my life by his love for the Church, the Blessed Virgin Mary, teaching and friendship. The last three years of this journey became difficult in many aspects, and I am bound to thank him very much for his kindness, thoughtfulness, and wisdom. Dr. Timothy Matovina has been an amazing professor and mentor since my coursework. Conversations with him and his questions to me have been essential. Dr. David Clairmont and his extensive scholarship has taught me how to connect to other religions, particularly regarding Marian devotion as related to the veneration of Bodhisattvas in Buddhism. Dr. Catherine Cavadini has been influencing and mentoring me since I arrived in South Bend, and from her, I learned how to become a precise scholar and reaffirm my passion for serving women and their vocations. I cannot thank her enough. Her mentoring and prayers have kept me going even when I thought I could not go further. I still remember her saying, "Keeping your chin up!" Again, I am grateful to each of these members of my dissertation committee for the invaluable conversations, collective wisdom, insights, and time to help shape and refine this work.

I thank the University of Note Dame, including the President, Fr. John I. Jenkins, C.S.C., for blessing me on my first day at Notre Dame and the late President, Fr. Theodore M. Hesburgh, C.S.C., for warmly welcoming me. For ten years, Notre Dame has transformed me to grow not only as a scholar but also as a Catholic. Thank you, Msgr. Dr. Michael Heintz, Dr. John C. Cavadini, and Dr. Theodore Billy for having confidence in me and supporting me even before starting the Ph.D. program. I thank Dr. Joseph Wawrykow, Dr. Gerald McKenny, Dr. J. Matthew Ashley, and Dr. Todd Walatka for their administrative efforts during my doctoral program. I thank all the professors and the people of the Department of Theology, especially those who teach and/or have had crucial conversations.

I would also like to thank the directors, the people, and benefactors of the McGrath Institute for Church Life, de Nicola Center for Ethics and Culture, and the Nanovic Institute for European Studies for providing much appreciated funding. It was only possible to conduct archival research with the assistance of those grants, which enabled me to complete this project. I thank the Graduate School, especially Dr. John Lubker, the Hesburgh Library, the Center for the Study of Languages and Cultures, and the Writing Center. I thank Dr. Logan Quigley for our friendship, the crucial conversations regarding English writing that he brought to my project, and for reading through my entire dissertation. I thank former Prof. Lisa Joy Oglesbee for our friendship and invaluable hours of conversation to help my English writing and speaking. Thank you, Dr. Louis MacKenzie and Ms. Cindy Alamargot, for editing my translation. I am benefited greatly from the editing of Dr. Catherine R. Osborne. This project would not have amounted much withouth a publisher. Special thanks are due to James D. Stock at Wipf and Stock Publishers for taking an interest in the manuscript, guiding it to publication. I also thank you, my readers, for the kindess of your attention to my first book.

While searching the sources, I experienced God's Providence through encounters with people. I am deeply indebted to a number of the people of God in Vietnam, Europe, and the United States. In Vietnam, I thank Archbishop Emeritus of Huế Étienne Thể N. Nguyễn, Archbishop Emeritus of Huế FX Hồng V. Lê, and Archbishop Joseph Linh C. Nguyễn for their time, support, and encouragement. I thank Bishop Joseph Trác C. Bùi, Rector of Saint Joseph Seminary of Sài Gòn, and Fr. Joseph Thứ

Acknowledgments

Hồ, P.S.S., Rector of Saint Sulpice Seminary of Huế, for allowing me to use their libraries. I thank you, Fr. P. Lợi V. Phan, Fr. Peter Vũ Nguyễn, Mr. Paul Chu Q. Trần, Sr. Maria Cúc T. Bùi, Sr. Maria Tuyệt T. Nguyễn, Sr. Agatha Sinh T. Lê, Sr. Anna Ngàn T.T. Đồng, and Fr. Px. Hiệu Trung Đào for helping to connect with the sources in Vietnamese language. In Europe, I thank the Vatican Apostolic Archive, the Vatican Apostolic Library (particularly Ms. Federica Orlando), the Propaganda Fide Historical Archives, the Archive of France-Asia Research Institute (the Archive of the MEP) (especially Ms. Brigitte Appavou), the Vietnamese Parish in Paris (especially Fr. Joseph Dũng A. Trần), Fr. Peter Hưng V. Nguyen, CM, and Fr. Markus Solo Kewuta, S.V.D. In the United States, I apprecite Fr. Jos. Chau Thanh Nguyen, Fr. Francis Hung Long, CRM, Fr. Dominic Phi Long, CSsR, Fr. Loc Nguyen, CSsR, Mr. Doan Ho, Mrs. Teresa Anh T. Nguyen, Mr. Quy Tran, and Deacon Jos Chuong Do for helping to connect with the sources.

I thank my former Directors in the MDiv Program: Msgr. Michael Heinz, Fr. Gary S. Chamberland, C.S.C., the late Dr. Janice Poorman, Prof. Stacy Noem, and my MDiv cohorts: Becky Ruvalcaba, Cassie Farrell, Claire Ziolkowski, Bridget Carey, Megan O'Brien Crayne, Philip Lomneth, Christopher Harrington, Fr. Brogan Ryan, C.S.C., Fr. Bryan Williams, C.S.C., Fr. Karl Romkema, C.S.C., and Fr. Michael Thomas, C.S.C., for their support and challenges that helped me to grow. I thank Holy Cross College for preparing me well to attend the University of Notre Dame, especially thanks to Brother John Paige, C.S.C, Fr. Michael B. Sullivan, C.S.C, Dr. Michael Griffin, Dr. David Lutz, Dr. Dianne Barlas, Dr. Louis Albarran, Prof. Edward Gareau, and Dr. Mathew Sherman.

Over the past years, my peers and colleagues have been an essential source of academic challenge and support. I thank you, Fr. Bruno M. Shah, O.P., Ph.D., Fr. Augustine Marie Reisenauer, O.P., Ph.D., Fr. Raphael Mary Salzillo, O.P., Ph.D., Sr. Patricia Idoko, Ph.D., Dr. Audrey Seah, Dr. John Lindblom, Dr. Kristi Haas, Dr. Hades Chavanne, Dr. Samantha Slaubaugh, Dr. Hansol Goo, Dr. Melissa Coles, Catherine Duggan, Amelia Ruggaber, and Jessica Keating Floyd. I am grateful for our friendship, the accountability, and the intellectual interest you all brought to my time at Notre Dame and writing. I also thank you, Sr. Helen Alford, O.P., Sr. Ellen M. Taylor, C.S.C., Sr. Joysline Lyngkhoi, C.S.C, the late Sr. Joanne Becker, Dr. Karla Bellinger, Dr. Becky Drury, Sr. Frances O'Connor, Sr. Edelquine Shivachi, Fr. Georges Massinelli, O.F.M., Ph.D., Fr. Andrew Hochstedler, O.F.M., Fr. RB Williams, O.P., Fr. Brian Van Hove, SJ., Sr.

Anna Joseph Nelling, OSF, Sr. Felicity Dorsett, OSF, Ms. Cheron Price, and Ms. Susan Coyne for your friendship and unwavering support.

I own a great debt of love and gratitude to Fr. Joseph Tinh V. Nguyen, Msgr. Jos Thang Pham, Fr. Bao Nguyen, SJ, Ph.D., Mr. & Mrs. Dat Tran and Nancy Bui, Mr. & Mrs. Hien-Tu Nguyen, Mr. & Mrs. Phuc Mai, Mr. & Mrs. Hung-Ha Doan, Msgr. Jos Van A. Nguyen, Ms. Quynh Do, Mr. & Mrs. Joseph and Mary Nguyen, O.D., Mr. & Mrs. Son and Anh Nguyen, MD, Mr. & Mrs. Peter and Ha Pham, the Lindblom family's baby Bridget, the Jos and Molly Gettinger family, and the Cavadini family members for your kind assistance, generous support and/or prayers. I also own a great debt of gratitude to the Dominican Sisters of Saint Rosa of Lima in Vietnam, the Congregation of the Sacred Heart of Jesus in Huế, the Dominican Sisters of Houston, the Sisters of the Holy Cross, the Sisters of St. Francis of Perpetual Adoration, the Adrian Dominican Sisters, the Dominican Friars of General Curia of the Order of Preachers at the Convent Santa Sabina, and the Priests and Brothers of General Curia of the Society of the Divine Word in Rome for their hospitality, especially for their worship of God, devotion to the Blessed Virgin Mary, and community life.

I must extend my deep gratitude to my family, especially, my beloved siblings, nephews, and nieces, for their love, encouragement, and generous support in all the ways I have asked for help. I am incredibly grateful to my sister Maria Trần Thị Duyên and my nephew Anthony Hoàng Trần Thành Trung for helping transport sources whenever and wherever I needed them from Vietnam as well as my sister Trần Thị Kim Oanh and her children, Kieu Anh and Anh Van, for their love and kind assistance. I am grateful to my youngest brother, Anthony Trần Đức Tiệp, for making himself available for conversation with me, especially during my time of desolation.

At this moment, I respectfully remember my loving people who rest in peace: my grandparents, my parents, my siblings, Bishop Joseph-Marie Cương T. Nguyễn, Fr. Anthony Hiệu V. Nguyễn, Sr. Maria Paul Nhiên T. Pham, Sr. Maria Magdalene Điểm Đào, Br. Richard Gilman, C.S.C., and Fr. Robert Pelton, C.S.C.; they were and still are my motivation.

Finally, I also own a great debt of gratitude to the late Fr. FX Truong Buu Diep, who is moving toward a possible beatification, and Saint Joseph at the Saint Joseph's Oratory of Mount Royal for bringing me to the United States to study.

Abbreviations

AAOH: The Archive of the Archdiocese of Huế
ACBCV: The Archive of Catholic Bishops' Conference of Vietnam
AMEP: The Archive of the Society of Foreign Missions of Paris
AOH: The Archdiocese of Huế
APF: The Archive of Propaganda Fide
CBCV: Catholic Bishops' Conference of Vietnam
MEP: The Society of Foreign Missions of Paris
NC-OLLV: The National Center of the Holy Mother La Vang
OLLV: Our Lady of La Vang
VAA: The Vatican Apostolic Archive

Introduction

OUR LADY OF LA Vang, also known as the Holy Mother La Vang, is the Catholic title of the Blessed Virgin Mary associated with Marian apparitions believed to have occurred at La Vang in Quang Tri, Vietnam, in 1798. The story of Our Lady of La Vang (OLLV) and the history of devotion to her demonstrate the importance of historical context for the development of the theology of OLLV. At the beginning of the persecution of Vietnamese Christians in 1798, OLLV appeared to a group of the suffering lay faithful of Dinh Cát/Quảng Trị province, who had fled to the jungle to avoid persecution. OLLV, holding the baby Jesus, appeared to old and young, men and women, most of them poor and powerless, after they had recited the rosary. Making herself part of the community of prayer, OLLV spoke words that empowered the gathered lay faithful to have trust and gave them the courage to endure suffering and hardship. She cared for their well-being by teaching them how to use local plants to cure their illnesses. She also affirmed their prayers and promised to be there for anyone who came to her. Finally, she spoke in a language and an idiom the local people could understand, easily remember, and pass on. I will present OLLV's story more fully in the first chapter, highlighting some of her unique elements. For example, she did not require anything from her supplicants; she simply empowered them to trust in God, promising she was, and constantly would be, there to help. Trust in OLLV even spread beyond the Christian faithful to others, locally at first, then nationally, and even internationally.

The story of OLLV, I argue, is also the story of the inculturation of the Catholic faith in Vietnam. This book shows that inculturation, though often wrongly regarded as simply a post-Vatican II concern, has in fact been happening all along—in Vietnam, in connection with the cult of OLLV. One prominent Vietnamese American theologian, for example, claims that this Vietnamese Mary is still the "Mary of privileges" and hasn't been affected by Vatican II.[1] But my research shows that, on the contrary, the title "Mother of the Church," a title that only fully came into its own with Vatican II and the subsequent endorsement of the popes, especially Pope Francis, was inculturated in the uniqueness of Vietnamese Catholic belief and practice from the time of OLLV's first apparition. "Our Lady Mother of the Church" is not a title of Marian privilege so much as it is a title of solidarity. What we see in the cult of OLLV is a piety and theology of Mary as "Mother of the Church," which, as it developed, also solidified an identity of Vietnamese Catholics as such. One reason is that, just as OLLV said she would, she inspired fortitude and endurance under persecution. The persecution of Christians in Vietnam lasted through nearly the entire nineteenth century in one form or another. As the official theology of Mary, Mother of the Church, developed more at Vatican II and in its legacy, it found a home in the hearts of Vietnamese Catholics where Mary had already been inculturated as ecclesial Mother.

Throughout the history of the devotion to OLLV, European titles were introduced to refer to her. "Our Lady Help of Christians" was officially named in association with her, but other titles, such as "Our Lady of Victory" and "Our Lady of Grace," have also been used less formally, or with artistic reference. But these titles, though originally extrinsic, were over time organically woven into the devotion to OLLV in such a way that they received their content from their unique Vietnamese context. Indeed, missionaries apparently introduced the title "Our Lady Help of Christians" because it seemed to correspond already to the piety that they were observing in the midst of persecutions, the persecutions in which their own lives were also at stake.

When the persecution of Vietnamese Christians finally ceased, the inculturation of these titles reaches a crescendo in the developments that led to the dedication of the shrine of OLLV as National Shrine and its church as a Basilica. In the time following Vatican II inculturation began to be a more explicitly expressed desideratum, and there was an acceleration of the process towards inculturated art and liturgy. But the story I have to tell about OLLV shows that the main work had already been done and the foundation laid in an organic development that took place

---

1. Phan, "Mary in Vietnamese Piety and Theology," 103.

over the span of two centuries of faithful adherence to the Gospel despite atrocious persecution, poverty and other obstacles. This heroic witness of faithful solidarity was formed in connection with devotion to OLLV.

Up to now, the only lengthy research work on OLLV, "Notre Dame de La Vang, Viet Nam, histoire et théologie: du message de Notre Dame de La Vang à la maternité de grâce de Marie et à la spiritualité de l'espérance," was a dissertation completed by Joseph-Marie Phong Thanh Trần in 2001. Although his title promised to explore the history and theology of OLLV, it does not offer a systematic account of the history of the devotion or its connection to a developing theology. In addition, though Trần discussed inculturation and OLLV's maternity, there is still a need for exploring in what way(s) the story of and devotion to OLLV was itself a story of a long process of inculturation with the apparition itself as a starting point, in a manner somewhat parallel to that of the apparition of Our Lady of Guadalupe in Mexico. There is still a need, in other words, to examine the crucial connections between the development of the cult of OLLV and inculturation such that she becomes a model of inculturation as well as a Mother to the Vietnamese people and the People of God as a whole.

This book demonstrates that OLLV is the ecclesial Mother of the Church in Vietnam and, at the same time, the ecclesial Mother of the universal Church. Her ecclesial maternity fulfills the teaching of the Second Vatican Council: the Blessed Virgin Mary (BVM) is the Mother of the Church, both local and universal. Accordingly, her ecclesial maternity reminds Vietnamese Catholics that the Church in Vietnam is part of the Universal Church. The inculturation of her maternity facilitates the connection between these two levels, local and universal. In telling this story, this book becomes the first research into the history and theology of OLLV to appear in English.

Method and Plan of Chapters

To carry out this project meant first to do extensive work locating and collecting sources, which are not easily available for OLLV who has been so little researched. I traveled to Vietnam twice during the course of this research, where I worked at the archive of the Archdiocese of Huế and the libraries of Saint Sulpice Seminary of Huế and the Saint Joseph Seminary of Sài Gòn. I met Mr. Paul Chu Quang Trần, who introduced me to many local Vietnamese sources on OLLV. I sought out documents on both history and theology from 1790 to the present. I also went on a pilgrimage to the National Shrine of the Holy Mother La Vang to pray, observe, and interview pilgrims and those who have served at the Shrine. I had conversations with many scholars who have written about OLLV. I also traveled to Europe twice. In France, I conducted research at the Archive of MEP, and I also met Fr. Joseph Dũng Anh Trần, who not only introduced me to the sources of the history of the Church in Vietnam but also allowed me to conduct research at the library of Giáo Xứ Việt Nam Paris [the Vietnamese Parish in Paris]. In Rome, I conducted research in the Vatican Apostolic Archive, the Archive of Propaganda Fide, and the library of the Vatican. In these archives, I sought documents related to southern Vietnam since the early nineteenth century.

I examined not only printed materials but also the handwritten materials in these archives pertinent to the history of the Church in Vietnam in general, Marian devotion, and the devotion to OLLV. I read the documents with an eye to comparing the history of the European Church that was sending missionaries to the situation of the Vietnamese Church. I also theologically evaluated the documents in the light of the bible, the Catholic tradition, and the magisterium's teachings on Mariology. Unfortunately, the COVID-19 pandemic prevented me from conducting even more archival research. I also had initially planned to do an ethnographic study of the thirty-second national pilgrimage itself by participating, observing, and interviewing; however, the pandemic shut down those plans because the national pilgrimage scheduled for 2020 was postponed until further notice, first due to the pandemic and subsequently due to major construction at the basilica.

Using these sources, I organized my work into five chapters. The first tells the story of the apparition of OLLV and explores the literature that bears witness to it. The second and third chapters explore the history of devotion to OLLV from soon after the apparition up to the present day. This historical exploration shows that the BVM has played a role in the economy of salvation for the Vietnamese people, who in their turn become, as it were, another OLLV for their neighbors. The fourth chapter unfolds the history of Marian titles related to the devotion to OLLV and investigates how the bishops of Vietnam impacted devotion to OLLV. This chapter reveals that OLLV's maternity fits into the developing teaching of the Church about the BVM. The fifth chapter surveys five Vietnamese theological commentators who wrote about OLLV following the apparition's two hundredth anniversary. On the one hand, most of those accounts reinforce reliable oral traditions of OLLV and the devotion to her inculturated in the hearts of the People of God. On the other hand, their accounts reveal the need for further theological development and education. Finally, a brief general conclusion contributes to the basic theology of OLLV, the ecclesial Mother of inculturated evangelization. It also encourages further research on the theology of OLLV and of pastoral ministry to pilgrims, both individual groups and national pilgrimages, at the National Center/Shrine of the Holy Mother La Vang.

1

The Story of the Apparitions of Our Lady of La Vang

POPE JOHN PAUL II first shared the story of Our Lady of La Vang (OLLV) with the Catholic world on June 19, 1988, the day the Pope canonized 117 martyrs in Vietnam.[1] In his homily, the Pope preached that the Vietnamese martyrs had initiated meaningful dialogues, liberated their people and their cultures, and preached the Catholic faith. They sought religious freedom to worship God first and only then to respect secular authority. In first obeying God and then observing civil authority, the Vietnamese martyrs shared the same experience as Christian martyrs around the world. The Pope also drew a parallel between the first three centuries of the early Church and the first three centuries of Christianity in Vietnam. Moreover, as the Pope emphasized, these martyrs displayed their Vietnamese Catholic identity, including a solid devotion to Mary, the Mother of Jesus.

On that same day in 1988, Pope John Paul II introduced the National Center/Shrine of OLLV to the Catholic world. In his daily Angelus address, the Pope invited pilgrims to Rome to learn about OLLV by telling her story in the context of persecution, sharing a brief history of her

---

1. John Paul II, "Homily on the Canonization of 117 Martyrs in Vietnam." Note that the term "the martyrs in Vietnam" refers to the 117 martyrs who were canonized into sainthood in 1988, including 11 Spanish Dominican preachers, 10 French missionaries, and 96 native Vietnamese Christians. The term "the Vietnamese Martyrs" refers to the latter group only.

The Story of the Apparitions of Our Lady of La Vang

shrine, and calling for the reconstruction of the Basilica of Our Lady of La Vang.[2] The Pope recounted that King Cảnh Thịnh had decreed the persecution of Christians in 1798, at which point a group of lay faithful fled to a wild mountain called La Vang in Dinh Cát/Quảng Trị province. Despite facing starvation, disease, and wild animal attacks, they remained hidden there. They gathered in the evening to pray, reciting the rosary to ask God for divine assistance. The Pope explained that, according to Vietnamese oral tradition, the Blessed Virgin Mary (hereafter BVM) appeared to these people many times while holding the baby Jesus, encouraging them to persevere and guaranteeing protection. Later, a shrine was constructed to mark the beginning of Vietnamese devotion to the BVM. The Pope pointed to two ecclesial decisions in 1961 that empowered devotion to OLLV. First, the Vietnamese bishops approved the Shrine of OLLV as the National Center/Shrine of the Holy Mother La Vang on April 13, 1961. Second, Pope John XXIII approved their request to elevate the Church of Our Lady of La Vang to the rank of a basilica on August 22, 1961. These episcopal and papal decisions, Pope John Paul II emphasized, offered enough justification to rebuild the Basilica of OLLV, which had been destroyed in 1972. The Pope further explained that devotion to OLLV, the Queen of Martyrs, at the Basilica would offer spiritual benefits to pilgrims and foster national unity, true civilization, and moral progress in Vietnam. June 19, 1988, thus not only marked the historical introduction of the Shrine of OLLV to the entire Church and encouraged the reconstruction of the Basilica but also inspired a new opportunity to reflect on the apparition story of OLLV.

Nearly a decade later, Pope John Paul II made another important impact on the devotion to OLLV. On December 16, 1997, the Pope wrote a letter to the Church in Vietnam at the beginning of the 200th Jubilee of the apparitions of OLLV (1798–1998).[3] He noted that OLLV had healed many people from "spiritual and physical tribulations." Moreover, the Pope pointed out that OLLV had lifted up her children amid their suffering from mental and physical ailments, saying, "Have trust, be willing to suffer hardship and sorrow. I have already granted your prayers. Henceforth all those who come to pray to me in this spot will see their wishes

---

2. John Paul II, *Angelus*.

3. John Paul II, "Letter to Cardinal Paul Joseph Pham Dinh Tung." Note that though the 200th jubilee of the apparition of OLLV took place from January 1, 1998, to August 15, 1999, its opening mass was celebrated from August 13–15, 1998. How the Pope impacted the devotion to OLLV will be discussed further in chapter 3.

fulfilled." OLLV's words, the Pope elaborated, are "a message of hope" that expresses how "the Mother of the Lord gave her children [a gift of assurance] in 1798." Further, OLLV's message of hope "still remains up to date." Although history records ups and downs, overall devotion to OLLV had continued to increase. For example, the Shrine of OLLV not only became the National Center/Shrine of the Holy Mother, but also "has been able to keep alive the tradition of pilgrimages." The Pope further taught that OLLV was the Heavenly Mother, to whom pilgrims "entrust their troubles and hopes." In OLLV, the Pope stated, the members of the church in Vietnam find "the welcoming presence of the One who gives them the courage to bear an admirable witness of Christian life." Through OLLV, the pilgrims grow in faith, hope, and charity. In other words, devotion to OLLV "is intrinsic to Christian worship" in a particular way in Vietnam, just as it is everywhere, as Pope Paul VI explained in *Marialis Cultus*.[4] Ending his letter, the Pope sent his Apostolic Blessing to all the members of the Church in Vietnam and in the Vietnamese diaspora "on this happy occasion of the second centenary of the apparitions of the Blessed Virgin." The Pope thus confirmed the Marian apparitions at La Vang as worthy of belief.

The following sections of this chapter provide a review of the literature on Our Lady of La Vang. I first examine the context of the apparition and then explore the accounts of the first scholars to write on this topic. The writings of later scholars are analyzed based on the in chronological order of publication.

The Context of the Apparition

The apparitions of OLLV took place during the persecution of Christians in Vietnam in 1798. Christianity was rejected by Vietnamese leaders soon after it arrived in Vietnam in the early sixteenth century. The first royal prohibition of Christianity is recorded in 1533. The document tells us, first, that a European missionary, a man named "I-ne-khu,"[5] had already evangelized Ninh Cường, Quần Anh, and Trà Lũ (in modern times, the Nam Dinh province). The action also tells us that the king saw the new

---

4. See *Catechism of the Catholic Church*, §971, citing Pope Paul VI, *Marialis Cultus*, §56.

5. "I-ne-khu" is most likely spelled phonetically.

religion as a threat, both heretical and superstitious.⁶ We know, therefore that there was tension between Christians and the Vietnamese kings and their officers from the beginning. Vietnamese rulers believed in Confucianism, favored Taoism, and accepted Buddhism; other religions, including Christianity, were considered heresy [tà đạo]. Persecution of Christian missionaries and their followers occurred as a result, although the extent of the persecution varied across time and space. In addition, the 1798 persecutions of Christians were linked to socio-political entanglements, as French missionaries increased their involvement in Vietnamese politics.

Despite this ban, many Vietnamese villagers followed Christianity even after the first missionary was expelled. In other words, though the persecution of Christians continued to occur, many Vietnamese people, especially the farmers and the poor, converted to Catholicism.⁷ They believed in Jesus Christ as their Savior, venerated the Blessed Virgin Mary, and loved the Church.

In addition to the religious conflict that emerged from the tension between indigenous belief and Christian faith, socio-political factors linked to the Vietnamese civil wars sparked further severe persecution and a series of massacres of Christians. Although the country was technically under the reign of the Later Lê Dynasty (1427–1788), the real national authority was in the hands of the Trịnh clan/lord (in the north) and the Nguyễn clan/lord (in the south). Those clans were also in conflict and fought one another, theoretically in the name of the king, to expand their power. Because the fighting made the lives of ordinary people miserable, they rebelled against the clans. Chinese involvement complicated these conflicts, and there were also many rebellions that sprang up during the second half of the eighteenth century.⁸

6. Phan, *Khâm định Việt sử Thông giám cương mục*, 33:5–6. Thanh Giản Phan (1796–1867) was a great counselor of the Nguyễn Dynasty and wrote this history at the order of the king, Tự Đức. It was completed in 1859; however, it was edited several times before the first printing in 1884. Most Vietnamese Catholic historians who study the history of the Church in Vietnam, such as Fathers Vincent Sinh Đức Bùi, Px. Hiệu Trung Đào and Anthony Sơn Ngọc Nguyễn, cite this source. See also Anonymous, *Hội Đồng Tứ Giáo*.

7. K. Nguyễn, ed., *Hạnh Các Thánh Tử Đạo Viet Nam* [*Virtues of Vietnamese Martyrs*], 13. Nguyễn was ordained for the Archdiocese of Ho Chi Minh City in 1980 and earned a D. Min at the Catholic University of America in 2004. Upon his return, he taught at Saint Joseph Seminary, and was ordained a bishop in 2008. For relevant sources, see A. Trần, "Witness of Faith."

8. K. T. Trần, *Việt Nam Sử Lược* [*A Brief History of Vietnam*] 1:89–92; 2:35–50;

During this political chaos, three farmer-brothers in Tây Sơn led a successful rebellion in 1771 and instituted the Tây Sơn Dynasty (1788–1802). The oldest brother was crowned king and took the title Quang Trung. He established a capital in Phú Xuân (in central Vietnam) and engaged in nation-building projects; however, he passed away in 1793. His seven-year-old son Nguyễn Quang Toản was crowned king and took the title Cảnh Thịnh. Under the reign of this very young king, the system of government became corrupt. King Cảnh Thịnh executed several of his officers without trial, which caused other officials to leave their posts and later turn against him. The Tây Sơn Dynasty was thus weakened. In those conditions, Nguyễn Ánh (1762–1820), a survivor of the Nguyễn clan, revolted against the king to regain power. With the support of outsiders, including the French bishop Pigneau de Béhaine, Nguyễn Ánh conquered the provinces of southern Vietnam one by one. After capturing Sài Gòn, Nguyễn Ánh prepared to destroy the Tây Sơn Dynasty and marched toward the capital (in central Vietnam). In response to this uprising, King Cảnh Thịnh grew afraid that the growing number of Christians would join Nguyễn Ánh's rebellion. To avert this threat to his dynasty, the king ordered a harsh persecution of Christians in 1798.[9]

King Cảnh Thịnh's decree was severe because it essentially sought to obliterate all missionaries, native clergy, and Christian adherents across the whole nation. In addition, the decree ordered the destruction of churches and Christian villages. When this wave of persecution began,

---

2:121–25. The Early Lê Dynasty reigned from 544–602, distinguishing it from the Later Le Dynasty, which reigned from 1427–1788. During the Later Lê Dynasty, Vietnam expanded south, and many civil wars took place. Kim Trọng Trần (1883–1953) was a Vietnamese literary scholar and politician, and the first to write two volumes of history of Vietnam in *chữ quốc ngữ* [the national script]. He published these volumes in Hà Nội in 1920, and they have been reprinted many times. This study cites the 1971 edition.

9. P. Phan, *History of the Catholic Church in Vietnam: Tome I, 1533–1960* (Long Beach: CTTT, 2000), 303–5; 319–24. Born in Huế, Father Phan (1926–2015) was a Redemptorist and probably the first Vietnamese historian to write the history of the Church in Vietnam in the current national script. His first volume was printed in 1959, and his second volume was printed in 1962. They were reprinted in 1965. He translated these texts into one volume in English and published it in the United States in 2000. This study uses the 2000 editions since they are translated into English. Also see Đ. Bùi, *The Catholic Church in Vietnam*, 1:441–46, 461. His three-volume work has had three printings, with the first in Saigon in 1972. This study uses the third edition, printed in Canada in 1997. For relevant information, see the Archive of the France-Asia Research Institute, belonging to the Missions Étrangères de Paris (MEP) and known as the Archive of the Missions Étrangères de Paris (AMEP), vol. 746, 691; Launay, *Histoire de La Mission de Cochinchine*, 3:251–56; T. Trần, *A Brief History of Vietnam*, 2:101–68.

many Christians fled in order to avoid being captured or killed. Peter Huỗn Phát Phan describes the punishment and execution of Christians that took place in 1798, which included imprisonments, torture, burnings, and beheadings. For example, Father Emmanuel Triệu Văn Nguyễn was imprisoned along with thirty-two lay male leaders of parishes, and then he was beheaded in public. Phan says: "For 40 days [Father Emmanuel Trieu] suffered from torments in prison: stocks around his neck, chains on all four limbs, several trials at court and three good beatings.... The execution site was at Bai Dau. Father Trieu calmly knelt, looking up and exposing his neck for the executing soldier to sabre.... His body was carefully buried by the faithful."[10]

In addition, Phan mentions that many religious women of the Congregation of the Lovers of the Cross were tortured, and their convent was destroyed.[11] It was during this persecution that the lay people of several parishes in Quảng Trị province escaped to a wild and forested mountain called La Vang. There the Blessed Virgin Mary appeared to them to encourage them to "have trust," to endure suffering and hardship, to affirm their prayers, and to promise to be there offering help to whomever comes to her.

The Marian apparition at La Vang marks the beginning of the tradition of OLLV in Vietnam. But more than this, devotion to OLLV became fundamental to the identity of Vietnamese Catholics. The following section explores the story of OLLV with a particular focus on the process of writing down the oral tale.

Literature Review of the Story of the Apparition of Our Lady of La Vang

For 225 years, the story of OLLV has been passed down through oral traditions, the stories of pilgrims, and written works. The first five written accounts include the following texts, ordered chronologically: 1) Jean-Louis Bonnand's "Un procès gagné–Une église à faire" (before 1892); 2) François Xavier Charle Patinier, "Mission Report" (1894); 3) Claude Bonin's "Notre Dame de La Vang" (1901); 4) Joseph Trang Văn Trần's

---

10. P. Phan, *History of the Catholic Church in Vietnam*, 306–7. There are several letters to account for Father Emmanuel's martyrdom. See Jean Labartette, AMEP, vol. 747.

11. P. Phan, *History of the Catholic Church in Vietnam*, 303–19; Đ. Bùi, *The Catholic Church in Vietnam*, 1:446–50. For a record of persecution of Christians, see AMEP, vol. 747, 21; 163–66. See also Dutton, *The Tây Sơn Uprising*.

Historical Narrative of Devotion to Our Lady of La Vang (around 1910s); 5) Dominic Cẩn Ngọc Hổ's *The Legend Poem of La Vang* (1929). When taken together, these accounts provide a holistic depiction of the story of the apparition of OLLV.

Interestingly, the earliest accounts do not tell the story of the apparition itself, but rather assume that the reader will understand the reference. Bonnand's letter is located at the Archive of the France-Asia Research Institute (AMEP).[12] As the pastor of Thanh-Huong church and probable overseer for the community of La Vang in Quảng Trị, Bonnand wrote this report to his superior in Paris. In it, he mentions that the Holy Mother had helped both Christians and non-Christians, and he and his companions had accordingly decided to formally re-establish the devotion to OLLV:

> Another story. To the great joy of Christians, we have decided to restore the cult of Our Lady of La Vang, of that Holy Mother whom even the non-Christians invoked with confidence and from whom they have several times received extraordinary favors.[13]

In this brief passage, Bonnand tells us two important things. First, the name of Our Lady of La Vang stands out. Bonnand and his companions believed that the apparition was the Holy Mother, that is, the Mother of Jesus, the Mother of God. Second, Bonnand tells us that OLLV's maternal help has been constant for *all* the Vietnamese people, both Christians and non-Christians. Although Bonnand does not mention the Marian apparition itself, his surviving letter, a primary source attesting to early Vietnamese Marian devotion under this name, is remarkable in the history of devotion to OLLV.

The context for the letter also matters. The exact date is unknown, but his letter was located in a collection box dated from 1886 to 1892. According to a record of his mission, Bonnand was the pastor of Thanh Huong (near Cổ Vưu and La Vang) in Quảng Trị from 1882–88. In this capacity, he probably oversaw the Christian community of La Vang. Collectively, this means the letter most likely dates to 1886–88.[14] It is

---

12. Bonnand, "Un procès gagné—Une église à faire," 694.

13. Bonnand, "Un procès gagné—Une église à faire," 694. The original quote is "Autre histoire. A la grande joie des chrétiens, nous nous sommes mis en tête de restaurer le culte de Notre Dame de La Vang, de cette bonne Mère que les païens eux-mêmes invoquent avec confiance et dont ils ont reçu plusieurs fois des grâces signalées." Also see V. Lê, Đức Mẹ La Vang, 30.

14. For a biography of Jean-Louis Bonnand, see AMEP, Documentation A Missionary 1475, https://irfa.paris/en/missionnaire/1475-bonnand-jean. For more detail of this source, see the introduction of this publication from 673–85.

undeniable that the condition of Vietnamese Christianity at that time was misery. Most churches and Christian villages had been burned or demolished during the Văn Thân Movement.[15] Material for rebuilding destroyed parish churches was limited. Moreover, at the time, La Vang was only a community of Christians; it was not yet a formalized parish. It is understandable that the pastors yielded authority for the construction to the Christian community at La Vang. The push to restore the rituals of OLLV and to quickly rebuild a church at La Vang suggests that OLLV was well-known among her children in Quảng Trị province. Bonnard was likely the first missionary to present written evidence for OLLV and report devotion to OLLV. His contribution offers powerful evidence that by the late nineteenth century OLLV was understood to be constantly helping the Vietnamese, both Christians and non-Christians.

At the AMEP, I also found evidence in the annual episcopal reports either quoting or mentioning the missionary François Xavier Charle Patinier (1850–1922) in relation to devotion to OLLV.[16] Arriving in Quảng Bình in 1875, Patinier soon served at Cổ Vưu parish, where he devoted himself to evangelization and strengthening the lay people. In his annual report in 1894, Apostolic Vicar Marie-Antoine-Louis Caspar quoted Patinier's report:

> Your excellency knows the little Christian community of La Vang located in the deep mountains. For many years now, the Blessed Virgin has been pleased to grant extraordinary favors to those who invoke her under the name Our Lady of La Vang. In 1885, the chapel was no more spared than the other churches in the district.[17]

---

15. The "Văn Thân Movement [Phong trào Văn Thân] was a nineteenth-century popular movement led by non-governmental scholars in central Vietnam. Their motto was "Demolish the Westerners; kill the heretics," i.e., the Christians. See T. Trần, *A Brief History of Vietnam*, 2:289–90. Note that most churches were built with wood. Instead of burning these, the movement repurposed the solid materials for other uses.

16. François Xavier Charle Patinier was ordained in 1875 and sent to the mission in the diocese of Cochinchine septentrionale. As a pastor of Cổ Vưu parish, he reconstructed the church in 1877. In 1885, this church was burned with four hundred lay faithful inside during the Văn Thân Movement. He completed reconstruction of this church in 1889.

17. Marie-Antoine-Louis Caspar, "Annual Report in 1894," AMEP, vol. 761, 61. The original quote is "Votre Grandeur connaît la petite chrétienté de La-vang, située dans la montagne. Depuis de longues années déjà, la sainte Vierge se plaît à accorder des faveurs extraordinaires à ceux qui l'invoquent sous le titre de Notre-Dame de La-vang." These writings are explored further in chapter 2.

The Christian community of La Vang, the new name of the BVM as OLLV, and the church itself all attest to a previous history of OLLV. Also, the report praises the help of OLLV. In the following annual report, the Bishop quoted Patinier again:

> Strike the shepherd and the sheep will be scattered; our sworn enemy followed this maxim to that expression; he endeavored to slander the leaders of Christian communities, especially those which had been newly founded, and without the special protection of Our Lady of La Vang we would have had to lament many losses.[18]

Though, like Bonnand, Patinier does not describe the apparition story, he not only invokes the faith of his flock is, but he also asserts his own belief in OLLV because of her powerful and constant help amid severe persecutions and massacres. He seems to assume the tradition is well-established and the story well-known. It is helpful to remember that the nineteenth century was a century with many Marian apparitions, and the name Our Lady of Lourdes, for example, was widely famous in Europe by this time. Here at La Vang in Vietnam, however, instead of evangelizing the local population to call on Our Lady of Lourdes,[19] the French missionaries bear witness to OLLV, as though adverting to the fact that there already was a local apparition tradition operative.

Claude Bonin (1839–1925) was the first scholar to contribute a brief but whole written story of OLLV when he published "Notre Dame de La Vang" in 1901.[20] This piece is considered the first written account of the story of OLLV. *The Legend Poem of La Vang,* which emerged from

---

18. Bishop Caspar, "Annual Report in 1895," AMEP, vol. 761, 65. The original quote is "Percute pastorem et dispergentur oves; notre ennemi juré suivait cette maxime à la lettre; il s'attachait à faire calomnier les chefs des chrétientés, surtout de celles qui venaient d'être nouvellement fondées, et sans une protection spéciale de Notre-Dame de La-vang nous aurions eu à déplorer bien des pertes."

19. Compagnon, *Le Culte de Notre Dame de Lourdes*, discusses the members of the MEP committed to spread the doctrine of the Immaculate Conception, and so also devoted to Our Lady of Lourdes.

20. Claude Bonin, "Notre Dame de La Vang" in *Annales de la Société des Missions-Étrangères*, no. 24. (Paris: MEP, 1901), 273–77. Bonin did not actually sign the article, for reasons that are somewhat unclear; however, Apostolic Vicar Antoine Caspar later said that he was quoting "the report of Father Bonin," and his text includes many elements from the article. It makes sense that this was written as a report by Bonin, who was the pastor of Cổ Vưu parish and administrated the La Vang community from 1895 to 1904 during the period of the church's dedication that he described. Father Joseph Trang Văn Trần also mentioned in his book that he had used an article by Father Bonin published in *Annales de la Société des Missions-Étrangères*.

The Story of the Apparitions of Our Lady of La Vang

oral traditions, was probably composed previously, over time, before the publication of "Notre Dame de La Vang," but it was not published until 1929.[21] Bonin's text is also held at the AMEP. He was appointed a pastor of Cổ Vưu parish in 1895 and held that position until 1904. He was also the administrator of the Church of La Vang, so he hosted the blessing of the chapel of OLLV and organized the procession of OLLV in 1900.[22] Bonin's account is structured into three major parts: original pilgrimage, extraordinary grace, and a solemn procession of OLLV and the blessing of the Church.

First, Bonin told the story of OLLV in detail according to the oral tradition. He described the location of La Vang in the midst of scrubland and only a few kilometers from Cổ Vưu parish in Quảng Trị province.[23] This was (and still is) a devout Catholic community and had many members who became martyrs. In this respect, the piece parallels both the historical documents of the Church in Vietnam and the homily that Pope John Paul II delivered during the canonization of the Vietnamese martyrs in 1988. Bonin recounted that, during the wave of persecution about a hundred years prior, many lay people of Cổ Vưu had fled from their villages to the jungle of La Vang, where the story of OLLV began.

Despite their suffering in the wild, the lay faithful still gathered in the evening at a meager shelter that served as a chapel where they could pray passionately. Bonin recounts that they prayed to "the Mother of God" every night for all types of assistance: meeting their urgent personal needs, protecting their lives, safety from wild animals, and religious freedom.[24] One night, after the group finished praying, a magnificent and

---

21. Hồ, "Introduction," *The Legend Poem of La Vang*. This study cites the second edition.

22. Bishop Caspar, "Annual Report 1900," AMEP, vol. 761, 90. Note that as a pastor of Cổ Vưu parish from 1895 to 1904, Bonin took care of the chapel of OLLV, continued the construction of the chapel of OLLV, and organized the ceremony celebrating its construction.

23. For more details, see V. N. Stanislas Nguyễn, *Linh Địa La Vang [Sacred Land of La Vang,]* 33–34. This work was reprinted with the same title (Carthage, USA: Trái Tim Đức Mẹ, 1978), and this study cites the later American publication. According to Stanislas Nguyễn, the local people in Quảng Trị, both non-Christians and Christians, lived by collecting wood and making charcoal to trade in towns. They often went as a group the area was a dangerous jungle where they might be lost and/or attacked by animals. They often worked for a week or longer, depending on whether they collected enough wood. Stanislas Nguyễn (1910–92) was ordained in 1942 as a priest of the diocese of Huế.

24. Bonin, "Notre Dame de La Vang," 274. Even today when the Vietnamese laity gather to pray, they often recite the rosary, though the Chaplet of Divine Mercy has also become well practiced.

beautiful lady appeared to them. Bonin's emphasis on the timing of the apparition—after the prayer was completed—suggests that OLLV was specifically answering their prayer.[25] She was dressed in white and surrounded by a radiance of brightness with two baby angels standing near her. Bonin adds that OLLV spoke to the lay faithful in a gentle voice: "My children, what you have asked of me, I grant you, and from now on, all those who will come here to pray to me, I will answer them."[26] Although the lady spoke with a soft voice, everyone heard her words, and—Bonin writes—they had been handed down through oral traditions from that moment onward. Bonin also mentions that the people have devoutly preserved this story because miracles have indeed been continuously performed, as OLLV promised.[27]

In the second part of his text, then, Bonin goes on to give a powerful account of the favors, graces, and miracles attributed to OLLV. He writes that many people claim that their requests had been granted, and as a result, many of those who received these favors converted to Catholicism, began devoutly practicing the Catholic faith, and/or began performing charity. Although Bonin does not state that OLLV appeared to non-Christians, he does report that non-Christians also received grace when they invoked OLLV and often converted to Christianity after receiving her gifts. One of the most frequently occurring miracles apparently involved infertile couples being able to have children after asking OLLV for help. Bonin gives his French audience some context when discussing this point, writing that, like the ancient Jews, Vietnamese couples consider childlessness a real misfortune and are proud of having large families.

Bonin lingers on one example. A non-Christian couple had a son after they prayed to OLLV, and they converted to Christianity. Later, during a period of Christian persecution, the husband told his wife that they should deny being Christians to save their lives. He intended that the denial would be verbal only, but his wife did not agree. Despite her hesitation, the husband decided to deny being a Christian, and the wife remonstrated with him, saying: "Since you only have a heart to deny

25. Just as the Israelites of the Old Testament suffered, cried to God, and were rescued, the lay faithful cried to the Blessed Virgin Mary during their persecution, said the Rosary, and received protection.

26. Bonin, "Notre Dame de La Vang," 274. The original quote is "Mes enfants, ce que vous m'avez demandé, je vous l'accorde, et désormais tous ceux qui viendront ici me prier, je les exaucerai."

27. Bonin's account of OLLV encouraging the lay faithful to endure suffering is written as a description rather than direct speech.

The Story of the Apparitions of Our Lady of La Vang

God, apostatize, let go, I agree, but before that, bring this child back to La-vang. The Blessed Virgin deposited it with us, because we promised her to live and die as good Christians. Since you don't want to keep your commitments, give the child back."[28]

Bonin records that the husband felt ashamed of himself, blushed, bowed his head, and remained true to his faith. He also states that when people received miracles, graces, or blessings, their subsequent devotion to OLLV was often expressed by performing the works of charity. Bonin's key example here is that when Father Bonnand and Father Patinier, his predecessors, called upon the lay faithful for donations to build the church of OLLV, they were generous in their response, donating materials or volunteering their labor to build the first brick church.[29] In short, Bonin claims, OLLV's miracles transformed the hearts of many people and encouraged them to be baptized and become living witnesses to the living God as devout Catholics.

Finally, Bonin offers a brief description of the blessing of the aforementioned brick chapel and of the solemn procession of the statue of OLLV.[30] Although he might not have trained to do "ethnography," Bonin nevertheless in effect performed one. As a host, participant, and observer of the procession, Bonin describes the ceremony magnificently and names major figures who were involved. For example, Apostolic Vicar Casper, who came from the diocese of Huế, joined in the procession and gave the blessing.[31] Bonin reports that the clergy, minor and major seminarians, and the lay faithful of that diocese were joyful during the procession. Under the direction of Father Izarn, the superior of the major seminary, marvelous songs and hymns were sung, and Father Patinier delivered a beautiful sermon. By combining their prayers with chanting, the lay faithful actively participated in the dedication of the chapel and the procession of OLLV. This attention to detail lends a sense of credibility to Bonin's report and the oral traditions that he carefully records.

28. Bonin, "Notre Dame de La Vang," 275. Translation mine. The original text is "Puisque tu n' as de coeur que pour renier Dieu, apostasie, lâche, j' y consens, mais auparavant, rapporte cet enfant à La-vang. La sainte Vierge l'a mis en dépôt chez nous, parce que nous lui avons promis de vivre et de mourir en bons chrétiens. Puisque tu ne veux pas tenir tes engagements, rends l'enfant."

29. In his report, Patinier said that the lay people of the La Vang community were joyful to volunteer in the construction of the church of OLLV. This is discussed further in the second chapter.

30. This is considered the first great pilgrimage to OLLV.

31. In his annual report in 1900, the bishop concluded by quoting a part of Bonin's article; see chapter 2 for further discussion.

Bonin also emphasizes the positive effect that the BVM had on the people who believed that she had kept the promise she made at La Vang. Bonin believed that just as OLLV protected the faithful's ancestors from persecution and lions and tigers alike, she now protected pilgrims from other type of dangers. He also recognized OLLV as the Mother of Jesus Christ when he wrote "Our Lady of La Vang give us many souls for Jesus Christ" and joined with the pilgrims in saying: "Our Lady of La Vang, pray for us!"[32] In ending his piece with these prayers, Bonin shows that he as well as his parishioners believed in the oral traditions of the apparition at La Vang and were convinced that OLLV was continuing to keep her promise by granting abundant favors.

Why did Father Bonin write this article? No one knows for certain, but he wrote the article in French despite being fluent in the Vietnamese language. It was published not in Vietnam but in Paris, where there was a strong devotion to Our Lady of the Miraculous Medal and Our Lady of Lourdes at that time, even as now. In addition, the Society of Foreign Missions of Paris (hereafter MEP) was committed to spreading the doctrine of the Immaculate Conception; therefore, its members promoted the cult of Our Lady of Lourdes. Despite being a member of the MEP, Bonin promoted devotion to OLLV. Bonin thus seems to be the first French clergy to introduce the full story of OLLV to his own people and to a wider audience so that they might become more aware of a remarkable ecclesial culture in a country that was quite distant from Europe. This seems to be a credible reason for Bonin to have written the story of OLLV. In doing so, Bonin defended the devotion to OLLV and affirmed that the Vietnamese Marian devotion was part of the life of the whole Catholic Church, just as much as the devotions practiced in Paris were.

Bonin was impressed by the pilgrims' love for OLLV and noticed that, despite their lack of comfortable accommodations, the pilgrims were joyful, dancing, chanting, walking in procession, and praying. Their enthusiastic participation perhaps demonstrated to him that Christianity had taken root in this culture and that its strength was connected to the tradition of the apparitions. Bonin himself also came to believe in OLLV through his pastoral investigations. When he visited the elderly or performed Last Rites for the sick, he writes, he asked them whether they had heard about the Marian apparitions. They all confirmed to him that they

---

32. Bonin, "Notre Dame de La Vang," 277. The original quote is "Notre-Dame de La Vang, donnez-nous beaucoup d' âmes pour Jésus-Christ. . . . Notre-Dame de La Vang, priez pour nous."

had indeed heard the story from their parents, grandparents, and the elderly.[33] Bonin therefore worked to contribute the necessary information that would be needed during the process to receive ecclesiastical approval of the Marian apparitions at La Vang.

Joseph Trang Văn Trần was probably the first Vietnamese scholar who contributed sources, probably in the mid-1910s, that proved to be important to the study of OLLV.[34] His key contribution is the account *Historical Narrative of Devotion to Our Lady of La Vang*.[35] Because Trần was born in the diocese of Huế, he inherited the devotion to OLLV and knew all of the oral traditions related to this figure. In his "Introduction," Trần identifies the sources that he used: 1) Bonin's article in French; 2) the oral poem tradition, which the lay faithful in Quảng Trị often read/delivered; 3) his interviews with elderly lay faithful and senior priests who lived near La Vang in Quảng Trị; and 4) his own experience.[36] Because Trần used so many primary sources, and he himself is a historical witness to the first great pilgrimage in 1900, his *Historical Narrative* is one of most helpful primary sources for the study of, in particular, the history of devotion to OLLV, despite a few limitations. In terms of structure, the *Historical Narrative* contains three sections, including two poems based on oral tradition, the narrative of the apparition, and a report of the abundant favors given.

33. For more detail, see V. Lê, *Our Lady of La Vang*, 9–11.

34. I cite the third edition. Regarding the first publication date, Léopold Michael Cadière mentioned that he did not provide an account because Trần's work was available. Cadière was an administrator of the church of OLLV from 1904–11. Trần's account went out of print but was republished in 1923; the AOH holds the second publication. Finally, the AMEP holds a third edition from 1930.

35. V. Trần, *Tự Tích Tôn Kính Đức Mẹ La Vang* [*Historical Narrative of Devotion to Our Lady of La Vang*]. Born in Huế, Father Joseph Trần (1882–1945) was ordained in 1910 and served in the diocese of Cochinchine septentrionale. In addition to being the founder of the Congregation of *Kim Doi* [Lovers of the Cross] and helping to reform the Congregation of Daughters of Our Lady of Visitation, he was zealous to evangelize, loved OLLV, and was committed to pastoral ministry. For more information, see the Archive of Archdiocese of Huế. Also see Ngọc Bích Lê, *Nhân Vật Giáo Phận Huế*, 1:326–28.

36. V. Trần, *Historical Narrative of Devotion to OLLV*, 3: "Các điều tôi kể lại sau đây, thì tôi muốn lấy các lời Cha Bonin. . . . một ít điều lấy trong văn La Vang dân xứ Quảng Trị hay đọc, lại hỏi thăm các Cha và các bậc kỳ lão có dạo ở Quảng trị gần La Vang, và những điều tôi thấy rõ tường tận" ("The sources I use include Father Bonin's accounts, the poem read among the lay faithful in Quảng Trị province, my own investigations among senior clergy and the elderly laity in Quảng Trị, especially those who lived near La Vang, and finally my own experience.") Trần mentioned that the poem was not collected and written down until 1929, which will be discussed after this review.

The first poem, "A La Vang Poem," comprises only eight verses.[37] Along with describing how OLLV appeared at La Vang located in a wild region of Quảng Trị, Trần states that the church was built, and that OLLV continually granted favors to all. His second poem, "A Poem Hailing Our Lady of La Vang," tells the story of OLLV in sixty-four verses. He begins by greeting OLLV as the Mother of God and describes La Vang as the place she chose to meet her Vietnamese children:

> Hail the Holy Mother of God,
> You have mercy on Nam-Viet in a hard life
> You have chosen La Vang, a wild jungle-mountain
> Having granted divine grace down to all people.[38]

The poem goes on to describe the context of persecution and the response, the apparition of OLLV, according to oral traditions. It then recounts that many people received OLLV's help, which echoed the accounts of Bonin and other narratives. The poem then focuses on the development of devotion to OLLV, how her devotees grew in trust and confidence, and how eventually the clergy and the bishop built a church dedicated to her. The end of the poem describes a procession of OLLV. In summary, Trần begins his account of OLLV with poetry, a traditional Vietnamese style for handing on wisdom, especially in the past centuries. Moreover, these two poems set an exciting tone, which seems to prepare the readers to engage in the story of OLLV and her abundant favors to everyone.

Moving on to the narrative of OLLV, then, Trần describes the context and the apparition of OLLV, essentially echoing the description in Bonin's article (which he used as a direct source). However, he emphasizes three important components of the narrative. First, he says that, in the story, the lay faithful claimed that the beautiful woman who appeared to them was the Mother of God, because she held the Baby Jesus in her arms. Second, Trần asserts that OLLV appeared *many* times and that non-Christians also saw her. Finally, his story emphasizes that OLLV chose La Vang as a place where she would grant favors to people. Trần also provided other significant details. For example, he says that

---

37. V. Trần, "La Vang Poem," in *Historical Narrative of Devotion to OLLV*, 4.

38. V. Trần, "A Poem of Hail Our Lady of La Vang," in *Historical Narrative of Devotion to OLLV*, 6.
"Kính mừng Đức Mẹ Chúa Trời
Đoái thương Nam Việt trong đời gian nan
Chọn nơi rừng núi La Vang
Ban ơn thiêng xuống khắp tràn nhơn dân."

the church was built upon the old floor of the previous church, where, according to the oral traditions, OLLV stood when she appeared to the lay faithful. He also repeated that "Our Lady of Help of Christians" was a title dedicated to OLLV,[39] mentioned a well dug to serve the pilgrims, and remarked on the rituals of OLLV, especially the triennial solemn pilgrimages and annual Lunar New Year pilgrimages.

In his account of OLLV's miracles, Trần emphasizes the abundant graces that the dignified OLLV granted to both Christians and non-Christians. He describes many of the cases that people reported in their petitions. One of the cases that Bonin reports in "Notre Dame de La Vang" (the one about the infertile couple who are granted a child) is also mentioned in Trần's story; however, Trần offers more information about the non-Christian couple, including their names and the name of their son, the name of their village, and where they lived. He also retells several cases that were also published in periodicals, such as *Southern Diocese Bulletin*.[40] Trần places particular emphasis on healings that occurred as the result of prayer and from using the leaves that surrounded the church of OLLV. Trần's narrative shows that by performing these types of favors, OLLV not only met the needs of her devotees, but also kept her promise. He emphasizes the healing powers of the leaves around the church,[41] which is reminiscent of the "leaves for healing" mentioned in Ezekiel 47:12 and the line from Revelation 22:2 that "the leaves of the trees serve as medicine for the nations." These points were significant for future theologies of OLLV.

While Trần wrote the poems that begin his work himself, another poem written anonymously as a memorial appears to have been passed down through oral tradition. This poem was collected, edited, and published by Dominic Cẩn Ngọc Hồ in 1929 (reprinted in 1932). Born in Huế, Dominic Hồ inherited the devotion to OLLV and knew the oral

---

39. Note that Christianity arrived in Vietnam in the sixteenth century when the national geography was stable. Therefore, when a church was built, it took the name of its region. This name is secular, so the church leaders often dedicated the church to a saint or the divine titles. A church was built at La Vang, so it is known as the Church of La Vang, and Bishop Louis Caspar dedicated it to OLLV under the Marian title "Our Lady of Help of Christians." For more details, see Peter Thang Duc Nguyễn, "A Title of the Church–A Name of Parish–Patron Saint of the Parish," https://www.simonhoadalat.com/HOCHOI/MucVu/128TuocHieuNhaTho.htm, accessed August 30, 2022. Chapter 2 examines the Marian title "Our Lady of Help of Christians."

40. Văn Trung Nguyễn, *Nam Kỳ Địa Phận*, 12–13, 38.

41. For more information, see Hải Quỳnh, *Chữa Bệnh Từ Cây Cỏ Vườn Nhà & Bài Thuốc Gia Truyền*.

traditions of OLLV, just as Trần did. Along with his own writings about OLLV since 1912, Hồ was the first scholar to collect, edit, and publish the memorial poem, which he titled *The Legend Poem of La Vang*.[42] He also added a short introduction in which he offered some interpretations of the text. Since its publication, *The Poem* has served as a valuable source in the study of OLLV.

Dominic Hồ says that *The Poem* tells the history of OLLV from the beginning of the apparitions to the first diocesan pilgrimage in 190[0].[43] He notes that no one knows who the original author of the oral poem was or when it was composed; however, he speculates that it might have been composed soon after 1900 because in addition to describing the entirety of the story of OLLV up to the dedication of the church, *The Poem* also discusses the procession of OLLV in detail. However, *The Poem* might have been composed over several periods (at least three). The first redaction would have been when the original pagoda was built under the early reign of King Minh Mạng around the 1820s; very soon after completed it was entrusted to Catholics, and became the first shrine of OLLV.[44] More may have been added to it when the shrine needed repair, including an account of a female draper to whom tremendous favors were granted.[45] Finally, *The Poem* reported the solemn celebration to dedicate the

---

42. Hồ, *La Vang Sự Tích Vãn* [*The Legend Poem of La Vang*], hereafter cited in English. Dominic Cẩn Ngọc Hồ (1876–1948) was born in Huế and attended An Ninh minor seminary in 1890. He then joined Phú Xuân seminary from 1896–1902. He was ordained to the priesthood in 1902. Ho might have thus participated in the dedication of the Church of OLLV as well as the procession of OLLV in 1900. Not only did he inherit a tradition of devotion to OLLV, but he was also a scholar who could write in French and Vietnamese. He wrote several articles and gave many homilies and sermons about OLLV. In 1935, he was ordained a bishop, becoming the second Vietnamese bishop. For more detail, see the Archive of the Archdiocese of Huế, Tiểu sử Linh mục Huế [Biographies of Clergy of Huế]. Also see Ngọc Bích Lê, *Figures of Diocese of Huế*, 2:131–41. Note that "Sự Tích" can be singular or plural nouns in the Vietnamese language. However, I chose a singular because this legendary poem echoes the oral traditions of OLLV. The fact is that this poem tells a long history of devotion to OLLV mixed with her story of apparition. Therefore, I translated "The" to highlight ancient Vietnamese culture, which often handed down lessons by composing poems and even passing on recipes.

43. See also Q. Trần, *Hành Hương Giáo Phận Huế* [*Pilgrimage to the Diocese of Hue*], 2:274. Trần first published at the website of the Archdiocese of Huế in 2000 with six volumes. Then he condensed them into three volumes in 2021. This study cites the new edition.

44. *The Poem* tells us that non-Christians also received abundant graces (lines 1–22).

45. *The Poem* tells us that a pastor wrote a letter to inform all Christians near and far that the sacred land of La Vang was returned to Christians (lines 83–92).

The Story of the Apparitions of Our Lady of La Vang

brick chapel and a procession to honor OLLV in 1900.[46] Hồ also admits, somewhat self-consciously, that there were several "unkind words" in *The Poem*, meaning expressions of hostility towards certain antagonists. Because he wanted to keep *The Poem* as it was, Hồ did not alter these instances to make the work less offensive. Instead, he writes, he only revised a few words for the sake of maintaining the poem's rhythm.[47]

Stylistically, *The Poem* is composed using thơ lục bát, which is similar to an alexandrine poem in French and an accentual syllabic style in English. This is one of the two Vietnamese classical poetry styles. The imagery, sound, rhythm, and density of *The Poem* made it easier to commit to memory and pass on. *The Poem* does not give any indication of time, includes many repetitions of descriptions of the apparitions, is long, and covers many different events. The piece can be divided into nine parts, including an introduction, an account of a construction of a pagoda under the supervision of non-Christian village heads, a process of entrusting the pagoda to Catholics, a legend of a female draper, a description of the apparition of OLLV, several miracles performed for both Christians and non-Christians, the construction of the chapel of OLLV, the procession of OLLV, and a conclusion. However, the reading of *The Poem* offered here divides it into three main parts: one that covers the story of OLLV as it unfolded up to the historical development of the shrine, a second that focuses on the abundant favors mingled with brief descriptions of the apparitions that do not include moments in which OLLV speaks, and a third that centers on the procession conducted in honor of OLLV.

The Poem begins with almost magical lines to describe a holy place. "*Trời*" [Mr. Heaven] created a wonderful place in a wild mountain, which was suddenly transformed into a shrine of "*Chúa Bà*" [a divine lady or goddess]. In Vietnamese indigenous belief, "*Trời*" and "*Chúa Bà*"[48] refer

---

46. Hồ, "Introduction," 1. For more details see M. Bernard, "La Vierge Marie au Viet-Nam," 168_–69; V. Lê, *Our Lady of La Vang*, 25.

47. Dominic Hồ did not provide an example; however, lines 35–39 mention a "lack of kindness." It is essential to point out that these lines describe the non-Christian village chiefs' dreams. In the dreams, they all see the Buddhas [Buddhist saints] appear and ask them to remove their statues because that area belongs to the Christian Lady. In the dream, the Christian Lady is described as having miraculous authority over the Buddhist saints and the pagoda.

48. "*Trời*" [Heaven] is a term used about a divine figure in Vietnamese indigenous religions. Worshipping goddesses is also a part of indigenous religions; however, it has been developed widely since the sixteenth century, when Confucianism and Taoism began dominating the system in Vietnam and subordinating women. Moreover, in Vietnamese indigenous religions, Heaven can have either positive or negative connotations,

to divine figures. These opening lines therefore introduce an interesting legend connecting longstanding indigenous belief to the apparition that would later occur on the site. Despite the wildness of the mountain, the area was named La Vang and became a place inhabited by human communities, symbolized by the existence of a banyan tree, one of the popular symbols of a village at that time. The first eight lines of *The Poem* read:

> Heaven gives birth to a miraculous place
> Suddenly, in the middle of the mountain, a temple of a goddess appears:
> Oral tradition recounts, there is a banyan tree
> Growing exuberantly in the middle of the mountain.
>
> In the daytime, cranes and phoenixes play around.
> At nighttime, tigers and panthers adore the spiritual palace.
> This place is quiet and serious.
> In the middle, between two fields, is La Vang village.[49]

These verses juxtapose the condition of La Vang before and after the arrival of the divine lady. *The Poem* then explains that the non-Christian villagers built "nền thờ vọng" [a foundation to worship] because this was a majestic place, where favors had been given.

The Poem describes how excited the non-Christian village chiefs were as they called upon people for donations to build a pagoda in return for abundant favors. The chiefs said that the generosity of donators would be rewarded:

> This is a majestic place,
> Whatever pagans beg for, their petitions come true.
> Pagan-villagers do not hesitate [to donate for the construction of a pagoda].
> The gods bless their generosity as their contribution.
>
> Those passing by this place should show respect;
> There dwells a divine presence, so miracles are often granted.
> Whoever goes to the middle of the mountains,
> There, whatever they pray for, peace is granted.

---

while "Chúa Bà" is primarily related to mercy and protection. In addition, the term "Chúa Bà" used in *The Poem* can refer to either "goddess" for Vietnamese non-Christians or the Blessed Virgin Mary for Vietnamese Christians. By using this term, *The Poem* shows an honest and gradual development of the chapel of OLLV. The fact that the people lived in the mountains also implies that they were poor, less educated, and lacking equipment, even in modern times. See N. Trần, *Cơ Sở Văn Hóa Việt Nam*, 140.

49. Hồ, *The Poem*, lines 1–8. Translation mine. I try in my translations both to keep close to the original meaning and to make sense in English.

The Story of the Apparitions of Our Lady of La Vang

> Those who collected wood and made charcoal
> All come to pray and petition.
>
> Our people work with fair effort,
> Gathering leaves and collecting wood to build a pagoda.[50]

These lines state that the non-Christian people built a pagoda by gathering leaves and collecting wood, materials available in the wild mountainous terrain. That means the pagoda was simple and relatively inexpensive. Because this area was a sacred place, everyone respected it when passing by. In *The Poem*, the pagoda is built because of the favors abundantly granted to people who prayed there.

Why do the non-Christians eventually hand over the shrine to Christians? *The Poem* explains this question when it describes the village chiefs experiencing nightmares:

> The village chiefs complete the construction, then go home,
> Pleased that the villagers worked hard.
>
> Having gone home delighted, now deep asleep, the village chiefs
> Suddenly dream in a thrilling manner:
>
> At the pagoda, gods and Buddhas are displeased.
> They appear to the village chiefs.
> The gods and Buddhas are cast outside.
> There, the Christian Lady reveals a miraculous authority.
>
> She enters [the pagoda] and fights so wildly
> that all gods and Buddhas flee.
> Her powerful voice spreads,
> Damages all incense, water bowls, and the shelter-temple.[51]

Just as they are in biblical stories, the dreams that appear in this poem are meaningful. The village chiefs are confused and frightened

---

50. Hồ, *The Poem*, lines 9–22. "Chức dịch" [non-Christian village chief] might mean both a head of a village and the village councils who rule the village. In the past, Vietnamese society was organized primarily into villages and citadels, including cities or towns. A village chief and his councils independently led each village. There were two types of village councils: one was well-educated, and the other comprised the elderly (see N. Trần, *Foundation of Vietnamese Culture*). When Christianity arrived in Vietnam in 1533, whole villages often converted; therefore, there were Christian and non-Christian villages. "Chức việc" refers to laymen in parish councils and distinguishes their leadership positions from non-Christian village chiefs. For more detail, see A. Trần, *Thoáng Nhìn Giáo Hội Công giáo Việt Nam*, 30–35.

51. Hồ, *The Poem*, lines 27–39.

when they wake from their dream because they thought what they had done was good, and do not understand why these omens should follow. When they realize that they all shared the same dream, they decide to go to the shrine for more information. When they arrive, they are shocked to see with their own eyes that the events that unfolded in their dream had in fact occurred.[52] After the village chiefs talk with one another, they recognize that the sacred site belongs to the Christian Lady:

> Together, they arrive just outside
> and see statues of gods and Buddhas laid down.

. . .

> Together, they have a serious discussion:
> It is better to entrust this pagoda to Christianity.

> They dismantle the pagoda, afraid that [the Christian Lady] is angry,
> But they fear to destroy it all because they calculate the wasted cost,

> Regretting to waste the villagers' labor,
> For three months of labor costs a lot of money.
> Buddhas are now not still, they thought.
> They intend to seek another place to construct a pagoda.[53]

They decide to hand the shrine over but first invite the lay leader of the Christian village of Thach Han and tell him the whole story:

> He arrives for a meeting in person.
> The chiefs tell their story and analyze it clearly.

> [They say]
> "There, incredible miracles are accomplished.
> They [the village chiefs] entrust the temple to your Christian religion.
> A thatched pagoda is completed.
> its garden is fenced around.
> Your religion receives it for the Lady,
> To care and nurture the banyan tree.[54]

---

52. *The Poem* reflects one of the Vietnamese perspectives on dreams, especially those which can be testified to.

53. Hồ, *The Poem*, lines 40–62. Given the wilderness location, construction of such a pagoda probably had a high labor cost.

54. In the past, every village had *"Cây đa- giếng nước- sân đình"* [a banyan tree, a well station, and a common house]. These became symbols of community. See N. Trân, *Foundation of Vietnamese Culture*.

> This place is the place of *"Chúa Bà"* [Our Lady]
> So, gods, Buddhas, and devils abstain."[55]

In these lines, *The Poem* depicts a peaceful transfer of the shrine from non-Christian to Christian. They also showcase the pastor, who received the news from the lay leader:

> The layman parish president accepts.
> Immediately, he informs his pastor about the entrustment.
>
> The pastor listens, smiling:
> *"Chúa Bà"* grants a miracle so that non-Christians may believe.[56]

These lines reflect that the non-Christians who occupied the sacred place and built a thatched shrine expressed tolerance towards the Christians. These lines also imply that the story of OLLV was told at the shrine. It is interesting that the priest also addresses the Blessed Virgin Mary as *"Chúa Bà,"* echoing the first lines of *The Poem* and reinforcing the heavenly power of the Marian apparition.

Having received authority over the shrine, the pastor is quick to dedicate it to OLLV. He appoints a person to take care of the shrine and writes a letter that recounts the story of OLLV to send to all Christian communities:[57]

> Now we[58] compose a poem,
> For the public to send to convents
> And to all parishes and dioceses.[59]
> Many generations have passed,
> and now the Blessed Virgin Mary appears again miraculously.
>
> Messengers receive the poem to deliver,
> Some go to *Nghe* [north], some go to the Citadel [south].

---

55. Hồ, *The Poem*, lines 68–76.

56. Hồ, *The Poem*, lines 75–80. This history of entrustment may imply not only that the apparition was well known, but also conflict about ownership of the sacred place.

57. In the past, and even during the twentieth century, one priest was expected to take care of several churches. In every church and chapel, the priest appointed a good layman as parish president to act as sacristan. See more in the decrees of the councils in Phố Hiến in 1760, Cái Sen in 1842, Kẻ Sặt in 1900, and 1912.

58. "Ta" can be either "I" or "We" and refers to someone who is aware of his or her own power.

59. "Nhà Chung" [common houses] might be diocesan or parish houses where *thầy giảng* lived. These were considered religious men who assisted pastors or bishops in the mission.

> People read the poem, which tells the narrative fully,
> All praise the name of the Holy Mother.[60]
> The story of Our Lady is known, near and far,
> Through the sea, through the rivers.[61]

Which story is that? *The Poem* does not specify or elaborate, suggesting that its intended hearers already knew the story of OLLV, which seems to be meant. *The Poem* states that abundant favors were granted to all the Vietnamese, both Christians and non-Christians, and it portrays OLLV as a sort of Vietnamese godmother.

As these favors continue to be granted and the shrine develops, the story of OLLV spreads, and people's confidence in OLLV grows as miraculous events occur. For example, when the thatched shrine of OLLV needs to be renovated, the layman who takes care of it reports to his pastor.[62] While the layman is away from the shrine, a miraculous event unfolds:

> When he is only halfway, he just goes to a rectory.
> At the pagoda, the Lady purchases fabrics [from a female draper passing by].
>
> Two women [Our Lady and the female draper] trade cloths,
> calculate the price of the five fabric rolls.
>
> The Lady has bought the fabrics to fix [the pagoda].
> She puts them into a box and seals it.
> Our Lady makes an appointment with the female draper
> To come back to receive payment at the rising of dawn.
> The two women have a longer conversation:
> These fabrics, I bought to sew curtains.
> As the conversation ends, the female draper wishes her goodbye, departing.
> At dawn, she returns to take the payment.[63]

As *The Poem* goes on to say, the female draper returns the following day to collect payment for the cloth, but when she meets the guard and states her purpose, he becomes angry and tells her to leave. She defends herself, however, and asks him to open the trunk where the Lady stored the fabric. When the guard opens the trunk, he finds the cloth and

---

60. In Vietnamese the literal word is "grandmother." Goddesses in Vietnam are called "grandmother" because Vietnamese culture has great respect for women, mothers, and grandmothers. This explains why they praise the Blessed Virgin Mother as the Holy Grandmother.

61. Hồ, *The Poem*, lines 83–92.

62. Hồ, *The Poem*, lines 93–96.

63. Hồ, *The Poem*, lines 97–108.

enough money to pay for the goods. This part of the narrative promotes the idea that OLLV appeared many times and, having chosen this place, cared for the needs of the people. After this marvelous event, *The Poem* depicts OLLV appearing multiple times as La Vang developed from the wilderness to a pagoda and ultimately into a shrine of OLLV:

> The poem says, "[in the name of] God, the Trinity
> [Our Lady of] Help of Christians, here is information:
>
> The Holy Mother appeared at a holy shrine,
> Holding the Holy Son, the Mighty God.
> The Holy Mother wears a golden crown, the most beautiful.
>
> . . .
>
> That is Our Lady, the Mother of God.
> She chose the quiet place in the midst of La Vang.
>
> . . .
>
> Oral tradition recounts: The Holy Mother appeared
> Holding the Baby Jesus, extremely majestic.[64]

The Poem states that the pastors eventually decide to build a brick church on the site and dedicate it to OLLV:

> Now then, we [the pastors] must write a letter,
> To advise the laity that they must take care of the paperwork.
>
> Listening to the letter, everyone is delighted.
> Having no money for donation, they readily volunteer their labors.
>
> They carry bricks, cement, and sand.
> They do not mind the long and rough road and hard work.[65]

The lay faithful are excited about the pastors' decision and volunteer to rebuild the church of OLLV. This time, the church is constructed with bricks, and the work is completed in 1900. Another example of collaboration between the pastor and the lay faithful occurs when the procession of OLLV is organized during the dedication:

---

64. Hồ, *The Poem*, lines 127–31, 181–82.
65. Hồ, *The Poem*, lines 233–38.

> The date of July thirteenth comes—such a beautiful day.
> The laity of Cổ Vưu parish ask their pastor for permission:
>
> "May we march in the procession of Our Lady?
> Around all neighborhoods, loving remembrance will be marked
> For a long time, Our Lady is placed at our church.
> Tomorrow, Our Lady will be brought to La Vang.
>
> Let's process with Our Lady to all neighborhoods [the villages around Cổ Vưu]
> so that Our Lady may visit our children and our relatives."
>
> The pastor listens to their heartfelt request.
> He approves, and it pleases them.[66]

Here, *The Poem* suggests that the active collaboration between the lay faithful and the clergy conforms to the model relationship of the shepherd and his sheep. Moreover, the clergy collaborated with them to prepare for the procession, as will be explored below.

Even though *The Poem* does not include a full description of the apparition and does not include the words "Our Lady of La Vang," it tells the history of the shrine clearly and incorporates the unique elements of the apparition consistent across its appearances: the Blessed Virgin Mary chose La Vang; she held the Baby Jesus; she was so beautiful; and she has appeared to both non-Christians and Christians many times. The Vietnamese people responded to her by building a pagoda. Why did non-Christians, rather than Christians, do such a thing? An answer will be provided in the second chapter. Another question, however, is why *The Poem* does not include the exact words "Our Lady of La Vang" despite having two descriptions of the Marian apparitions. The answer likely rests in the fact that *The Poem* was limited in its amount of detail because it assumed knowledge of them. It is also possible that her words were well remembered and that the faithful, even the Vietnamese people, valued actions (in this case, the healings) more than words, as the oral traditions suggest.

The Poem mentions the abundant favors that were given to Christians and non-Christians alike within the blended descriptions of the apparitions of OLLV, which do not include any moments where she is speaking directly. The tale of the church's building occupies a great deal of the text, including the legend of the female draper. The favors that OLLV grants seem to dominate *The Poem*. In the story, OLLV answers all

---

66. Hồ, *The Poem*, lines 255–64.

types of human needs, and many people claim that their petitions have been granted. For example, *The Poem* includes the following description of OLLV's favors:

> Our Lady is authority and wisdom,
> The dead are raised and live normally.
>
> Someone goes bankrupt, loses their path,
> They fall into poverty and cry out to Our Lady.
> Our Lady protects, consults, and
> leads them to peace as she promised.
>
> If across the sea, someone sails,
> And meets a stormy sea, they cry out to Our Lady;
> Our Lady calms the waves and rebukes the winds.
> Whoever trusts, despite a hundred miseries, will be well.
>
> Whatever misfortunes, how far distant or whatever circumstances may come,
> Whoever, non-Christians or Christians, their petitions are heard.
>
> Whoever has a disease or disability,
> Comes to the shrine to pray, and the miracle is granted.
>
> Whoever has a distorted mouth or twitching hands,
> Whoever has asthma or a cough, all are recovered.[67]

Lines 159 through 164 also repeat that many people from near and far, and even those who are unable to come to La Vang, trust OLLV and have their petitions granted:

> Many people who are suffering,
> Despite being incapable of coming, their petitions are granted
>
> As long as they cry to the Holy Name,
> Asking Our Lady at the shrine for help.
>
> Whoever bequeaths gifts or money,
> Sends it there, their petitions are granted, they are at peace.[68]

In addition to discussing these miracles, *The Poem* often reminds us, or at least signals, that the apparitions and the sacred land of La Vang are connected. In other words, the Holy Mother chose La Vang as *the*

---

67. Hồ, *The Poem*, lines 165–80.
68. Hồ, *The Poem*, lines 159–64.

place to express her maternal love, care, and protection to her Vietnamese children.

The Poem also mentions instances of healing that arise from contact with the leaves on the site and describes the custom of picking up leaves from the grounds surrounding the church of OLLV. This act reflects the trust and confidence that people have in OLLV and her ability to heal them. Devotees believe that there is no better medicine:

> Many people pick banyan tree leaves,
> Others pluck grasses to take with them.
> No medicine is as effective in recovery
> As the leaves and grass around the shrine of Our Lady.
>
> . . .
>
> Whatever grows on grounds surrounding the Church:
> Leaves of myrtles, tamarind, indigo, and binary at La Vang are good.
> Whatever leaves, whatever grasses
> They take home, boil, and drink, the disease disappears.[69]

As previously noted, the descriptions of the apparitions and the reported miracles were held to be sufficient, in the context of Vietnamese culture, to prove the presence of the Blessed Virgin Mary at La Vang.[70] In *The Poem*, it sounds like the apparition was made credible and preserved in memory because of the abundant favors that OLLV granted. These, in other words, were just as important as the original apparition, because they demonstrate that OLLV continued to keep her promise.

Finally, *The Poem* describes the celebration and procession that took place in the diocese of Huế once the church of OLLV was erected. Many members of the diocese, including the lay faithful and their pastors, participated. Marian devotion had been commonly practiced among Vietnamese Catholics since the earliest missionaries arrived in Vietnam.[71] Also, European religious congregations, such as the Order of Preachers and the Order of Friars Minor, were especially devoted to the Blessed

---

69. Hồ, *The Poem*, lines 185–88; 191–94; 319–20.

70. There are several Marian shrines in Vietnam that were initially established when people claimed to received favors from Our Lady there; see Đức Mẹ Việt Nam [*The Holy Mother of Vietnam*], https://sites.google.com/site/memariavietnam, accessed December 30, 2020.

71. See Terres, "Le culte de la Sainte Vierge au Tonkin Oriental," 141–64. Joseph Terres was the Bishop of the Diocese of Hai-Phong during 1875–1906. See Ngọc Ấn Martin Lê, "La dévotion Mariale au Việt Nam," 264–350.

The Story of the Apparitions of Our Lady of La Vang

Virgin Mary. For Vietnamese converts, it seems fair to say, the main content of their faith was the Creed and devotion to the Blessed Virgin Mary.[72]

After 1886 the persecution decree was revoked, making it possible for Vietnamese Christians to live with considerably more freedom and less fear. Despite the poverty of the faithful, a brick church of OLLV was built, with the lay faithful donating and volunteering their labor for the construction of the church despite the many obstacles that they faced. Given that the recent emergence of religious freedom overlapped with the construction of the first brick church dedicated to OLLV, the lay faithful and clergy were extremely excited about the dedication and procession, an event that is also described in Bonin's article. After six years of difficult work, *The Poem* reports that the lay faithful were elated to see the finished church:

> Six years, days, and months have gone by,
> The brick church, now, is complete.[73]

The Poem describes how the lay faithful from villages and citadels prepare to express their thanksgiving to God for the appearance of the BVM at La Vang:

> Everywhere, down to the sea, up to the mountains,
> Villagers and citadel people, all are participating.
>
> They practice hymns, songs, and dance.
> Composing musical players, they practice performing.
>
> They are dressed in noble outfits.
> Náp, sticks, flags, paddle fans, parasols, noble parasols, and lamps are ready.[74]
>
> They create musical plays, and they practice for several months.
> All hearts are waiting for July thirteenth.[75]

---

72. For more information, see John Paul II, "Homily on the Canonization of Vietnamese Martyrs"; K. Nguyễn, *Virtues of Vietnamese Martyrs*.

73. Hồ, *The Poem*, lines 239–40. These lines directly reference a report that Patinier submitted to his bishop in 1894. This is important data because it shows the connection between the French and Vietnamese languages.

74. "Náp, hèo, cờ, quạt, lọng, tàn ba đăng" are a group of the items used in a ceremony of either kingships or indigenous religious processions.

75. The Vietnamese people, including Vietnamese Catholics, calculate dates according to the lunar calendar.

> In some places, the laity are so excited,
> They add a flower dance and stick dance teams.[76]

Just as the clergy and the lay faithful are excited to rehearse performances for the ceremony, they are also delighted on the day that the ceremony takes place. They overcame all obstacles to join the ceremony:

> The participants go on foot, other drive boats,
> On roads, on rivers, they come according to their condition.[77]

The Poem emphasizes the diversity of parishes that participate in the ceremony, including the pastors and their parishioners. They perform many plays and musicals and even compete with one another:

> The flower teams and lamp teams have been practicing for a long time.
> Now they perform for competition and for joy.
>
> Whoever joins, whatever teams,
> Lamp teams or *náp* teams, all are invited to make petitions day and night.
>
> Whatever parish sings hymns well
> Is rewarded or encouraged in the contest.
>
> *Cổ Vưu* and *Ngô Xá* parishes' trumpet teams
> Perform and dance; their complement is the first reward.
>
> *Phủ Cam* parish's teams play flutes to adore the Eucharist.
> The drums, organs, bamboo flute, and bamboo percussion teams play quite well.
>
> *Bố Liêu* parish's team sings hymns beautifully.
> With good voices, they chant beautiful hymns.
>
> *Kẻ Văn* parish's team performs with flags and images
> Beautifully and all are pleased.[78]

These passages discuss not only how many parishes, but how many people of the diocese participated. Their sense of excitement echoes Bonin's impression of how much the lay faithful love OLLV. *The Poem* continues:

---

76. Hồ, *The Poem*, lines 241–52.
77. Hồ, *The Poem*, lines 53–54.
78. Hồ, *The Poem*, lines 267–80.

> From major roads to wilderness[79]
> Two sides of magnificent groups take walks magnificently.
> The drums, gongs, firecrackers teams play,
> They recite, their beautiful singing pleases the ears
>
> The distance of procession is around seven miles
> Two lines stretching almost half of the distance.
>
> The pastors had just celebrated Masses[80]
> They all line up in liturgical vestments to march in the procession.
> The bishop is in the middle of the procession.
> Major seminarians and minor seminarians march in an orderly way.
> At six in the morning, the bell is rung,
> and a magnificent palanquin appears, clearly seen.
>
> Cổ Vưu parish's teams are in order.
> They escort the palanquin and put the statue of the Holy Mother on it.
> The sun rises just high enough
> to shine brightly on the face of the Holy Mother.
> The clouds fly as if walking on the sky,
> covering the sky and making the temperature cool.
>
> In experiencing that, everyone realizes
> that grace is granted by the Holy Mother.[81]

As these passages show, the devotion to OLLV incorporated a variety of pious practices, including the rosary, musicals, performances, processions, and chanting, along with uniquely Vietnamese customs. It is also important to note that at the dedication, devotion to Our Lady under the title "Our Lady of Help of Christians" was strong—for example, the use of the title "Help of the Christians" in the context of God's love and the apparition in line 128. In fact, this title had been part of the practice of devotion to the Blessed Virgin Mother in the diocese since the early nineteenth century.[82]

Finally, the faithful's love of OLLV is depicted as inspiring the clergy, especially the French clergy. Line 256, for instance, states that the lay

---

79. Note that "wilderness" implies La Vang because the area was a jungle.

80. At the time, Mass was celebrated in the Latin language, which most of the lay faithful did not understand. See Dutton, *The Tây Sơn Uprising*.

81. Hồ, *The Poem*, lines 293–310. La Vang in Quảng Trị is usually hot in August when the three-year pilgrimage occurs. The cooler temperature also returned again during the twenty-eighth national pilgrimage to OLLV in 2008.

82. See Q. Trần, *Pilgrimage to the Diocese of Huế*, 1:174–76.

faithful successfully received permission from their pastor, who we can assume is Bonin, to have a procession.[83] The Poem's tone imparts a sense of thanksgiving and rejoicing, and its final lines hint towards a future filled with heartfelt remembrance:

> Once again, they invite one another into the sanctuary in order to give thanks.
> Despite departing, the pilgrims do not want to leave.
>
> Graces are granted abundantly.
> When someone goes on this pilgrimage, they remember it forever.[84]

In ending with an emphasis on the lay faithful's remembrance, The Poem suggests that they will continue telling the story of OLLV and expressing their devotion. The participants will recall the dedication of the church and the solemn ceremony of the procession and return home with a renewed sense of devotion. By the end of The Poem, embarking on a pilgrimage to OLLV becomes an important part of strengthening faith during daily trials.

When comparing the works of Jean-Louis Bonnand, François Xavier Charle Patinier, Claude Bonin, Joseph Trang V. Trần, and Dominic Cẩn Ngọc Hồ, several elements are constant, despite inconsistencies. These components include the apparitions, the history of the shrine, the cult of OLLV, the name OLLV, and the title "Our Lady of Help of Christians." Taken together, these commonalities offer important information for researching the history and development of devotion to OLLV.

Even though there is a wealth of oral traditions around OLLV, some skepticism still exists as to whether the apparition really happened. In a critique of the Marian apparitions at La Vang, Xuân Đắc Nguyễn, a non-Christian Vietnamese American scholar, published an online article titled "Seeking Understanding of the History of the Church of La Vang through Christian Sources" in 2008.[85] Nguyễn denies the story of the apparition OLLV because there is no written documentation from the first century of the apparition, and what is preserved is in what he deems unworthy sources. One of the issues that he raises has to do with the property of the Basilica of Our Lady of La Vang. Based on several lines of The

---

83. Hồ, The Poem, lines 256–64.

84. Hồ, The Poem, lines 320–24.

85. Xuân Đắc Nguyễn, "Tìm hiểu lịch sử Nhà thờ La Vang qua các nguồn tư liệu của Thiên Chúa Giáo" ["Seeking Understanding of the History of the Church of La Vang through Christian Sources,"] January 11, 2008, https://sachhiem.net/TONGIAO/TOAKHAM/NguyenDXuan.php, accessed 8 September 2019.

Legend Poem of La Vang, Nguyễn concludes that the Buddhist laity were kind, while the Blessed Virgin Mary was cruel, because of the violent actions of both OLLV and the Catholics who took control of the pagoda and renovated it into a church.[86] He argues that many scholars ignore *The Poem* because it portrays OLLV as unkind. He notes that most Catholic historians ignore the apparition; for example, two well-known Catholic clergy scholars, Léopold Michel Cadière and Peter Huồn P. Phan, did not write about the story of OLLV.[87] He also mentions that two Buddhist monks sued the Catholics in an attempt to take back the pagoda.[88] This leads Nguyễn to conclude that OLLV was only a legend and not a real historical figure, and to condemn the Catholics for violently taking over the pagoda and renovating it into a church.

However, as M. Bernard's work (as explored below) shows, this is not the only possible reading of *The Poem*. His interpretation is that the pagoda was built when persecutions made it impossible for Christians to gather at the site. Thus, it was claimed for Buddhist practices. Nguyễn's interpretation also does not mention *The Poem*'s commitment to an inclusiveness of all who come to pray, no matter who they are, gains credibility as it is reflected even in current devotion. Furthermore, as M. Bernard mentions, *The Poem* clearly states that the donation of the site occurred because the village chiefs had the same dream. This is powerful evidence because Vietnamese culture has always placed great emphasis on dreams, especially when several people have similar dreams.[89] Moreover, Nguyễn ignores sources that were created after the first pilgrimages in both French and Vietnamese. Although he quotes lines 35–36 of *The Poem* in order to demonstrate that OLLV and the Catholics were violent, these lines describe the dreams of three village leaders. Line 70 also states that the village leaders collectively decided to donate a pagoda to Christians because they, as line 75 states, agreed that La Vang is the place of OLLV. *The Poem* recounts a peaceful transition, and there is no reason to discount this evidence. *The Poem* presumes the readers already know the

86. Xuân Đắc Nguyễn, "Seeking Understanding," 2.11.

87. Xuân Đắc Nguyễn, "Seeking Understanding," 1.

88. Xuân Đắc Nguyễn states that Buddhist monk Thích Chơn Tế in Huế and Buddhist monk Thích Phước Châu in Quảng Trị sued Catholics by sending their request to the Vietnamese government. Nguyễn does not provide a date, but see "Hòa thượng Thích Chơn Tế gửi thư cho Giáo hoàng Bênêđíctô thứ 16 Vatican City," 2005, https://phathocdoisong.com/hoa-thuong-thich-chon-te-gui-thu-cho-giao-hoang-benedicto-thu-16-vatican-city.html. It is unclear what happened or the outcome.

89. Van Chung Nguyễn, *Giải Mã Giấc Mơ*. This perspective echoes biblical narratives. For example, Saint Joseph and the magi had prophetic dreams in Matthew's Gospel.

story of the apparition and so would understand the prior claim on the site that the dreams seem to recognize.

Although Nguyễn claims that Léopold Michel Cadière and Peter Huôn P. Phan did not recount the story of OLLV, they actually did. Cadière not only affirmed the apparition handed among both French missionaries and the Vietnamese clergy and faithful, but also investigated, which will be analyzed below.[90] Phan, too, narrated the apparition of the BVM at La Vang in 1798. He mentioned the persecution of the Christians, the investigation into the apparitions, and the history of the story of OLLV in both his Vietnamese and English publications.[91] My review of Nguyễn's article has led me to affirm not only the credibility of the story of OLLV, including the miracles she has granted to all the Vietnamese people who cry out to her, but also to discern the influence of what seems to be current tension between some Buddhists and Catholics. *The Poem* may reflect this conflict at an earlier point in time or may be retrojecting it backwards in time. After the non-Christian village chiefs entrust the pagoda to the Christians through a layman parish president, the latter informs his pastor. After listening to the report, the pastor credits those same dreams as the miracle of OLLV.

The following sections analyze the writings of scholars who recount the story OLLV, the history of the pilgrimages, the cult of OLLV, and the healings that took place. The texts were authored by individuals who were French, American, Vietnamese, and members of the Vietnamese diaspora. Most of them were also clergy.

As a well-respected and widely known scholar of science, the Vietnamese cultures, and religions and Christianity in Vietnam, Léopold Michel Cadière (1869–1955) was a French member of the Society of Foreign Missions of Paris.[92] He was sent as a missionary to Cochinchine septentrionale in 1892. His "Souvenir" ("Memoires") strengthens the tradition of OLLV by first investigating the history of devotion to OLLV, then studying the rituals employed in the cult of OLLV, and finally providing descriptions

---

90. Cadière's "Souvenir" mentions his study of the history of OLLV and devotion to her (The AMEP, vol. DH. 430/06, 39–48).

91. See P. Phan, *History of the Catholic Church in Vietnam*, 305–19. Phan preached the story of OLLV at the Thống Nhất Theater in Sài Gòn on February 18, 1959; this was published under the title "*Đức Mẹ và Dân Tộc Việt Nam*" ["The Holy Mother and the Vietnamese Nation"] in *Our Lady of Perpetual Help Magazine* 119 (Sai-Gon: CTTT, April 1959), 105–7.

92. The Society of Foreign Missions of Paris [Société des Missions Etrangères de Paris] is a Roman Catholic mission established in 1658–63 for evangelizing Asian countries. See https://missionsetrangeres.com.

of the great pilgrimage that took place in 1910.[93] After teaching at An Ninh seminary and working in pastoral ministry at several parishes, Cadière was appointed pastor of the church of Cổ Vưu in 1904 as the successor of Father Bonin. In taking this position, he also oversaw the Church of OLLV. While carrying out his ministry there, Cadière investigated the apparition of OLLV, did ethnographies of the rituals of and devotion to OLLV, and organized the triennial pilgrimages. He met the faithful, including the old and young among the lay faithful as well as native priests and missionaries, in particular his predecessors Fathers Patinier, Bonnand, and Bonin. Cadière declared that "They [all] spoke to me about the apparition."[94] Cadière did not write down what he heard; however, he committed himself to further study about the history of the pilgrimages to OLLV. This implies not only that the oral traditions of La Vang were continuing to be handed down by devotees, but also that Cadière believed what he was being told.

Cadière went on to study devotion to OLLV by first interpreting the name "La Vang," by examining miracles including healings and the birth of a child, and by reporting on local rituals. Cadière argued that "La Vang" might come from either the name of a plant (spelled "Lá Vằng") or from a word for a leaf that has changed to a yellow color (spelled "Lá Vàng"). He concluded that it probably derived from the second meaning, because when the Blessed Virgin Mary appeared, she stood on grass that transformed into yellow leaves. As a scientist, Cadière also researched the instances of healing that emerged from herbs around the church. Because the Vietnamese use many types of plants to treat illness or disease, Cadière doubted the miraculous character of the healing. However, he observed that a native priest offered blessings for the leaves on the grounds of the church. Many pilgrims, however, did not bring their leaves to be blessed because, they said, "if the herbs heal, it is because OLLV granted that. No need to have them blessed."[95] Moreover, it was believed that "OLLV grants children."[96]

---

93. Léopold Michel Cadière, "Souvenir," AMEP, vol. DH. 430/06, 39–48. This brief work mentions his childhood and vocation to the priesthood, then turns to a fuller record of his experiences as a missionary in the diocese of Huế since 1892. He remained there until his death in 1955.

94. Léopold Michel Cadière, "Souvenir," AMEP, vol. DH. 430/06, 39. The original quote is, "On me parla d'une apparition."

95. "Si les plantes guérissent c'est que Notre Dame de La Vang leur donnait cette vertu. Inutile donc de les faire bénir. C'est sans doute le raisonnement que se faisaient les pèlerins" (Cadière, "Souvenir," 44–45).

96. "Notre Dame de La Vang accorde aussi des enfants."

As a pastor, Cadière probably helped to develop the rituals of OLLV which he recorded. These rituals included the annual pilgrimage, which takes place on the first new days of the Lunar New Year, and the triennial pilgrimage, which takes place every three years in August. Cadière, it appears, was good at collaboration. According to his memoirs, when he received the new mission at Cổ Vưu in 1904, he was told to prepare the triennial pilgrimage. He provided no details about this pilgrimage except to credit Father Bonin, who helped him with the task, since he had little experience in this area. He further provided more details about the triennial pilgrimage in 1910. For example, he informed the faithful about the pilgrimage and led the local people to decorate the Church. Through collaboration, Cadière made it accessible for a diverse range of pilgrims to come to participate in the solemn procession; he worked with the train system to add more trips and a more conveniently located stop, allowing many more people to go on pilgrimage. Finally, Cadière involved himself in the devotion to OLLV not only as an organizer but also as a devotee. He ordered a palanquin to carry the statue of OLLV in procession, seeking to participate in Vietnamese culture. Although this attempt was unsuccessful due to the expense, his work displayed his engagement with and belief in OLLV. Furthermore, he also directed, edited the painting of the church of OLLV, including an image of Our Lady of Victory dedicated to her (fig. 1), and ordered multiple printings.[97]

In "Souvenir," Cadière contributed three necessary pieces of evidence to reinforce the history of OLLV. First, Cadière is probably the first writer to claim to have scientifically investigated the history of devotion to OLLV and to recognize that the oral tradition of OLLV has been handed down among the local people and French missionaries. (He says that he had not, however, attempted to write the story of OLLV herself because his friend, Father Joseph Trang V. Trần, had already published it.) Second, his contribution fills a gap in the history of triennial pilgrimages to OLLV. None of the other early accounts, and no recent scholars, have mentioned the second and the third triennial pilgrimages. While describing the triennial pilgrimage in 1910, he mentions that, during his time there (1904–10), he hosted three triennial pilgrimages.[98] This sug-

97. Cadière, "Souvenir," 40–41; See A Pastor of Co Vuu, "Ảnh Tượng Đức Chúa Bà La Vang bằng giấy."

98. "Par suite, de l'incidence des années de processions, j'eus, pendant les six ans que je passai à Cổ Vưu, à organiser trois de ces grandes processions" (Cadière, "Souvenir," 45).

gests that the second great pilgrimage took place in 1904 and the third one must have taken place in 1907.

Fig. 1: The first brick church of Our Lady of La Vang, c. 1900 (AAOH).

Cadière's third contribution is in specifying that Bonin was the person who set up the cult/rituals of OLLV, which includes annual[99] and triennial pilgrimages as well as other Marian solemnities and memorials, for two reasons. First, if Bishop Caspar established the cult/rituals of OLLV at the first Great Pilgrimage, as most previous scholars have stated in their accounts, then Bonin was supposed to have hosted the second one in 1903. However, according to Cadière, this second pilgrimage did not happen until 1904. In his annual report in 1902, moreover, Bishop Caspar himself wrote that Bonin set up the cult/rituals of OLLV "because the lay faithful were devoted wholeheartedly to OLLV."[100] Previous work has assumed that Bonin proposed the rituals of OLLV and that the bishop approved them. This evidence seems to show harmonious collaboration between the episcopate and clergy. In sum, as an investigator and an eyewitness of early twentieth-century devotion to OLLV, Cadière affirmed her story passed on among the faithful and provided vital information to fill a gap in the history of devotion to OLLV.

Another relatively early French clergyman who discussed OLLV was François Arsène Lemasle (1874–1946). He was a member of the MEP as well as a missionary of Cochinchine septentrionale and was later appointed apostolic vicar. Like his predecessor Cadière, Lemasle did not provide a description of the Marian apparition at La Vang. He did, however, defend the cult of OLLV by saying that it was similar to the practice of Marian devotion in France. He believed that, just as France was named the kingdom of Mary, so too was "Annam."[101] Lemasle emphasized that OLLV chose La Vang and that she attracted Vietnamese people to that site. He also pointed out that, in the Vietnamese context, the ability to grant favors is linked to divine characteristics, meaning that OLLV's miracles pointed to her heavenly origins.

A third French writer, J.B. Roux (1875–1955), helped strengthen the oral and written traditions of OLLV by authoring three articles on the subject. Roux was a member of the MEP and began serving as a missionary for Cochinchine septentrionale in 1898. After serving in the diocese of Huế for thirty-four years, he began publishing about OLLV. Roux

---

99. The annual pilgrimages are performed every Lunar New Year and every August.

100. Bishop Caspar, "Annual Report," 1902, 101.

101. Lemasle, "Pèlerinage de Notre Dame de La Vang." In the mid-nineteenth century Vietnam was usually divided into the regions of Tonkin (north,) Annam (central), and Cochinchine (south). Moreover, the French often used "Annam" to refer to Vietnam as a whole.

The Story of the Apparitions of Our Lady of La Vang

certainly believed in the Marian apparitions at La Vang; however, he also suggested that some information might have belonged to the original oral traditions, and some was likely added later by devout lay faithful. His articles include accounts of the Marian apparitions, the magnificent pilgrimages, the cult of OLLV, and the custom of picking leaves from the plants surrounding the church of OLLV. His first article, "Le Grand Pèlerinage de Notre Dame de La Vang," was published 1932 and became an important source for the study of OLLV.[102] In this piece Roux reaffirms the Marian apparition at La Vang, which he verifies happened under the reign of the Tây Sơn Dynasty. He also emphasizes that the Holy Mother chose La Vang as the place in Vietnam, specifically, where she would grant abundant favors to those who trusted her:

> What is evident is that the Blessed Virgin chose this solitary valley for her foothold in Annam, as she chose others in various countries of the world. It is she who attracts the crowds there, and she delights in distributing her spiritual and temporal graces abundantly.[103]

These powerful passages not only helped build on the work of J.B. Roux's predecessors but also motivated him to contribute a second article, which was published in 1935. Here, Roux pointed out that "the statue of Notre Dame de La Vang is the image of Notre Dame des Victoires"[104]—probably the first French writer to mention this. Before passing away, Roux wrote one last piece in 1954, in which he repeats the apparition of OLLV and the history of the cult of OLLV. In a new context, the beginning of the Vietnam War, he could only hope that the pilgrimages would take place again after having stopped due to World War II and the First Indochina War, although the Shrine was now located in non-Communist South Vietnam. His accounts ultimately reinforced the story of OLLV, especially among French missionaries, and they emphasized that OLLV revealed her maternal love to the Vietnamese people in the historical context of their indigenous culture.

102. Roux, "Le Grand Pèlerinage."

103. Roux, "Le Grand Pèlerinage," 833. The original quote is "Ce qui est de toute évidence c'est que la Ste Vierge a choisi ce vallon solitaire pour son pied à terre en Annam, comme elle en a choisi d'autres en divers pays du monde. C'est elle qui y attire les foules, et Elle se plaît à y distribuer abondamment ses grâces spirituelles et temporelles."

104. Roux, "Pèlerinage à Notre-Dame de Lavang," 788. The original quote is «La statue de Notre Dame de La Vang est l'image de Notre Dame de victoires: ici comme a Paris, Marie est bien le refuge des pécheurs."

J.B. Hướng, a Vietnamese priest in the diocese of Sài Gòn who made the pilgrimage to La Vang, wrote a series of articles, "Going to Visitation of the Holy Church of Our Lady of La Vang," in early 1923.[105] Apparently, Fr. Trần's *Historical Narrative of Devotion to Our Lady of La Vang* was out of print. While waiting for the second edition, Hướng wrote his articles to serve those who wanted to learn about OLLV and who planned to go on pilgrimages. By quoting Trần's account, J.B. Hướng reinforced his version of the story and his account of the cult of OLLV. His description of the journey shows that La Vang was still wild and underdeveloped. Although J.B. Hướng did not provide new details to the story of OLLV, his accounts demonstrate that devotion to her had passed well beyond the border of the diocese of Huế.

In 1938, Joseph-Marie Thích Văn Nguyễn composed a poetical prayer, "A Prayer to the Holy Mother La Vang."[106] Its fifty lines recount Nguyễn's prayer during his pilgrimage to OLLV. His poem has three themes, and the first two lines are repeated as the last two lines of his prayer. First, the poem equates the theology of OLLV with the theology of Mary. Lines 3–6 and 13–14 are Nguyễn's profession of faith: OLLV is the Mother of the Son of God; she is holy and far beyond the rest of creation; at the same time, she is rich in mercy and close to everyone; and OLLV is the Mother of God, and so too, the mother of all humans. These four elements are the fundamental theology of Mary, who is the Mother of Jesus Christ, Mother of God, and Mother of all humanity, as well as being merciful. Lines 7–8 declare that she chose to appear at La Vang, and since her arrival there, not only is the land transformed but also her grace has been constantly given. She has become well known among the Vietnamese people, Christians and non-Christians, who come from both

---

105. Hướng, "Đi Viếng Cung Thánh Đức Mẹ La Vang" ["Going to Visit the Sanctuary of Our Lady of La Vang."]

106. Văn Thích Joseph-Marie Nguyễn (JMT), "Lời Cầu Cùng Đức Mẹ La Vang." According to the archive of the Archdiocese of Huế, being born into a devout Buddhist and middle family in Huế, JMT was highly educated in accordance with Confucianism and Taoism. A promising future waited for him. However, having gone to a Catholic school in Huế, Nguyễn converted to Catholicism when he was twenty years old. This shocked his parents and extended family. Soon after that, he joined a seminary and was ordained a priest of the diocese of Huế; this was extremely difficult for his parents. Later, his sister, who was a Buddhist nun, converted as well and joined the Congregation of Lovers of the Holy Cross of Huế. Finally, his parents were baptized by him almost at the end of their lives. A translation note: "Lời Cầu" can be both singular and plural. I chose the singular to express the one trust in OLLV and also distinguish this from 1998's "The Prayer to Our Lady of La Vang," which will be discussed in chapter 3.

north and south to La Vang. In dense poetic form, Nguyễn thus mingles Mariology and OLLV in his prayer.

Second, Nguyễn invokes OLLV to respond to numerous needs. He prays for himself to be at peace, to have fidelity to God in his vocation, to avoid temptation and sins, to maintain his practice of virtues and the Ten Commandments, to develop the right worship of God, to adore OLLV, and to have a peaceful death. His prayer to OLLV is also for others, including his parents, the peace of his nation, evangelization, and the mentally and physically vulnerable. Another beautiful aspect of his prayer is that it provides a space for those who may use his prayer to pray to OLLV before concluding his prayer.

Third, Nguyễn's prayer demonstrates the mother-and-child relationship he perceives between OLLV and himself. He says he loves and believes in OLLV—the Mother of Jesus Christ, God, and humanity—who is always there to intercede for him. Therefore, he gives thanks to her right after his petitions. Coming to the end of his pilgrimage, he is to return to his daily life with his strong trust in, gratitude to, and remembrance of OLLV. In his last two lines, which repeat the first two lines, he greets her ("Hail the Holy Mother La Vang") and asks her to listen to his prayers. Nguyễn's poetical prayer is evidence of how longstanding Vietnamese pedagogy had handed on the tradition of OLLV.

Our Lady of La Vang, a book edited by Mathew Thành Văn Lê and published in the mid-1950s, provides important evidence about the oral traditions, testimonies, and accounts of the Marian apparition at La Vang.[107] Mathew Lê used many sources we have already encountered: the oral traditions of OLLV (*The Legend Poem of La Vang*), the testimony of Father Claude Bonin, the writings of Father JB Roux, Dominic Cẩn Ngọc Hồ's "Homily," Bài Hữu Nguyễn's "Explanation of the term 'La Vang,'" and a variety of historical narratives based on the oral traditions. Additionally, Mathew Lê also provides the history of the devotion and references a collection of extraordinary favors attributed to OLLV.[108]

Mathew Lê contributed three important elements to the story of OLLV: he reports more detail on how Bonin investigated the Marian apparitions

---

107. V. Lê, *Đức Mẹ La Vang* [*Our Lady of La Vang*.] The original publication was the work of Father Kinh Linh Nguyễn, an administrator of the Church of OLLV from 1948–55. As his godson, Father Mathew Lê (1919–99) edited and published it in 1955. He was born at Trí Bưu (Cổ Vưu), so his ancestors witnessed the Marian apparition at La Vang in 1798. He inherited not only strong faith, but also the traditions of devotion to OLLV. See the Archive of the Archdiocese of Huế.

108. V. Lê, *Our Lady of La Vang*, 45–71.

at La Vang; the history of the devotion; and miracles or special graces. Lê records that Father Bonin, who served as the pastor of Cổ Vưu from 1891 to 1911, interviewed the sick Mrs. Xa Thoai, a parishioner of Cổ Vưu who was nearly one hundred years old. Lê describes their conversation:

> 'You are going to depart to the particular judgment. You have to tell the truth about whether you heard when you were a child that the Blessed Virgin Mother appeared at La Vang and promised that whoever comes to La Vang to pray, the Blessed Mother will grant their petitions and teach them how to use leaves from the surrounding garden to cure disease. Have you heard about it?' In reply, she, who is devout and honest, says, 'Yes, Father. When I was a child, I heard my parents and the elderly people who said all those things. [Our] parents and grandparents told us about the story of OLLV.'[109]

Furthermore, Mathew Lê attested to two other elements of the oral traditions: 1) the Holy Mother appeared to the lay faithful who hid at La Vang due to persecution; 2) the appearance of the Holy Mother occurred around one hundred years before the first diocesan pilgrimage in 1900. Lê concluded, in agreement with Roux, that the apparition of OLLV probably occurred under the reign of King Cảnh Thịnh sometime around the time of that the decree of Christian persecution came into effect in August or September 1798. Asking why no record existed from the time of the apparition and why there was not yet ecclesial approval of the apparition, Mathew Lê pointed to three possible reasons. First, he argued, Christians continued to suffer for a long time because the persecution lasted from the Marian apparitions to the late nineteenth century, making it difficult to see how written records could exist. Second, OLLV did not expound or commend any particular new doctrine. Third, the process of formally approving the Marian apparitions requires thorough evidence and investigation. It was impossible to open a formal church investigation into the Marian apparitions at La Vang given the difficulties imposed by a century of persecution.

However, the history of OLLV still shows evidence of a continuous devotion. For Lê, the context of Christian persecutions played an important role by causing the lay faithful in Quảng Trị to flee into La Vang. Moreover, Lê also mentions that when the lay faithful gathered to pray, they often said the rosary and cried out to the Holy Mother for help.[110]

109. V. Lê, *Our Lady of La Vang*, 10–11.
110. V. Lê, *Our Lady of La Vang*, 10–19.

Mathew Lê shared a description of the apparition just as the scholars before him, emphasizing especially that OLLV held the Baby Jesus and stood next to a banyan tree. Also, he frames Our Lady's speech in a way that emphasizes the sense of comfort and encouragement that the faithful felt after hearing her. He describes how this encounter assisted them to endure suffering, as well as helping them to cure disease.

Furthermore, Mathew Lê argues that devotion to OLLV took place soon after the apparition despite the severe persecution of Christian. He recounts that the first thatched chapel burned in 1885 during the Văn Thân revolution and that the second thatched chapel was built over its foundation soon after that. Lê also mentions the well that was dug in 1903 under direction of Father Cảnh and states that the construction of the first brick church dedicated to OLLV began in 1886 under the direction of Bonnard, Patinier, and Bonin. (Like Joseph Trang V. Trần, Lê states that the blessing of church and solemn procession of OLLV took place in 1901; however, these events actually took place in 1900, as demonstrated above.) The devotions to OLLV were established, including a solemn procession that took place every three years, an annual August procession, a pilgrimage on Lunar New Year, and the use of the title "Our Lady of Help of Christians."[111] Moreover, Mathew Lê discusses the rebuilding of the church of OLLV in 1924 and its completion in 1928, and he provides a list of great pilgrimages up to 1938. He also describes the preparation for the great pilgrimage in 1955 after a suspension of nearly twenty years due to World War II and the First Indochina War.[112]

Finally, one third of *Our Lady of La Vang* presents a list of reports of the people who claimed that their petitions were answered after they went on a pilgrimage to La Vang or prayed to OLLV. Several of these stories are also mentioned in the previous works and are probably dependent on them—for example, the miracle of the female draper.[113] Other stories in this collection mention the dreams of the village chiefs found in the "Legend Poem of La Vang," the healing of a man from the leaves that grew at the shrine, the astonishing death of a man named Mr. Tho who set the shrine of OLLV on fire in 1885, and other descriptions of favors and acts of healing that were credited to OLLV.[114] This collection

---

111. V. Lê, *Our Lady of La Vang*, 24–34.

112. V. Lê, *Our Lady of La Vang*, 36–45.

113. The collection of these accounts of OLLV's favors is credited to Kinh Linh Nguyễn, the pastor of the church of OLLV between 1948 and 1955.

114. V. Lê, *Our Lady of La Vang*, 19–24.

makes clear that Vietnamese people, both Christians and non-Christians, believed that OLLV continued to grant petitions long after the apparition.

Since Vietnamese church leaders chose the shrine of OLLV as the National Marian Center and Pope John XXIII approved their request to elevate the Church of Our Lady of La Vang into a Basilica, academic interest in OLLV has grown.[115] The site and its history have attracted the attention of a diverse group of scholars, including Vietnamese individuals who have served as clergy in the diocese of Huế, Vietnamese laity, Vietnamese scholars living in the United States, and a handful of non-Vietnamese researchers. In 1961, two major publications emerged. The first was a monthly magazine called *Our Lady of La Vang*, created by Archbishop Peter Thục Đình Ngô. In this periodical, the story of OLLV was told in accordance with the oral traditions. In addition, scholars discussed relevant devotions, liturgical events, and Catholic history. For example, several articles discussed the ritual of blessing the Church of OLLV that elevated it to the rank of Basilica, such as Sơn V. Nguyễn, "What Is a Basilica?" and Toàn V. Trần, "What Is a Church?"[116] Another widely read publication from this period was Khiêm Đình Phạm, *Our Lady of La Vang is the Queen of Victory*.[117]

Xuân Ly Băng composed "La Vang Sacred Land" in 1962.[118] As one of the richest poems on La Vang, Ly Băng tells the story of OLLV by first describing the landscape and specific features around of the sacred land of La Vang. Each thing he sees or hears, such as a forest of purple myrtles, streams, a bell tower, and hymns being sung, calls readers' attention to his telling of the history of La Vang. He depicts a chaotic history of Vietnam in which, during persecutions of Christians, suffering people had to sneak into the wild forest to pray every sundown. He describes the Marian

---

115. John XXIII, *Magno nos solatio*, 381–82; Ngô, "The Invitation." I will discuss this point further in Chapter 3.

116. S. Nguyễn, "Vương Cung Thánh Đường là gì?" and T. Trần, "Nhà Thờ là gì?."

117. Đ. Phạm, Đức Mẹ La Vang là Nữ Vương Chiến Thắng. Phạm portrays OLLV as being triumphant over illness, human hearts, and enemies. He emphasizes that because she is Our Lady of Help of Christians, OLLV helps the faithful overcome all types of obstacles. He also compares the story of OLLV with a history of "Notre Dame de Victoires" so that the readers may be persuaded that history repeats itself. By reflecting on the history of "Notre Dame de Victoires," Phạm encourages his readers to grow in hope and deeper devotion to OLLV.

118. Xuân Ly Băng, "La Vang Thánh Địa" ["La Vang Sacred Land"], 9. Xuân Ly Băng is the pen name of Monsignor J.B. Lê Xuân Hoa from the Archdiocese of Huế.

The Story of the Apparitions of Our Lady of La Vang

apparition as a beautiful woman in a white dress, holding the Baby Jesus, in radiant light, who appeared at one of these sunset gatherings.

> With sweet and gentle words, OLLV says:
> Stand firm, my children, in faith [and] hope,
> Endure suffering [in faith,] peace in hearts
> Deep notes, [your] petition to Mother,
> Whoever come to cry out, from now on
> Mother will release anxiety, in this place
> Mortal hands break the leaves of the sacred garden
> See divine healing once illness.[119]

Xuân Ly Băng continues that, though the vision then vanished, the nation of Vietnam from then on belonged only to the Holy Mother. He describes how, since abundant grace has been given, many people, both Christians and non-Christians, return over and over again to La Vang. Not only are the people devoted to her, but also elements of the natural world in that region—the old forest, baboons, and purple myrtle—all witness the Holy Mother; whoever encounters OLLV may wonder at the beauty of the Divine. He ends his poem by showing his readers, moved by the story, entering the sacred land, and themselves pondering the divine beauty. Through this poem, written just a year after the solemn pilgrimage to OLLV, Xuân Ly Băng reinforced the tradition by including elements of the culture of the middle region of Vietnam to describe the landscape of La Vang. His poem proposes that the Holy Mother of God has transformed this landscape and strengthens the witness to the tradition of OLLV.

One of the most important non-Vietnamese scholars writing in French was M. Bernard, who published "La Vierge Marie au Viet Nam" in 1969, in a venue that made the story available to European Catholics.[120] In addition to giving a description of the apparition, Bernard presents the history of the basilica. He records that in the three Buddhist villages near La Vang (Cổ Thành, Thạch Hãn, and Ba Trù), the people heard about the apparition of a Thiên Mụ [Heavenly Lady] under a banyan tree and of miraculous healings for those who came to pray. During the persecution of Christians that occurred under the reign of King Minh Mạng (1820–40), the villagers built a pagoda in honor of Buddha. Bernard stated further that while Christians were unable to go to La Vang, non-Christians kept

---

119. Xuân Ly Băng, "La Vang Thánh Địa," lines 48–54.
120. Bernard, "La Vierge Marie au Viet-Nam."

up the traditions of pilgrimage. However, he reports the story that the heads of the three villages eventually donated the pagoda to the Catholics because they all had the same dream twice in which the buddhas told them to remove their statues from La Vang. The site belonged to the Christian Lady, who was more powerful than they.[121]

In the tense midst of the Vietnam War, Stanislas Ngọc Văn Nguyễn, a Vietnamese priest of the Archdiocese of Huế, published *Sacred Land of La Vang* in 1970 to reinforce the oral tradition and affirm continuing strong devotion to OLLV throughout almost two hundred years.[122] His contributions go back to the sources mentioned already, but Nguyễn offered at least three important contributions of his own to the developing tradition: he used *The Poem* to understand and verify the apparition of OLLV; he provided two lists of villages in Dinh Cát/Quảng Trị province to show that the La Vang village was established after the apparition; and he affirmed the devotion to OLLV under the title "Our Lady of Help of Christians" not only as the primary and official title of the Basilica of OLLV, but also as being in practice in the early nineteenth century.[123]

Martin Ấn Ngọc Lê was probably the first member of the Vietnamese clergy who did not belong to the diocese of Huế to offer an account of OLLV. He explored this topic in a section of his dissertation completed in 1977.[124] This work presents the story of OLLV using several sources mentioned above. He also demonstrates that Christology and Mariology had been taught together ever since Catholicism's emergence in Vietnam, and

---

121. Bernard, "La Vierge Marie au Viet-Nam," 169.

122. S. Nguyễn, *Sacred Land of La Vang*, 3.

123. S. Nguyễn, *Sacred Land of La Vang*, 46–47.

124. Martin Lê, "La dévotion Mariale au Việt Nam." Born in Gia Dinh, Sài Gòn, Lê (1946–2019) studied in Rome in 1967 and completed his dissertation in 1977; however, he was unable to return to Vietnam until 2012. In his dissertation, Lê traces the history of Marian devotion in Vietnamese Catholicism. One of his contributions is his argument about how early Christian missionaries influenced Vietnamese converts regarding devotion to the BVM. He also reinforces the unique relationship between the BVM and Jesus Christ. In addition to giving accounts of the stories of OLLV, Our Lady of Trà Kiệu, and Our Lady of La Mã Bến Tre, Lê provides several Vietnamese paintings of the BVM with the Baby Jesus based on diverse Vietnamese subcultures. He argues that Vietnamese Catholics strongly devote themselves to the BVM because she is the Mother of Jesus. This shows that Vietnamese Mariology is rooted in Christology, and therefore the story of the apparition of OLLV should be deeply studied because of the context in which the apparition appeared and the historical reality in Vietnam. Just as the preaching of the Good News is one of the primary tasks of the Church, he writes, the urgent needs of preaching Marian devotion must be facilitated in academic and pastoral ministry, especially in Vietnam.

The Story of the Apparitions of Our Lady of La Vang 51

although he does not use this term, he argues that Marian devotion may be a starting point for inculturation. For example, he provides a list of Vietnamese paintings of the Blessed Holy Mother and the Baby Jesus that incorporate Vietnamese hairstyles and traditional clothing. These pieces of Christian art, he claims, help Vietnamese people integrate the depiction of the mother-child relationship into their own ecclesial cultures. This seemed to be the earliest collection of Christian art that presents Catholicism using Vietnamese appearances, concepts, and perspectives.

To prepare for the 200th jubilee of the apparition in the 1990s, a pair of Vietnamese-language publications about OLLV appeared, one in Vietnam and the other in the United States. However, their content seems to be dependent on the sources reviewed above.[125] Also in honor of the 200th jubilee of the apparition of OLLV, the Archdiocese of Huế published *The Sanctuary of Our Lady of La Vang* in 1998.[126] Though short, this account discusses the Marian apparition and covers key historical events that occurred in the development of the devotion to OLLV. It also includes several documents written by Pope John Paul II and the Vietnamese bishops that share consistent elements but provide different presentation on the apparitions of OLLV. The work provides two explanations about the name "La Vang" and mentions the decree of King Cảnh Thịnh against the Christians in 1798. It recounts many familiar details of the story, and phrases the apparition's words as follows:

> Các con hãy tin tưởng, hãy vui lòng chịu đựng đau khổ, Mẹ đã nhận lời các con kêu xin. Từ nay về sau hễ ai chạy đến cầu khẩn cùng Mẹ ở chốn này Mẹ sẽ nhận lời ban ơn theo ý nguyện.[127]

---

125. In 1994, Joseph Hội Văn Nguyễn published *Tìm Hiểu Về Đức Mẹ La Vang* [Seeking Understanding of Our Lady of La Vang]. In this work, Nguyễn presents his readers with the context behind the history of the story about OLLV, confirms that the traditions of OLLV were passed down through the generations, and recounts the legends that occurred in the context of persecutions. The other account is Hồng Phúc's *Đức Mẹ La Vang và Giáo Hội Công Giáo Việt Nam* [Our Lady of La Vang and Catholic Church in Vietnam.] It was published in the United States in 1998. His work incorporates important elements of the story, including the context of the persecution of Christians, the apparition, a brief history of the devotion, and important figures who were involved and/or went on pilgrimages to OLLV. Although this publication does not present any information that cannot be found in the sources examined above, it is still important because Hồng Phúc himself was a devotee of OLLV, and he worked to pass down the oral traditions of OLLV through his writing.

126. Archive of the Archdiocese of Huế, *Thánh Địa Đức Mẹ La Vang* [*The Sanctuary of Our Lady of La Vang.*]

127. Archive of Archdiocese of Huế, *The Sanctuary of Our Lady of La Vang*, 8. I quote the Vietnamese version because it is key that OLLV spoke the Vietnamese

> Children, have trust, be willing to endure suffering. Mother [I] have already granted your prayers. Henceforth, all those who come to pray to Mother [me] in this spot Mother [I] will listen and grant them according to their wishes.

In reiterating these words at the beginning of the jubilee, the Archdiocese of Huế encouraged pilgrimage. Interestingly, some additional words have been added to OLLV's address, as compared to previous written accounts: "Children, have trust, be willing to suffer hardship and sorrow." These words were part of the descriptions of the apparitions but were not a part of OLLV's speech as presented by earlier scholars. However, these words do echo the account given by Pope John Paul II. These additional words remind us that the oral traditions of OLLV varied, and, at the same time, the words of OLLV and the descriptions of the apparitions were coherent enough that the story of OLLV continues to be handed down in a consistent form.[128]

Paul Chu Quang Trần is one of the best-known scholars of OLLV in the late 20th century. Being born in Huế, he inherited the tradition of OLLV. He created a collection of sources on OLLV and also composed poems about OLLV. The first of these was written in 1970 after going on the 1970 pilgrimage to OLLV. In 1998, he began to study the history of OLLV. He admitted that his work is as simple as a collection of sources; however, as we will see, he provides important contributions to the history of OLLV. For example, he was able to prove that the first great pilgrimage, the blessing of the building of the church, and the first solemn procession took place in 1900 rather than 1901 by comparing three elements: 1) the episcopal annual report in 1900, (2) the moon calendar of 1901 and 1900, and (3) *The Poem*.[129]

Trần also composed his second poem, "A Golden Page of Sacred Blood" in 1998, 200 years after the apparition of OLLV.[130] His forty verses display the history of persecution of Christians in the territories of the middle of Vietnam, where the sacred land of OLLV belongs, since the

---

language, making her comprehensible to the lay faithful. In Vietnamese culture, one often addresses others based on relationship. For example, a mother and child address one another as "mother" and "child" instead of "you" and "I."

128. For another 200th jubilee publication see Roco Do Tự Nguyễn, *Đức Mẹ La Vang: 200 Năm*. This work provides, among other things, a list of the solemn pilgrimages.

129. Q. Trần, *Pilgrimage to the Diocese of Huế*, 2:274. This is discussed in the following chapters.

130. Q. Trần, "Trang Vàng Huyết Lệ," 32–33.

The Story of the Apparitions of Our Lady of La Vang

beginning of the rejection of Christians in the seventeenth through the nineteenth centuries. He mentions the names of national leaders who ordered the persecutions and the names of locations and vulnerable Christians in the middle of Vietnam. Remarkably, the opening of the poem contains four lines that introduce martyrs, persecutions, and places of execution and, at the same time, express hope because the blood of martyrs made the land sacred. Like the Lord's "cup," their sacrifice becomes sweet fruits for others. The six last lines are uplifting:

> Blood of martyrs is [like] drops of treasure, great pearls
> The halo has glinted the crown
> the blood of martyrs pours down the sacred land
> [Their] cup of martyrdom in the past, now becomes sweet.
>
> Reading the martyr history, it is moving.
> The victory of the Holy Mother, we humans praise.

Those verses not only describe the martyrs in Vietnam, but also reinforce a theology of martyrdom. Furthermore, Trần connects the Marian devotion to the Holy Mother's help in times of difficulty. Although he does not recount the apparition of OLLV in this poem, he alludes to the huge number of the faithful who were martyred in central Vietnam. He sees the powerful help of OLLV acting through the ending of persecution and the strong witness of the martyrs. His poem is theologically significant: as it presents the three centuries of trials that the Christians went through, it suggests that OLLV conforms Christians to Christ, who empowers them to become Christ for one another.

Recently, scholarly interest has focused on OLLV. One of the first major research projects conducted around the topic of OLLV was a 2001 dissertation by Joseph-Marie Phong Thanh Trần.[131] This will be taken up in chapter 5. Meanwhile, I want to mention a few more recent pieces of interest. Hưng Quang Nguyễn's 2010 "Our Lady of La Vang and Trà Kiệu in Vietnam Seen from the Non-Christian Viewpoint" argues that following the Vietnam War, the Hanoi authorities eventually forbade the veneration of Our Lady of La Vang and of Trà Kiệu because the Catholic devotion to Our Lady became linked to "political motivation."[132]

---

131. "Notre Dame de La Vang, Viet Nam, histoire et théologie."
132. Q. Nguyễn, "Our Lady of La Vang," 71. Quang Hưng Nguyễn is an Associate Professor at the National University of Hanoi, Vietnam.

The un-welcoming of the Hanoi authorities toward veneration of Lady of La Vang and Tra Kieu is not without the cultural-religious reasons. The cultural-religious factors alone could not cause directly conflicts between Catholic Church and authorities, but they can play a definite role to increase or otherwise to dissolve those.[133]

According to Nguyễn, the veneration of Our Lady began as pure devotion but eventually became a political tool linked to anti-Communist motives. But this study itself is not without political motivation.

In 2019 Sister Maria Tuyết Thị Nguyễn published *Lạy Mẹ La Vang, Con Yêu Mến Mẹ* [*I Bow to the Mother La Vang, I Love You*] to share her childhood experience growing up near the shrine and living a consecrated life in her home diocese.[134] Maria Nguyễn is the first female author to publish a book about OLLV, which is a collection of her forty-two articles published outside of Vietnam.[135] She says, "I wrote the articles based on my experiences as a participant at the events at [the National Center of the Holy Mother] La Vang and prayed with the People of God before our gentle Mother at the Sacred Shrine of OLLV."[136] Her hope is that La Vang will become a place to nurture spirituality and faith of all her children, a place without religious discrimination. She hopes La Vang might become a center of formation to train not only ministers but also a united ministry for the whole nation.[137] One of her contributions is a reflection on a history of "The Prayer to Holy Mother La Vang."[138] This will also be taken up in chapter 5.

This chapter has offered an overview of the literature on the Marian apparition itself at La Vang in Quảng Trị, Vietnam. This review shows

133. Q. Nguyễn, "Our Lady of La Vang," 71.

134. Maria Tuyết Thi Nguyễn, *Lạy Mẹ La Vang, Con Yêu Mến Mẹ*.

135. Maria Nguyễn is a religious Sister of the Congregation of the Lovers of the Holy Cross of Huế. Her family immigrated to Quảng Trị, close to the Sacred Shrine of OLLV, in 1954, which also means that she grew up near the Shrine of OLLV. "OLLV is close to my heart," she said. She began to compose poems on OLLV, passing them on to her religious community, in 1998. Her articles were later posted at "Ben Me La Vang" ["Close to Me La Vang"], a newsletter for Vietnamese Catholics in the United States, and reposted at the website "Dân Chúa Châu Âu" ["The [Vietnamese] People of God in Europe"], which is gathers and serves Vietnamese Catholics who live in European countries (https://danchua.eu/). Sr. Mary Kim Anh Thi Tran, Interview with Sister Maria Nguyễn.

136. Sister Mary Kim Anh Thi Tran, Interview with Sister Maria Nguyễn.

137. Maria Nguyễn, *Lạy Mẹ La Vang, Con Yêu Mến Mẹ*, 115.

138. This account is further examined in chapter 5.

that the tradition of OLLV has been continuously handed down and built up in three ways: through oral channels, through Marian devotion at La Vang in Quảng Trị, especially pilgrimages, and later through written scholarship. OLLV is a living Vietnamese tradition that seems to reflect the tradition of the church. The following two chapters will explore the 225 years of the tradition of OLLV through the development of the devotion to OLLV from the beginning of the apparition to the present day.

2

The History of the Devotion to Our Lady of La Vang

THIS CHAPTER SEEKS TO understand more fully how devotion to OLLV became a fundamental part of the identity of Vietnamese Catholics. This history is divided into three periods, with the first two periods covered here. The first, from 1798–1900, focuses on the local community and parish level, where we find the dawn of devotion to OLLV among the lay faithful and their pastors in Quảng Trị province. The second period, from 1900–61, is focused on the diocesan level—that is, devotion to OLLV under the care of the Bishop of the Diocese of Huế. Finally, the third period, which is treated in the next chapter, centers on the period from 1961–2022 at the national level to examine the development of devotion to OLLV through the great pilgrimages that occur every three years. Each section examines critical context and introduces relevant sources and scholars as well as Vietnamese church leaders and the Popes who significantly impacted the devotion to OLLV at any of these three levels.

This present chapter explores devotion to OLLV as it became inculturated within Vietnamese history and culture. It concentrates on how the devotion strengthened Vietnamese Christians to stand firm in their faith during trying times. As already noted, the first historical record of persecution against Christians in Vietnam was in 1533, shortly after missionaries first arrived in the area, and stemmed from political and religious conflict. However, the most severe sanctions against Christianity, those in 1798, were also linked to socio-political entanglements. The depth of the religious and political concern about Christians led to a series of terrible persecutions and even massacres.

Fig. 2: The first two dioceses were established in 1659: Tonkin in the north and Cochinchine in the south. Source: Author edit of Wikimedia Commons, https://commons.wikimedia.org/w/index.php?title=File:Vietnam_map.png.

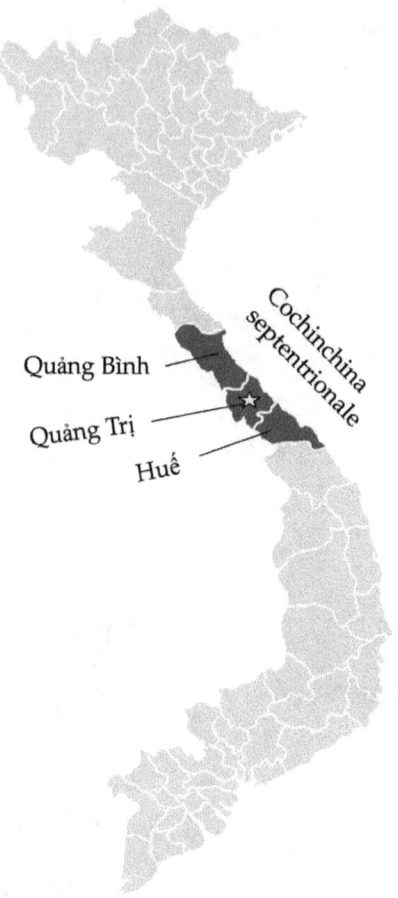

Fig. 3: La Vang belonged to the diocese of Cochinchine septentrionale, established in 1850. Source: Author edit of Wikimedia Commons, https://commons.wikimedia.org/w/index.php?title=File:Vietnam_map.png.

The First Period of the History of Devotion to OLLV (1798–1900)

During this period, which begins immediately after the apparition and extends to the blessing of the new church and the first great pilgrimage, OLLV was venerated under the Marian title "Our Lady of Help of Christians." The area of La Vang belonged to the diocese in Cochinchine;

it was known as upper Cochinchine because of its location in the center of Vietnam (fig. 2). Then, beginning in 1850, it belonged to the newly established diocese of Cochinchine septentrionale (fig. 3).[1]

Socio-Religious-Political Factors and the Circumstances of Christianity

In general, Vietnam was marked by extreme political chaos during the eighteenth and nineteenth centuries. The victory of the Tây Sơn brothers ended the reign of the Later Lê Dynasty and established the Tây Sơn Dynasty (1788–1802). This short-lived dynasty was ended by Nguyễn Ánh when he forced King Cảnh Thịnh out of Phú Xuân. Nguyễn Ánh was crowned in 1802 and took the title King Gia Long, marking the beginning of the longer, but far from peaceful, Nguyễn Dynasty (1802–1945).

Restrictions, persecutions, and massacres of Christians continued until the end of the nineteenth century. Although King Gia Long (r. 1802–20) did not decree that Christians should be persecuted, he did order restrictions in 1803. He consecrated himself as the patriarch of all religions but claimed that Christianity was a foreign religion that was secretly evangelizing in Vietnam. However, the restrictions did not prevent people from practicing their faith. Moreover, King Gia Long decreed in 1806 that local authorities were not allowed to give Christians' permission to repair damaged buildings. or build new ones.[2]

Gia Long's three immediate successors and their local officials continued restrictions and revived persecutions of Christians increasingly between 1820 and 1862. They believed this religion contradicted their native beliefs and practices. Along with the ancestor cult, they, like many Vietnamese people, observed Confucianism, Taoism, and Buddhism.[3] Therefore they often viewed other religious beliefs unfavorably, and they overestimated Christianity as a danger to their own religious observation. Violent persecution of Christians occurred continuously under Minh Mệnh (r. 1820–41), Thiệu Trị (r. 1841–47), and Tự Đức (r. 1847–83). They favored Confucianism most of all and viewed Christianity as "tà

---

1. For more detail see Bùi, *The Catholic Church in Vietnam*, 2:12.

2. Louvet, *La Cochinchine Religieuse*, 2:16–19. For more details, see Stanislas Nguyễn and Joseph Nguyễn, *Lịch Sử Giáo Phận Huế*, 176–77. Note that Buddhists were allowed to renovate old buildings.

3. For more detail, see Nguyễn and Hoàng, *The History of Buddhism in Vietnam*.

đạo" [wrong religion].⁴ For them, destroying Christianity meant protecting their national traditions.

During the reign of Minh Mệnh, for example, many missionaries were killed, and thousands of Christians were imprisoned, exiled, or executed. As a follower of Confucianism, the king viewed Christianity as an obstacle to his policies and dangerous for his dynasty. A significant part of his royal strategy thus involved defending Confucian beliefs and defeating Christianity. He prohibited missionaries from evangelizing in the name of Jesus. Jean-Louis Taberd (1794–1840) described in a letter how the decree was framed: "All Europeans residing in the nation who preach the name Jesus and put themselves as the leaders of the religion, who deceive and abuse the people, are guilty of a great crime and deserved to be strangled."⁵ The situation intensified as the king and his officers grew increasingly afraid of the influence of Christianity, which they viewed as a threat to their authority. To stop his people from following Christianity, Minh Mệnh established another series of sanctions.

The "thập điều" [ten regulations] were delivered in 1834. Seven of these regulations were against Christians, and whoever violated them was executed.⁶ While facing these conditions, Christians needed to be strengthened in their faith, hope, and love, especially because missionaries and the episcopacy were unable to function in their pastoral ministry. One question that remains to be answered about this period is how the missionaries were still able to, in some way, continue their work despite these conditions, and why most of the faithful persevered and even strengthened their trust in God and the protection of the Holy Mother.

---

4. For more details, see T. Trần, *A Brief History of Vietnam*, 2:186; Louvet, *La Cochinchine Religieuse*, 2:41; Bùi, *The Catholic Church in Vietnam*, 2:16; Trương, *A Story of Vietnam*, 131–35.

5. Taberd, "Vicaire apostolique de la Cochinchine," 470. The original quote is "Tout Européen résidant dans le royaume, qui s'y fait un nom [Jésus], et se met à la tête d'un parti qui trompe et abuse le peuple, se rend coupable d'un grand crime, et mérite d'être strangle." Taberd arrived in Cochinchine in 1820 and at Cổ Vưu in Quảng Trị in 1821. He was appointed apostolic vicar in 1827; however, he could be not consecrated until 1830. Only three years later, he had to leave the nation due to the serious persecutions. Realizing that he could not return to Cochinchine, he appointed Étienne-Théodore Cuenot as his coadjutor in 1835, and the latter became an apostolic vicar in 1840 when his predecessor passed away. For more details, see AMEP, "Documenting a Missionary: TABERD," https://irfa.paris/missionnaire/0340/, accessed January 21, 2022.

6. For more detail, see Louvet, *La Cochinchine Religieuse*, 2:47–118; T. Trần, *A Brief History of Vietnam*, 2:186, 2:196; Bùi, *The Catholic Church in Vietnam*, 2: 48–65; AMEP, "Biographies of the Missionaries"; *Annales de la Société* (1898): 36–39 and (1900): 238–46; and *Annales de la Progagation de la Foi* (1826–27), XVII, 456, 463, 467, 476.

The History of the Devotion to Our Lady of La Vang

King Thiệu Trị, Minh Mệnh's successor, reigned only six years. Although he disliked Christianity, King Thiệu Trị did not move against it until 1847, the last year of his reign, when a French businessmen shot at a Vietnamese ship. In his order in response, Thiệu Trị simply repeated what his predecessor had issued and said that he would take the persecution of Christians seriously.[7] This religious-socio-political context became even more chaotic when the French invasion of Vietnam began in 1858, a situation that intensified persecution.

In these tense circumstances, King Tự Đức assumed the throne and established many additional harsh decrees. For example, in 1861, the king issued *Sắc Lệnh Phân Sáp*, one of his most stringent orders. This decree, which consisted of five statements, ordered the exile of Christians from their villages. They were to be stripped of their property, and family members were even to be separated by sending them to different non-Christian families. Moreover, the Christians' right cheeks were inscribed with "tả đạo" [wrong religion], and their left cheeks were inscribed with the name of the place where they were exiled.[8] The cruelty of this decree was intended to degrade the dignity of the person by intentionally violating Vietnamese cultural sensibilities. First, it destroyed the family bond. Second, this decree's most sinister quality was that it forced neighbors to oppress their neighbors. Third, the decree played on Vietnamese sensibilities by teaching that Christianity preached against Vietnamese traditions, including the practice of ancestor piety. Given that Christians faced these conditions in the middle of the nineteenth century, how is it possible that the lay faithful were able to go on a pilgrimage to La Vang or even remain Christians?

In fact, during this time, entire parishes and Christian villages were destroyed, and their members were either burned or drowned. While analyzing the Christian persecutions that took place in Annam from 1820–62, J. B. Roux recognizes the strong faith of both the clergy and the faithful:

> Under the kings Minh Mang, Thieu Tri, and Tu Duc, from 1827 to 1862, the capital of Annam witnessed, so to speak without interruption, the heroism of the pastors and the faithful, affirming by their deeds and their words, before Caesar himself or his

---

7. Tuck, *French Catholic Missionaries*, 31–33.

8. Bùi, *The Catholic Church in Vietnam*, 2:419–20; Louvet, *La Cochinchine Religieuse*, 2: 171–211, 2:247–98; AMEP, "Learn about a Missionary," https://irfa.paris/en/en-learn-about-a-missionary. Etienne Theodore Cuenot was a victim of the executions in 1861.

representatives, that when it comes to the Christian faith, it is better to obey God.[9]

Like the early Christians, the Vietnamese Christians led extremely difficult lives during this period because of their faith. Becoming true disciples of Christ, they lived their faith, hope, and love through their words and deeds as they faced the choice between life or death. Identically with the ancient martyrs, they were willing to obey national leaders but put God first.[10]

Furthermore, due to socio-political conflicts primarily linked to the French invasion, anti-French movements also arose, and their followers massacred Christians, burned their houses, and dismantled or fired their churches until as late as 1886.[11] For example, the Văn Thân movement stood out as responsible for particularly violent instances of aggression against Christians, especially in central Vietnam. The motto of the Văn Thân was *"bình tây-sát tả"*—"demolish the French, kill Catholics."[12] In particular, Cổ Vưu in Quảng Trị province was a region where some of the bloodiest persecutions took place in 1885. That year, around four hundred Christians in Cổ Vưu were massacred while in a church where they had taken refuge.[13] Around two hundred lay faithful were burned in front of the shrine of OLLV.[14]

Another example is the Cần Vương movement. Patrick JN Tuck explains the goals of the movement's leader, Thuyết Thất Tôn: "He called for the massacre of collaborating mandarins, the destruction of commercial districts surrounding major towns, and above all for the wholesale

---

9. Roux, "Prisons et Prétoires du Vieux Hué," 173. The original quote is "Sous les rois Minh Mang, Thieu Tri et Tu Duc, de 1827 à 1862, la capitale de l'Annam a été témoin, pour ainsi dire sans discontinuer, de l'héroïsme des pasteurs et des fidèles, affirmant par leurs actes et leurs paroles, devant César lui-même ou ses représentants, que quand il s'agit de la foi chrétienne il vaut mieux obéir à Dieu qu'aux hommes."

10. For more detail see K. Nguyễn, *Virtues of Vietnamese Martyrs*.

11. See Bùi, *The Catholic Church in Vietnam*, 2:381–531; Louvet, *La Cochinchine Religieuse*, vol. 2. The Treaty of 1862 granted national religious freedom.

12. The Văn Thân Movement's legacy was "bình tây-sát tả" or "dẹp người Pháp, giết người Công giáo." It sought to save the country from French invasion, beginning in 1864 in the middle of Vietnam. For more details, see Stanislas Nguyễn and Joseph Nguyễn, *The History of Diocese of Huế*, 319–86.

13. For more details, see Jabouille, "Une page de L'histoire du Quang-tri septembre 1885." Jabouille was a French resident administrator in Quảng Trị province at that time.

14. See more, The Archive of the Archdiocese of Huế.

extinction of Christian villages."[15] As a result, thousands of Christians were killed or massacred. As historical records show, these brutal persecutions took place throughout the nation, but most especially in central Vietnam. Kim Trọng Trần records that "Eight French clergy and more than twenty thousand Vietnamese Christians living in the middle of Vietnam were murdered from the end of June to August in 1885."[16] Moreover, Apostolic Vicar Louis Caspar reported in a 1885 letter that the total number of martyrs in his diocese Cochinchine septentrionale was rising as more than seven thousand Christians had been massacred. He offered an account of the violent persecutions in several letters.[17]

In its last years the Nguyen Dynasty broke down and became increasingly chaotic. King Dục Đức only reigned for three days, July 20–23,1883, and in this same year, King Hiệp Hòa reigned for four months, July 30-November 29, 1883. King Kiến Phúc reigned for eight months, 1883–84, and King Hàm Nghi reigned less than a year during 1884–85.[18] In these circumstances, Christians were still seen as a major threat. But the prospect of French rule did not necessarily help Christians either. There, anti-clerical and anti-ecclesial measures also occurred in waves, especially during 1870–1940.[19] If French authorities did not favor Catholics in their own country, how could they favor them in Vietnam?

In sum, the period between 1798 and 1900 was complicated and marked by a variety of setbacks and disasters for Christians in Vietnam.[20] Yet even so missionaries, clergies, religious women and men, and many of the lay faithful persevered. As a result, the history of the Church in Vietnam has a record of about 130,000 martyrs, most of whom (about 90,000) were executed during the nineteenth century. Of the 117 martyrs canonized in 1988, 111 were executed in the nineteenth century and

---

15. Tuck, *French Catholic Missionaries*, 205–6; for more details, see pp. 215–20.

16. T. Trần, *A Brief History of Vietnam*, 2:326.

17. These letters can be found at AMEP, vol. 760, 303; 304. For more detail, see Bùi, *The Catholic Church in Vietnam*, 2: 519–21; Stanislas Nguyễn and Joseph Nguyễn, *The History of Diocese of Huế*, 338–73. In 1887, the French took authority over all of Vietnam, and the official persecutions of Christians ended despite Christians continuing to be killed sporadically. Also, apostolic vicars began to submit many reports of the martyrs for a process of beatification toward canonization. See, for example, Launay, *Les trente-cinq vénérables serviteurs de Dieu*.

18. T. Trần, *A Brief History of Vietnam*, vol. II.

19. See Gibson, *A Social History of French Catholicism*.

20. See Buttinger, *The Smaller Dragon*, 270–385; Taylor, *A History of the Vietnamese*, 398–483; Tuck, *French Catholic Missionaries*, 5–258; and Trương, *A Story of Vietnam*, 107–53.

the other 6 in the eighteenth century.[21] But why were these Vietnamese Christians willing to die for their new beliefs?

A short answer can be found in Pope John Paul II's homily on the canonization of 117 martyrs in Vietnam. Along with their strong faith, the Pope preached, the Vietnamese martyrs had a deep devotion to the Holy Mother. In other words, Marian devotion strengthened the martyrs' conviction, helping them persevere to the point of death. Alongside the persecutions and massacres of Christians, then, they saw that OLLV was coming to help. It is understandable that the story of OLLV was unable to be preserved in written form throughout a long century of ups and downs (mostly downs). However, her story was preserved in the hearts of the lay faithful who witnessed her and passed down the story orally. Devotion to OLLV cultivated strong faith in these descendants that empowered them as Vietnamese Christians to endure martyrdom, and, in contrast to the nationalist political movements, to be formed in an inculturated religious identity. This devotion persisted continually after the Marian apparition, which was itself an occasion of encouragement in the midst of persecution. Moreover, amid the records of martyrdom, we find written evidence of constant devotion to OLLV under the Marian title "Our Lady of Help of Christians."

Devotion to Our Lady of La Vang During 1798–1900: Spirited Local Devotion

The devotion to OLLV emerged in the historical context summarized in the previous section. During this period of persecution, OLLV revealed herself to the lay faithful as their maternal protector and helper. In response, lay faithful and their leaders not only persevered in their obedience to God but also devoted themselves to her. That the persecutions did not end did not deter their devotion. As with other geographical Marian titles and names such as Our Lady of Lourdes, of course, the apparition did not identify herself under the title used later. However, when Marian devotion entered a "golden age" around the second half of the nineteenth century, she seemed to approve the name OLLV by granting favors to those who invoked her under that name.[22] Exploring the archival record

---

21. T. Vũ, *Dòng Máu Anh Hùng*, 5; Bùi, *The Catholic Church in Vietnam*, 2:411–500.

22. The Marian apparitions of Our Lady of Miraculous Medal in 1830, then the Marian apparitions at Lourdes, and the discovery of Louis de Montfort's manuscript "True Devotion of the Blessed Virgin Mary" strengthened Marian devotion, which

The History of the Devotion to Our Lady of La Vang 65

of Marian devotion during this time period is thus important when examining the historical development of devotion to OLLV. Records from the diocese of Cochinchine (Quảng Bình, Quảng Trị, and Huế provinces; see fig. 2) demonstrate that the historical development of devotion to OLLV has roots in wider Marian devotion.[23] This section introduces the region of La Vang and the French missionaries who oversaw that territory as well as their archive, located in Paris. Ultimately, it argues that the devotion to OLLV has roots in a local "Association of Our Lady of Help of Christians," which eventually became explicit devotion to "OLLV."

As with many other locations of Marian apparitions, La Vang was not a land hospitable to human life before the BVM appeared. Instead, it was a wild area encompassing jungles and mountains where the poor local people in Quảng Trị came to chop firewood and make charcoal for a living. On an eighteenth-century map of Vietnam, La Vang is located in Dinh Cát [Quảng Trị] province, situated close to Phú Xuân (modern-day Huế), where the Tây Sơn Dynasty (1778–1802) shifted the capital. It was then further developed by the Nguyễn Dynasty.[24] From 1659–1844, La Vang belonged to the Catholic diocese covering the south of Vietnam, which was named Cochinchine (see fig. 2). From 1844–50, it briefly belonged to a diocese in the east of southern Vietnam, Cochinchine Orient. From 1850 onwards, however, La Vang belonged to the northern diocese of southern Vietnam, which was named Cochinchine septentrionale (see fig. 3).[25] In this discussion, I use the names (upper) Cochinchine for the period 1798–1850 and Cochinchine septentrionale from 1850–1900.

For French sources on OLLV, the Archive of the Society of Foreign Missions of Paris (MEP) is especially relevant. Established in 1658, the MEP was a Roman Catholic organization of clergy and lay faithful who dedicated themselves to becoming and supporting missionaries in Asia.

---

led to the beginning of the "golden age" of Marian devotion. Also, the local Bishop of Tarbes, Bertrand-Severe Laurence, venerated the Blessed Virgin Mary in Lourdes at first, then Our Lady of the Rosary, and only then under the name Our Lady of Lourdes. See Lasserre, *Our Lady of Lourdes*.

23. This information can be found at the Archive of Archdiocese of Huế; in Stanislas Nguyễn and Joseph Nguyễn, *The History of Diocese of Huế*, 217–18; and AMEP, "The MEP in Vietnam: An Overview (1664–1975)," https://irfa.paris/en/zonesgeographiques/vietnam-2. Note that the nation and many provinces have been renamed over time. See Phan, *Mission and Catechesis*, 6–7nn2, 4, and 5.

24. See Trương, *A Story of Vietnam*, 1–130.

25. See Bùi, *The Catholic Church in Vietnam*, vol. II. Cochinchine septentrionale became the Diocese of Huế in 1924 and the Archdiocese of Huế in 1960.

Located at 128 rue de Bac in Paris, the headquarters continues to preserve a physical archive, "The France-Asia Research Institute" (hereafter AMEP), as well as a website. The physical archive of the AMEP preserves their manuscripts, which mainly consist of handwritten letters and copies of annual reports, etc.[26] AMEP also provides a variety of sources, some of them in printed form, including the biographies of its members, as well as other pertinent biographical information. Many members of the MEP were sent to Vietnam between 1659 and 1960, and they collaborated with other missionaries there to evangelize and build the Church in Vietnam. Two of the MEP's co-founders, Lambert de la Motte and François Pallu, were appointed the first apostolic vicars in Vietnam in 1659.[27] They were put in charge of the territory located in central Vietnam along with several other regions after Jesuit and Franciscan missionaries started to leave during the second half of the eighteenth century. This territory is what became Cochinchine septentrionale in 1850. The accounts of French missionaries are important because they were eyewitnesses to events in Quảng Trị province. As missionaries, they were also themselves subject to persecution, which did not deter them. In difficult and dangerous circumstances, they loved the Vietnamese people and they observed and recorded the strong devotion to the Holy Mother that the lay faithful and even non-Christian villagers expressed.

As we have seen, a strong starting point for the study of the history of the devotion to OLLV is the celebrations held in Cochinchine septentrionale, including the erection of the Church of OLLV and the procession of OLLV in 1900. In his annual report in 1900, the Apostolic Vicar of Cochinchine septentrionale, Bishop Louis Marie Antoine Caspar (1841–1917), mentions Claude Bonin's account of the erection of the

---

26. For the history of the Société des Missions Etrangères de Paris, see https://missionsetrangeres.com/une-breve-histoire-des-mep/?lang=en. For an overview of the archive, the AMEP, see https://irfa.paris. Although the MEP stopped sending missionaries to Vietnam in 1975, its Institution still supports the Church in Vietnam by providing education to Vietnamese clergy. Several Vietnamese bishops and archbishops were educated at the seminary of the MEP. See J. Trần, *Thoáng Nhìn Giáo Hội Công giáo Việt Nam*, 401–608.

27. Not only were Lambert de la Motte and Francois Pallu co-founders of the MEP, but they were also made the first apostolic vicars in Vietnam when Pope Alexander VII established the Catholic mission in Vietnam on September 8, 1659. At the meeting of the Catholic Bishops' Conference of Vietnam at the Diocese of Hai Phong in 2019, the Vietnamese bishops decided to work for the possible beatification of three bishops and several Vietnamese martyrs. Two their candidates were de la Motte and Pallu (Archive of CBCV, "Biên bản họp" ["Meeting Record"], October 2019).

church and the procession of OLLV. In addition to other religious activities, Caspar's report also mentioned a sermon by Fr. Charles Patinier (1850–1922),[28] which reported a century-long tradition of pilgrimages to OLLV."[29] A hundred years of pilgrimage would mean, of course, that devotion to OLLV began immediately after her apparitions in 1798. In addition to missioning at Cochinchine septentrionale as pastor of Cổ Vưu in 1878 and as chief pastor in Dinh Cát/Quảng Trị province in the 1880s-1890s, Patinier became a part of the Christian communities in Quảng Trị province. There he experienced not only the massacre of Christians but also the protection of OLLV, so he must have known the oral tradition of OLLV well. His sermon provides a historical and spiritual record of continuous Marian devotion at La Vang.

Jean Labartette (1744–1823) became one of the most important figures in the history of devotion to OLLV. He was a missionary in Dinh Cát/Quảng Trị and served as the apostolic vicar of Cochinchine from 1799–1823. In 1773, Labartette was sent to Cochinchine; in 1776 he went to Dinh Cát, where no missionary had been for thirty years. Labartette suffered hardships during the terrible persecutions in Dinh Cát and was arrested twice. He was also nearly arrested in May 1798 and had to live in a cave for some time. Moreover, he spent a long time in upper Cochinchine, in central Vietnam, specifically at the Church of Cổ Vưu in Quảng Trị province. His letters were addressed from Cổ Vưu and written while he oversaw Cochinchine, whose territory included the archdiocese of Huế, the modern-day Archdiocese of Ho-Chi-Minh, and the region of Cambodia. The events that Labartette describes highlight the importance of the Cổ Vưu community.[30] In other words, Labartette was likely familiar with the story of OLLV.

28. Patinier was sent to Cổ Vưu in Quang Tri in 1875, and probably knew the tradition of OLLV from the immediate descendants of the original visionaries.

29. Caspar, "Annual Report in 1900," 90; Bonin, "Notre Dame de La Vang," 276. The original quote is "M. Patinier adresse à la foule un sermon émouvant dans lequel il retrace l'historique du pèlerinage qui remonte à près de cent ans." Another episcopal report in 1910 mentions Patinier's sermon, which will be examined later. In a 1659 bull, Pope Alexander VII asked the apostolic vicars to write him annual reports about the mission. The first two apostolic vicars belonged to the MEP, so they also sent copies to their superiors in Paris.

30. Several of Labartette's letters were addressed from Cổ Vưu and dated 1778. For example, he wrote a letter dated 1784 that reported how the lay faithful in Quảng Trị suffered from civil war and oppression. For more details, see Jean Labartette, "Letter," AMEP, vol. 746, 29–31. For the mission of Labartette, see Launay, *Histoire de La Mission de Cochinchine*, 3:490–95. See also AMEP, https://irfa.paris/missionnaire/0240-labartette-jean.

In several of his letters, Labartette expresses the lay faithful's devotion to the BVM. For instance, in a letter dated 1800, Labartette discusses a folk religious custom called "Lạy Xác" [Bowing Down to Dead Body] and then describes an instance when a Christian refused to dishonor an image of the Holy Mother when ordered to do so by an officer. He preferred instead to accept any type of torture.[31] This event is also mentioned in the biographies of the Vietnamese martyrs. In addition to reciting the rosary, many martyrs refused to tread on images of the Crucifixion or the Holy Mother because it signaled a renunciation of faith. As these examples illustrate, honoring images of the BVM was part of the lay faithful's devotion.

Labartette also provides other important information relevant to the history of devotion to OLLV. In 1806 he wrote as the apostolic vicar of Cochinchine, and on behalf of European missionaries, asking the Pope to permit him to establish the Association of Perpetual Devotion to the Blessed Virgin Mary. He makes three major arguments. First, the apostolic vicar and the European missionaries were promoting the establishment of a Marian Association. Second, they were asking for something that was already approved and practiced among Western countries. Finally, the apostolic vicar pointed out that Marian devotion leads to conversion, and that the devotion was a key tool for evangelization: "[I] hope that the Association will greatly benefit the rituals [of the Blessed Virgin Mary] by promoting and accelerating the salvation of souls."[32] Although Labartette does not mention the Marian apparition at La Vang, his letter affirms intense Marian devotion in the area in which it was alleged to have occurred, namely, upper Cochinchine. In addition, we know that during the 1798 persecution he stayed at Cổ Vưu often. Those realities suggest that he knew the apparition and hoped that an Association of Perpetual Devotion to the BVM would formalize the emerging devotion to OLLV, strengthening the lay faithful as a group. Perhaps because it was "only" lay faithful who witnessed it, and no clerical authority, and because in addition they were poor and illiterate, he did not feel a report of the apparition would be received as anything but unsubstantiated rumor, and not itself a sufficient reason to form an Association.

There are two other noteworthy points about this letter. One is that the letter is dated 1806, only eight years after the apparitions, and the

---

31. Labartette, "Letter," AMEP, vol. 747, 9–16.
32. Labartette, "Letter," AMEP, 1806, vol. 747, 327.

other is that, in his territory, Labartette had to deal with a variety of pastoral issues, including mixed marriages, formation for the priesthood, and indigenous religious customs. The fact that he asked to establish the Association of Perpetual Devotion to the BVM thus demonstrates that this request, even amid those other complex pastoral concerns, seemed essential to his diocese, making this letter an important document in the study of the emergence of the devotion to OLLV.

Moreover, political chaos in Europe, particularly France, Italy, and the Vatican, also indirectly affected the development of Marian devotion in upper Cochinchine during the early nineteenth century. The Church was also facing persecution in France because of the French Revolution and subsequent anti-Catholic sentiment, and ongoing European upheaval included, among other things, the Napoleonic Wars and the unification of Italy into a secular state and the reduction of the papal states to the Vatican. The MEP continued to send missionaries to Vietnam, but perhaps the supply seemed tenuous. As a result, Labartette established a seminary to train local priests.[33] He also had to ask for guidance about local customs, such as the cult of ancestors, funeral ceremonies, and marriages, which could seem to be in tension with Catholic teaching.[34]

Subsequently, we do have evidence of strong Marian devotion through the Association of Our Lady of Help of Christians. For instance, in two of his letters, Jean-Joseph Audemar (1757–1821) discusses Marian devotion. In 1809, Audemar wrote a letter to his friends, one of whom was Cardinal Boiret, the Prefect of the Propaganda Fide in Rome. In addition to sharing about his mission in upper Cochinchine, Audemar asked Boiret for many holy cards so that he could deliver them to the members of "Nhà Chúa" [House of God] and an Association of Notre Dame auxiliaries:[35]

---

33. In the early nineteenth century, most Catholics were illiterate; not only basic education but Latin was required for seminarians to be ordained. Therefore, although apostolic vicars were supposed to train local priests, according to Labartette, there were three missionaries and eighteen Vietnamese priests. See Stanislas Nguyễn and Joseph Nguyễn, *The History of Diocese of Huế*, 179.

34. Labartette asked Propaganda Fide for pastoral direction by sending 69 questions; see AMEP, vol. 747, 307. For the answer he received see AMEP, vol. 747, 331.

35. Jean-Joseph Audemar, "Letter," AMEP, vol. 747, 599–601. Audemar was sent to Cochinchine as a missionary. He became superior of the seminary Phuong-ruou in the middle region of Vietnam, and he was appointed coadjutor to the Apostolic Vicar of Cochinchine in 1817. His biography can be found at AMEP, https://irfa.paris/missionnaire/0320/.

> Ah! If I would dare to ask you again to provide me with small images for the associates of the brotherhood or an Association of Our Lady Help of Christians, I would need a few thousand. In about two months we received here more than two hundred people who wanted to be enrolled in this society.[36]

Many people devoted themselves to the Holy Mother by joining the Association of Our Lady of Help of Christians. Although we do not know precisely when this Association was founded, its members apparently devoted themselves to the Holy Mother in the upper Cochinchine, reminiscent of the request made in Labartette's earlier letter.

In another letter dated 1811, Audemar states that the lay faithful impressed him because of their resilient fidelity and deep devotion to the Blessed Virgin. He also again requested thousands of holy cards with images that depict either the Crucifixion or the Holy Mother with the Baby Jesus:

> Monsignor, if you could provide me with three or four thousand images representing the Crucifixion or the Blessed Virgin with the Child Jesus in her arms. . . . Above all, I would like a lot of medals with the figure of the Blessed Virgin holding the Child Jesus in her arms. Please forgive my importunity.[37]

Unlike many other Marian apparitions around the world, in the Marian apparitions at La Vang, the BVM is described as holding the Baby Jesus. The Church had long showed devotion to images depicting the BVM with a child as a way of teaching, defending, and revering its claims about her: that since Jesus has two natures, so too the BVM, as the Mother of Jesus, is also the Mother of God. Audemar's letters show that Marian devotion, practiced under the Marian title Our Lady Help of Christians and connected to the image of the Mother of Jesus holding the baby Jesus, as she was alleged to have appeared at La Vang, was devoutly practiced in upper Cochinchine during the early nineteenth century.

---

36. AMEP, vol. 747, 600. This original quote is "Ah! Si j'osais vous prier encore de me procurer de petites images pour les associés à la confrérie, ou Société de Notre Dame auxiliatrice. Il m'en faudrait quelques milliers, dans deux mois environ nous avons reçu ici plus de 200 personnes qui ont voulu se faire enrôler dans cette Société."

37. His letter can be found in AMEP, vol. 747, 647. This original quote is "Ah! Monsieur, si vous pouviez me procurer trois ou quatre mille images représentant notre Seigneur en croix, ou la Sainte Vierge avec l'enfant Jésus entre les bras. . . . Je voudrais surtout beaucoup de médailles avec la figure de la Ste Vierge tenant l'enfant Jésus aux bras. Pardonnez, s'il vous plait, mes importunités."

The History of the Devotion to Our Lady of La Vang

Unfortunately, the Vatican Apostolic Archive and the Archive of the Propaganda Fide are missing significant correspondence from 1800 to 1814 due to the French invasion, and I could not find a letter directly answering Labartette's request. However, reading between the lines of the existing letters, I suggest that Pope Pius VII might have guided the apostolic vicar to establish an "Association of Our Lady of Help of Christians" instead of an "Association of Perpetual Devotion to the Blessed Virgin Mary" for two reasons. First, Christianity in Vietnam at that time faced persecution; the faithful needed divine help. Second, at the beginning of his papacy in 1800, Pope Pius VII devoted himself to the divine help and the help of the Mother of God. As the early nineteenth century unfolded, he developed this devotion in the context of being threatened by Napoleon, then exiled in 1809. The Pope could not return to Rome until 1814. He adored the Eucharist and recited the rosary every day. He eventually established a feast day for Our Lady of Help of Christians on May 24, the day he returned to Rome. There is reason to think, therefore, that his response to Labartette was positive and that he probably counseled Labartette to establish an Association of Our Lady of Help of Christians, meaning that the devotion to OLLV under that title began within recent memory of the apparition.[38]

As we saw above, oral tradition records the first shrine was built by non-Christians, dedicated to the Buddha, around 1820–30, though soon after its construction, the non-Christians entrusted it to Christians.[39] As mentioned above, under the reign of King Gia Long, the law forbade new construction of religious buildings and renovation of Christian churches. This law, however, would have fallen unevenly on Christians relative to Buddhists.[40] After the King passed away, the non-Christian villagers constructed the first shrine, usually called the Buddhist pagoda. They were able to build the shrine for two reasons. First, Buddhism was considered a national religion in Vietnam, and the Vietnamese dynasties observed it respectfully, except during the reign of King Gia Long. Second, OLLV needed time to gain the ordinary people's trust, and the reign of King Gia Long allowed that to occur as many people experienced OLLV's help. We know that by 1809 there was a flourishing devotion to the BVM in the area near the site of the apparition. The evidence from

---

38. See the VAA. This will be further discussed in chapter 4.

39. Archive of the Archdiocese of Huế, *Our Lady of La Vang*, 9.

40. Louvet, *La Cochinchine Religieuse*, 2: 18, 19. Tran, *Pilgrimage to the Diocese of Hue*, 1: 284.

the archives corroborates the evidence from *The Poem* regarding early devotion there. We know too that the story of OLLV, probably spread among neighbors by Christian devotion, inspired non-Christians to ask for her help. The non-Christians also received OLLV's help. Because OLLV granted graces abundantly, the non-Christians interpreted her as a Buddhist Lady or goddess. They therefore built a shrine to honor her. La Vang was still a wild area. The local people of Quảng Trị did come to collect wood, but no one was living there, and it belonged to no one at that time. When it became possible, those of the local people who could build a shrine did. Constructing a shrine corresponds to the Vietnamese manner of responding to divine help.

It is quite plausible that the non-Christians were able to build when the Christians were not. Most of the faithful were poor, and like many ordinary people they did not know how to read or write. That the faithful fled to La Vang under persecution means they were under extreme duress. They left their homes as hostages to fortune, and it is likely they were ruined. When they returned, probably when King Cảnh Thịnh was defeated, they had to rebuild their village life. They would not, most likely, have had the resources to build a shrine at La Vang. We have evidence that they were unable to rebuild a shrine after it was burned as late as 1885.[41] After this later wave of persecution, it took the help of the French missionaries to coordinate the faithful to donate their labor, and Father Patinier had to appeal for donations in his native country to build the church of OLLV in 1894.[42] We know that those Christians who witnessed the apparition recognized Our Lady as the Mother of Jesus, whom she was holding. By some mechanism, represented in *The Poem* by the simultaneous dreams that each of three Buddhist village leaders had, the Buddhist leaders were persuaded that it was a Christian Lady who had appeared, and the shrine was transferred peacefully to the Christians.[43] There is no mention of any hostile act—for example, of the Buddhist statues being destroyed (though in the dream they were symbolically overturned). Since Our Lady did not play favorites, one could imagine that the Buddhists had as much to gain by attributing the favors they received to their rightful source. In any event, it is certainly one of the

---

41. AMEP, vol. 761, 61; Archive of the Archdiocese of Huế, *The Sanctuary of Our Lady of La Vang*, 10.

42. AMEP, vol. 761, 61.

43. Hồ, *The Legend Poem of La Vang*; Bonnand, "Un procès gagné—Une église à faire," 694.

unique features of the inculturation of devotion to Mary in the Vietnamese context that it was not closed off from non-Christians and that this inter-religious openness continues even to the present time.

Along with the violent persecutions of Christians under the reigns of the Kings Minh Mệnh, Thiệu Trị and Tự Đức (1820–83), devotion to OLLV was sustained and further developed under the Associations of Our Lady Help of Christians, in particular from 1850 onwards when the diocese of Cochinchine septentrionale was established. The apostolic vicar encouraged Marian devotion. For example, François Marie Pellerin (1813–62), the first apostolic vicar of the diocese of Cochinchine septentrionale, encouraged his clergy to strengthen Marian devotion by teaching lay faithful how to participate in the Association of Our Lady Help of Christians along with other Catholic associations.[44]

Moreover, Pellerin's successor Joseph Hyacinthe Sohier (1818–76) marked an important layer in the history of devotion to OLLV. After a long period of official persecution, Vietnamese Christians enjoyed a short time of peace after the 1862 Hòa ước Nhâm Tuất [Treaty of Sai Gon.][45] During this period a Christian community at La Vang was established, probably by Sohier.[46] There is also evidence that he intended to build a seminary, convents for religious women, a home for retired priests, and an orphanage at La Vang even though it was a remote and dangerous region. Although his construction plan failed, it signals the otherwise somewhat inexplicable importance of the La Vang territory.[47]

Soon after 1862, devotion to OLLV was also expressed through more publicly organized pilgrimages to La Vang. Born in a Christian village of Cổ Vưu, FX. Thìn Thiện Lê (1805–78) was not only a good doctor but also a devout Catholic.[48] Lê was born at Cổ Vưu in 1805, just seven years after the Marian apparitions; his parents must have been among the faithful who experienced OLLV's appearance at La Vang. He was appointed Ông Trùm [lay leader] of the Church of Cổ Vưu and oversaw

44. Stanislas Nguyễn and Joseph Nguyễn, *History of the Diocese of Huế*, 222; Q. Trần, *Hành Hương Giáo Phận Huế [Pilgrimage to Diocese of Huế,]* vol II, 24–28. AMEP, vol. 760, 51; "François PELLERIN" in Documentation a Missionary, 0485. https://irfa.paris/missionnaire/0485-pellerin-francois/.

45. Q. Trần, *Pilgrimage to Diocese of Huế*, 2:117–18. Tự Đức gave up three provinces to French in 1862 under the peace treaty.

46. See Q. Trần, *Pilgrimage to Diocese of Huế*, 2:157–58; Stanislas Nguyễn and Joseph Nguyễn, *History of Diocese of Huế*, 289–90.

47. Stanislas Nguyễn and Joseph Nguyễn, *History of Diocese of Huế*, 289.

48. See Launay, *Les trente cinq venerables Serviteurs de Dieu*, 147.

other parishes in Quảng Trị province. He and his wife were imprisoned with other Christians under the anti-Christian decrees issued by Tự Đức in 1861. His wife died during their imprisonment, and he was released in 1862 as a result of the peace treaty. Under the guidance of the pastor of the Church of Cổ Vưu, Lê organized pilgrimages to La Vang.[49] It was still quite dangerous to go to La Vang at that time, and the pilgrims had to take sticks and gongs to protect themselves from wild animal attacks.

Obviously, the pilgrimages to La Vang became an essential element of the spiritual journey of the local parishes in Quảng Trị province. For example, born at Cổ Vưu, diocesan priest Dõng Văn Đặng (1871–1932) testified to the lengthy history of the Marian devotion at La Vang. As a senior clergyman, he still remembered that when he was an altar boy, he accompanied Fr. Ignatius Huấn Văn Lê, the pastor of Cổ Vưu from 1880–83, on pilgrimage to La Vang a couple years before the Văn Thân movement again attacked Christians.[50]

Furthermore, the strong devotion to OLLV becomes clearer and more visible over time under her own name. As mentioned, another series of massacres of Christians took place in 1885. The Văn Thân Movement's death toll in Dinh Cát, for example, totaled around 4,642.[51] Afterwards, however, the devotion to OLLV spread more openly, and as we have seen this is when the name "Our Lady of La Vang" was first mentioned in print: "To the great joy of Christians, we have taken it into our heads to restore the cult of Our Lady of La Vang, the good Mother to whom the pagans invoked themselves with confidence and from whom they have received several times extraordinary favors."[52] Since the name OLLV is mentioned as a cult to be *restored*, not instituted, it seems clear that her name must have been venerated in practice earlier. The series of massacres of Christians likely interrupted established rituals of the cult of OLLV. In addition to prompting OLLV's constant help, the result of these massacres seems to have been an effort to continue deepening the devotion to OLLV.

49. Andrew Lê, "Nhìn lại gương mặt Lương y Lê Thiện Thìn." This is a part of a reliable gia phả [genealogy] of the Lê family. See also FX Nguyễn, *Testimony of Hope*, 4.

50. See Stanislas Nguyễn, *Sacred Land of La Vang*, 41; Mathew Lê, *Our Lady of La Vang*, 25.

51. Louis Caspar, annual report in 1885, AMEP, CR 1885, 96–100.

52. Bonnand, "Un procès gagné—Une église à faire," 694.

Moreover, under the name of OLLV, Bonnand further called for donations to build a temporary church because the previous one had burned down during a rebellion:

> To replace the poor straw hut temporarily erected on the ruins of the chapel burned down by the rebels, we made a collection in the whole district. The parishes of Thanh Huong and Cổ Vưu have given generously, and we have received in rice or cash more than six thousand ligatures and serious promises for next year.[53]

This letter provides evidence that a chapel of OLLV existed before 1885 and that a temporary chapel was built to replace it when the former one was burned down. It also shows that the parishioners surrounding La Vang were devoted enough to OLLV to joyfully receive the news of a revival and to participate in it.

In sum, Bonnand's letter demonstrates that the Marian apparition at La Vang had clearly been "approved," at least locally, as it is a custom of the approved Marian apparitions that the place where the BVM appeared becomes part of her title. This letter also indirectly indicates OLLV's constant help to all those who trust in her as she promised in 1798. Bonnand's letter also testifies that OLLV had granted favors of motherly care to non-Christians, as though this too were a well-known aspect of her maternal care. OLLV had become the mother of the suffering Christians and Vietnamese people through her care of them.

After the persecutions of the eighteenth and nineteenth centuries finally came to an end, the history of devotion to OLLV began to involve the bishop and his whole territory of Cochinchine septentrionale. The tradition of La Vang was handed down by Charles François Patinier, the first member of the clergy to mention devotion to OLLV specifically while writing to his bishop. As a member of MEP, Patinier was sent to Cochinchine septentrionale in 1875, about seventy-seven years after OLLV's apparition. This meant he worked with the generation raised by the visionaries who saw OLLV in ministries at Cổ Vưu parish and in Quảng Trị province. Patinier soon rebuilt churches that were under his care. He renovated the church of Cổ Vưu in 1877, which was burned in

---

53. Bonnand, "Un procès gagné—Une église à faire," 694. The original quotation reads, "Pour remplacer plus dignement la pauvre paillote provisoirement élevée sur les ruines de la chapelle brûlée par les rebelles, nous avons fait une quête dans tout le district; les paroisses de Thanh Huong, Co Vuu se sont généreusement signalée, et nous avons reçu en riz ou en sapèques plus de six mille ligatures et des promesses sérieuses pour l'an prochain."

1885 and then fully rebuilt it in 1889. He also worked on the reconstruction of the church of La Vang sometime between 1889 and 1891, at which point he returned to France for health reasons. In an 1894 report, Patinier mentions a Christian community at La Vang and the powerful name OLLV, under which the Blessed Virgin granted abundant favors. In the same report, Patinier shares a brief history of the Christian community at La Vang and its church:

> In 1885, the chapel was no more spared than the other churches in the district. When the peace was finally restored, I hastened to rebuild the little sanctuary, but in a completely provisional way, while waiting for sources and for less troubled times. Father Bonnand, who replaced me during my stay in France, actively took care, with the help of Father Gontier, of the definitive reconstruction of this chapel.[54]

Patinier's report confirms both that a small, temporary shrine was constructed in honor of OLLV, as Bonnand also mentioned, and that these French missionaries had positive responses to the local devotion to OLLV.

In the same report, Father Patinier says while he was recovering his health in France, he collected donations for the construction of the church of OLLV. Upon his return, Patinier directed the construction, and he writes that the members of the church of OLLV were excited to participate in the project: "Each family will be honored to participate in this good work and will send their contribution. Long live Our Lady of La Vang."[55] His assertion that the lay faithful were delighted and volunteered to help with the construction aligns with how this event is portrayed in *The Legend Poem of La Vang*.

Patinier continued to invoke OLLV by this name in his letters. For example, the apostolic vicar Louis Caspar described an account that was included in Patinier's report in 1895:

> 'Strike the shepherd and the sheep will be scattered' [Matt. 26:31]; our sworn enemy followed this maxim to that expression;

---

54. AMEP, vol. 761, 61. The original quote is: "En 1885 la chapelle ne fut pas plus épargnée que les autres églises du district. La paix a peine rétablie, je m'empressai de relever le petit sanctuaire, mais d'une façon tout à fait provisoire, en attendant des ressources et aussi des temps moins troubles. M. Bonnand, qui m'a remplacé pendant mon séjour en France, s'est occupé activement, avec l 'aide de M. Gontier, de la reconstruction définitive de cette chapelle."

55. AMEP, vol. 761, 61. The original quote is: "Chaque famille tiendra a honneur de participer à cette bonne oeuvre et enverra son obole. Vive Notre-Dame de La-Vang."

The History of the Devotion to Our Lady of La Vang

he endeavored to slander the leaders of Christian communities, especially those which had been newly founded, and without the special protection of Our Lady of La Vang, we would have had to lament many losses.[56]

This document is evidence of a settled devotion under the name OLLV by the end of the century. As previously mentioned, Quảng Trị province was one of the regions most affected by the persecution of Christians. While serving as a missionary there, Patinier experienced this violence and witnessed the maternal protection of OLLV. The information that Patinier provided about the local tradition was indirect evidence of at least local approval of the Marian apparitions at La Vang, leaving the question open for any further investigative process or for a later Pope like John Paul II to cite the words of OLLV approvingly.

The tradition of La Vang became fully visible in its modern form in 1900 when the Church of OLLV was erected and the first formally organized public procession of OLLV took place. Louis Caspar (1841–1917) was sent to Cochinchine in 1865 and served as the apostolic vicar of Cochinchine septentrionale from 1880–1907. During that time, he became one of the most influential figures in the story of OLLV. Like Labartette, Caspar experienced the late-nineteenth century persecution and massacres of Christians. His territory was a particular hot spot during this time. Furthermore, as the head of the diocese, Bishop Caspar blessed the building of the church and joined the procession of OLLV in 1900. Caspar was joyful, giving thanks to God and OLLV for her maternal protection. As his 1900 annual report stated:

> For a long time, Christians have been calling for the inauguration of the new sanctuary of La Vang and the consecration, so to speak officially, of the pilgrimage that has been established in honor of the Blessed Virgin. Finally, this year, the reconstruction work having been completed, we were able to satisfy, I would not only say the devotion of the faithful of Quảng Trị province, but also all the Catholics of the Mission.[57]

---

56. AMEP, vol. 761, 65. This original quote is "[Patinier wrote] Percute pastorem et dispergentur oves; notre ennemi juré suivait cette maxime à la lettre; il s'attachait à faire calomnier les chefs des chrétientés, surtout de celles qui venaient 'd'être nouvellement fondées, et sans une protection spéciale de Notre-Dame de La-vang' nous aurions eu à déplorer bien des pertes."

57. AMEP, vol. 761, 90. The original quote is "Depuis longtemps, les chrétiens réclamaient l'inauguration du nouveau sanctuaire de La Vang et la consécration, pour ainsi dire officielle, du pèlerinage qui s'est établi là en l'honneur de la très sainte Vierge.

No reports of the apparition suggest that OLLV requested the building of a church. The inauguration of a church in her honor was, instead, a response to her maternal love. Bishop Caspar reports that the whole diocese rejoiced in participating in the ceremony. A diverse set of individuals, both French and Vietnamese, had collaborated in the new church's construction.

Bishop Caspar encouraged all the members of his community to be joyful because the BVM was in their midst: "Finally, a great joy, which is also a powerful reason for hope, was given to the Apostolic Vicar and his clergy at the blessing of the chapel erected at La Vang, in honor of Mary, to replace the old one destroyed in the torment of 1885."[58] It was on this occasion that Father Patinier delivered his moving sermon about the previous century of historical pilgrimages to La Vang. Bishop Caspar not only presided over the erection of the church and walked in the procession of OLLV, but also mentioned the ceremony in his annual report that year. From that point onwards, devotion to OLLV was not only observed by the devotees of Quảng Trị province, but also the whole diocese of Cochinchine septentrionale. In addition, most scholars consider that Bishop Caspar endorsed the cult/rituals of OLLV, including annual Lunar New Year pilgrimages and pilgrimages that occurred in annual August and August every three years. He also used the title Our Lady of Help of Christians and installed a statue named "Our Lady of Victories" at the church (see fig. 1). However, the cult was established when the Bishop approved those rituals promoted by Fr. Claude Bonin.[59] Through these decisions and actions, Bishop Caspar informally communicated approval of the Marian apparitions at La Vang. One more step that remained to be taken was to open investigation toward the formal Vatican approval.

In summary, lay faithful in central Vietnam devoted themselves to the BVM under the title Our Lady of Help of Christians before the name OLLV is attested in print. The Marian Association of Our Lady of Help of Christians developed through episcopal encouragement. Early

---

Cette année enfin, les travaux de reconstruction étant terminés, on a pu satisfaire, je ne dirai pas seulement la dévotion des fidèles du Quảng Trị, mais encore celle de tous les catholiques de la Mission."

58. AMEP, vol. 761, 90. The original quote is "Enfin, une grande joie, qui est aussi un puissant motif d'espérance, a été donnée au Vicaire apostolique et à son clergé, lors de la bénédiction de la chapelle érigée à La Vang, en l'honneur de Marie, pour remplacer celle qui fut détruite dans la tourmente de 1885."

59. Stanislas Nguyễn, *Sacred Land of La Vang*, 67–68; Joseph Trần, *Historical Narrative of Devotion to Our Lady of La Vang*, 15; Cadière, "Souvenir," 45.

The History of the Devotion to Our Lady of La Vang

veneration of OLLV also seems associated with the image of the Holy Mother with the Baby Jesus. These devotions continued to persist in Cochinchine septentrionale after 1850 and strengthened the faithful's ability to stand firm during the subsequent persecutions. Collectively, this suggests that devotion to OLLV began soon after her apparition under the Marian title Our Lady of Help of Christians. The 1900 solemnity was not only to give thanks to OLLV but also to move on to a new era in the history of the devotion to OLLV: the diocesan level.

The Second Period of the History of Devotion to OLLV (1900–61)

The second period in the history of OLLV was free of persecution, and the rituals of devotion to OLLV developed in many ways. Still, for most of the years between 1900–1961, Vietnam was under French colonial control, and just as French administrators did not favor Catholics in their own native country, so too they were disfavored in Vietnam. Also, many ideological nationalist groups emerged to combat both French domination and Catholicism. Towards the end of this period World War II (1939–45) and the First Indochina War (1945–54) caused significant misery in Vietnam. The Second Indochina War, also known as the Vietnam War, was especially disruptive.[60] The civil war, which also served as a proxy war for the United States and the Soviet Union, sharply divided Vietnamese people. Despite the interruption that these events occasioned for the great pilgrimages, the rituals/cult of OLLV continued to grow.

Two events tied to the history of Christianity in Vietnam also had an impact on the cult of OLLV. First, a National Marian Year was celebrated in 1959 to celebrate the 300th anniversary of the establishment of the first two dioceses in Vietnam. During this time, the bishops entrusted the nation to the Immaculate Conception of the Blessed Virgin Mary and promised to dedicate a worthy church to her. Second, the hierarchy of the Church in Vietnam was formally established in 1960.[61] This establishment turned out to be one of the most important drivers of the national devotion to OLLV. Ironically, during the division caused by the Vietnam War, devotion to OLLV became even stronger. In the following section

---

60. See Buttinger, *The Smaller Dragon*, 423–69; Taylor, *A History of the Vietnamese*, 484–578.

61. Bùi, *The Catholic Church in Vietnam*, 3:501–3; 301–5; Tuck, *French Catholic Missionaries*.

I explore the factors that either hindered or promoted the cult of OLLV during the first half of the twentieth century and discuss how devotion to OLLV developed throughout this period.

The Context from 1900–61: Socio-Religious-Political Factors

Throughout the French colonial era Christianity was freely practiced by law. However, many nationalist groups emerged to contest the French colonial administration, especially in Tonkin (northern Vietnam) and Annam (central Vietnam). Historian Joseph Buttinger summarizes the period from 1900–40: "During these four decades, the French had to deal with numerous strong waves of Vietnamese resistance in various forms, but they remained always firmly in control of the whole country... The economic development of Vietnam... made Indochina France's 'richest colony.'"[62] Although the French administration was able to suppress the movements, this resistance foreshadowed national independence.

Japanese forces invaded Vietnam during World War II; 1944–45 brought suffering and starvation to the country. The great pilgrimages to OLLV had to be suspended, but the annual pilgrimages that took place during the first days of the Lunar New Year and individual pilgrimages still continued. The subsequent First Indochina War was primarily fought between the French and the Viet Minh, one of the most prominent Vietnamese nationalist groups. After experiencing Chinese domination and other invasions, many Vietnamese people willingly participated in the call for national sacrifices. After the Viet Minh won the First Indochina War at the "Battle of Điện Biên Phủ," the Genève Conference decided that the decolonized Vietnamese government would be divided in two (see fig. 4). The area of Vietnam located to the north of the 17th parallel was to be under the Communist regime or Democratic Republic of Vietnam, with a capital at Hanoi. The area located to the south of the 17th parallel was controlled by the Republican Party of Vietnam and had its capital at Saigon.[63]

---

62. Buttinger, *The Smaller Dragon*, 423. Some examples of the nationalist groups that emerged include Phong trào Đông du (1905–9), Đông Kinh nghĩa thục (1907), Mưu khởi nghĩa ở Huế and Khởi nghĩa của binh lính và tù chính trị Thái Nguyên (1917), and Phong trào cách mạng (1920–30). See Trương, *A Story of Vietnam*, 154–26. Many pieces of literature produced during this time express the misery of the ordinary people. For example, a 1937 novel called *Tắt Đèn* by Tố Tất Ngô tells the story of an innocent young village couple who are exploited in many areas of life.

63. For the history of Vietnam during the second period of the history of OLLV, see Buttinger, *The Smaller Dragon*, 423–69; Taylor, *A History of the Vietnamese*, 484–582; Tuck, *French Catholic Missionaries*, 258–304; Trương, *A Story of Vietnam*, 156–275.

The History of the Devotion to Our Lady of La Vang

Fig. 4: The 17th Parallel was the border during the Vietnam War. La Vang was near the border, but on the southern side. Source: Author edit of Wikimedia Commons, https://commons.wikimedia.org/w/index.php?title=File:Vietnam_map.png.

War persisted in Vietnam because division arose over different approaches to decolonization. While the Democratic Republic of Vietnam favored the Communist system, the Republican Party of Vietnam preferred Western culture and economic systems. Buttinger summarizes the situation when he says that "Vietnam, in gaining full national independence, lost its unity together with the hope that the end of colonialism would bring also an end to oppression of all Vietnamese."[64] The largest demonstration of protest against the communist government ever to occur took place in 1954 when a large number of people, including Christians, left the north for South Vietnam. According to Vincent Sinh Đức Bùi, 71.4 percent of the Catholic laity lived in the northern dioceses prior to 1954, but after the migration this ratio reversed: now 77.7 percent of Christians in Vietnam were living in the southern dioceses.[65] Peter Hansen created a table that shows the number of laity and clergy from the ten dioceses in the north that moved to the south in 1954.[66]

	Total Lay Departures	% of Laity Migrating	Total Priests Departures	% of Priests Migrating
Hà Nội	50.000	33.4%	115	55.6%
Hải Phòng	60.000	52.3%	79	80.6%
Vinh	57.080	31.7%	70	39.3%
Bùi Chu	150.000	71.7%	150	77.7%
Hưng Hóa	8.000	11.8%	23	28.4%
Bắc Ninh	38.000	55.9%	60	75.0%
Phát Diệm	80.000	72.7%	139	87.4%
Thanh Hóa	18.500	20.6%	64	88.9%
Thái Bình	80.000	57.1%	79	70.6%
Lạng Sơn	2.500	50.0%	14	58.3%

This mass migration of clergy and laity made the national division appear to be narrowed down to a conflict between the Communist party and Christianity.[67]

Christians in Vietnam came to feel that "Miền nam tự do" [the South (was) freedom], and "Miền bắc Cộng sản" [The North (was) Communist].[68] These expressions reflect the deep divisions that existed between the two regions of Vietnam. In this context, J.B. Roux raised

---

64. Buttinger, *The Smaller Dragon*, 464.

65. Bùi, *The Catholic Church in Vietnam*, 3:214; Buttinger, *The Smaller Dragon*, 465.

66. Hansen, "Bắc Đi Cú," 180. See also P. Phan, *History of the Church in Vietnam*.

67. For more details, see Bùi, *The Catholic Church in Vietnam*, 3:240. Most of the migrants were Catholics, including clergy, religious women and men, and the lay faithful. This wave of immigration was likely influenced by the Church's perspectives on the Communist party. See Pius XI, *Divini Redemptoris*; Pius XII, *Ad Apostolorum Principis*.

68. See Buttinger, *The Smaller Dragon*, 464–69; P. Phan, *The History of the Catholic Church in Vietnam*, 1:35–37. For general circumstances (1954–60), see pages 58–84.

the question of whether a great pilgrimage to OLLV should take place in 1955: "Next year will again be a year of pilgrimage. Will it take place at Lavang? The hearts are torn between fear and hope."[69] His words highlight that even the clergy were uncertain about the changing situation; however, the solemn pilgrimage to OLLV was indeed organized in 1955, as the Bishop of Huế reported:

> His Excellency Bishop Urrutia writes that 1954–55 was the first year of peace since 1946. It was the year of reorganization of Christianity in the south of the 17th parallel. The Marian year of 1954 ended with a great feast on December 8 at the sanctuary of La Vang.[70]

While the Vietnam War restricted the Church in the northern area of the country, it brought religious freedom in the region south of the 17th parallel. Also, though La Vang was situated very close to the border in Quảng Trị province, only the people living in the southern part of the country could go on the solemn pilgrimages to OLLV that took place in 1955. They prayed to OLLV for families to be united and for peace and unity across the nation.

In 1959, a National Marian Year was celebrated in honor of the 100-year anniversary of the Marian apparitions at Lourdes and the 300-year anniversary of the establishment of the first two dioceses in Vietnam. Pope John XXIII sent Cardinal Gregoire Pierre to preside over the Marian congress.[71] The National Marian Year only took place in southern Vietnam, again due to the Vietnam War, and its celebrations played an important role in the lives of Christians and the decisions of the bishops in the Republican Party of Vietnam. One of the pastoral ministries of the bishops in southern Vietnam was to invoke the Blessed Virgin Mary and dedicate a worthy place to venerate the Immaculate Conception. Because

---

69. Roux, "Notre-Dame de Lavang," 306. The original quote is "L'année prochaine (1955) sera de nouveau une année de pèlerinage. Sera-ce a Lavang qu'il se déroulera? . . . Les cœurs sont partagés entre la crainte et l'espoir."

70. Jean Baptiste Urrutia, "Mission report in 1955" at the IRFA online, https://irfa.paris/en/ancienne_publication/rapport-annuel-1955/region-sud-indochine/, accessed on January 1, 2022. The original quote is "L'exercice 1954–1955, écrit S. Exc. Mgr Urrutia, a été la première année de paix depuis 1946. Elle a été l'année de la réorganisation des chrétientés au Sud du l7e parallèle. L'année mariale 1954 s'est terminée par une grande fête, le 8 décembre, au sanctuaire de Lavang."

71. Bùi, *The Catholic Church in Vietnam*, 3:501–2; P. Phan, *History of the Catholic Church in Vietnam*, 881–87, in particular page 886.

of these duties, the bishops in southern Vietnam decided to discuss issues related to OLLV at a later point during their meetings.

Fig. 5: The hierarchy of the Catholic Church in Vietnam was established in 1960. Source: Author edit of Wikimedia Commons, https://commons.wikimedia.org/w/index.php?title=File:Vietnam_map.png.

Moreover, the establishment of the hierarchy of the Church in 1960 also pushed the devotion to OLLV into a new era. By this time, most church leaders and bishops were not European but Vietnamese. Three archdioceses were established: Hà Nội (north), Huế (in the middle), and

Sài Gòn (south) (fig. 5).⁷² During the Vietnam War, the territory of the Archdiocese of Hà Nội belonged to the area controlled by the Democratic Republic of Vietnam, while the territories of Huế and Sài Gòn belonged to the region under the authority of the Republic of Vietnam. During the Vietnam War, there was no communication between the Archdiocese of Hanoi and the two other Archdioceses.

Situated in Quảng Trị province, the shrine of OLLV still belonged to the archdiocese of Huế. It was located in South Vietnam but only about twenty miles away from the 17th parallel. In other words, the shrine of OLLV sat at a divisive and dangerous border during the Vietnam War. After a couple of meetings, the bishops of both Archdioceses in South Vietnam decided to dedicate the sanctuary of OLLV to the BVM as the Trung Tâm Thánh Mẫu Toàn Quốc La Vang [the National Center of the Holy Mother La Vang]. They also decided to make a request to the Holy See to elevate the Church of OLLV to the rank of a minor basilica.⁷³

Devotion to Our Lady of La Vang (1900–1961): Delightful Diocesan Devotion

Rituals of devotion to OLLV had continued to become more popular over the first half of the twentieth century despite the interruptions that occurred between 1939 and 1954. Under the care of the French bishop, the bishop of the diocese of Huế, and the clergy, devotion to OLLV grew stronger and spread out beyond the diocese. The more pilgrimages took place, the more crowded each became. Also, many favors and healings were credited to OLLV, and the sanctuary of OLLV became a center for joyous and hopeful pilgrimage that touched the hearts of many Vietnamese people.⁷⁴ This account of the second period of the history of devotion to OLLV explores three important dimensions: the emergence of new publications about OLLV, the rituals of devotion to OLLV, and the construction and improvements to the grounds of OLLV over time.

During this time, publications on the story of OLLV and many other topics related to her emerged in both French and Vietnamese. A number of periodicals were published out of France and Vietnam, many

---

72. John XXIII, *Venerabilium Nostrorum*. See Bùi, *The Catholic Church in Vietnam*, 3:302–5.

73. See Stanislas Nguyễn, *Sacred Land of La Vang*, 103–6.

74. See footnote 114, page 98.

of which can be found both in the Archives of IRFA (AMEP) as well as the archives of the diocese of Huế and other southern dioceses. Few of the individuals who wrote about OLLV were lay faithful; most were French missionaries and Vietnamese clergy. They were the apostolic vicars, missionaries, pastors of parishes of the diocese of Huế, or members of religious congregations, and all witnessed the veneration of OLLV. Their written work promulgated the devotion beyond the diocese of Huế, which caused an increasingly diverse group of people to participate in the great pilgrimages.

I have already reviewed two of the first articles published in French, namely Claude Bonin's 1901 "Notre-Dame de La-Vang" and Léopold Cadière's "Souvenir."[75] François Arsène Lemasle, who served as a pastor of Cổ Vưu and became the apostolic vicar of the diocese of Huế in 1938, further investigated the cult of devotion to OLLV. During his pastoral ministry, he encountered a seminarian of the diocese of Qui Nhơn who went to OLLV for thanksgiving. Lemasle's 1914 article on the pilgrimage defended the use of the name OLLV and discussed the development of the cult of OLLV through 1913.[76] It opened with the saying "regnum Galliae, regnum Mariae"—"the nation of France, is the nation of Mary." Speaking for himself and his French confreres, Lemasle wrote that "coming from the 'kingdom of Mary,' the missionaries feel comforted to see the cult of OLLV developing among the Anamneses Christians."[77] Apparently, Vietnam was also a kingdom of Mary. Just as the Mother of God was venerated in France, so too was she venerated at La Vang in Quảng Trị, Vietnam.

Among the slightly later French writers, J.B. Roux's work was important for reasons discussed in the first chapter. His final article, 1954's "Notre-Dame de Lavang," was published soon after the Genève Conference ended and less than a year before his death. In this piece, Roux tried to ensure that his readers, new French missionaries in the context of this hot region of the Cold War and of decolonization, would understand the story of OLLV and how it would affect their pastoral ministry.[78] At the

---

75. Bonin, "Notre Dame de La Vang"; Cadière, "Souvenir."

76. Lemasle, "Pèlerinage de Notre Dame de La Vang," 52.

77. Lemasle, "Pèlerinage de Notre Dame de La Vang," 49–52. The original quote is "C'est une bien douce consolation pour les missionnaires qui viennent de 'royaume de Marie' de voir le culte de Notre-Dame de La-vang se développer parmi les chrétiens annamites."

78. Roux, "Notre-Dame de La Vang," 299–306.

same time, a significant number of publications about OLLV were being printed in the Vietnamese language, including periodicals, chapters, and books. Many different Catholic periodicals were created, such as *Nam Kỳ Địa Phận* [Southern Diocese Bulletin], *Đức Mẹ Hằng Cứu Giúp* [Our Lady of Perpetual Help], *Tông Đồ* [Mission], *Vì Chúa* [Because of God], *Trái Tim Đức Mẹ* [The Heart of the Holy Mother], *and Sacerdos* [Priesthood Magazine]. Three periodicals in particular were frequently cited. First, under the care of the apostolic vicars, *Southern Diocese Bulletin* (hereafter *NKDP*) was a Catholic weekly bulletin based in the south of Vietnam from 1908 to 1945. *NKDP* mainly printed articles that addressed topics related to OLLV. In addition to presenting the story of OLLV and describing solemn pilgrimages, the periodical printed testimonies about the many favors and cures that she granted after devotees prayed to her. Second, *Our Lady of Perpetual Help* was published monthly under the care of the Redemptorist Province in Vietnam. At the start of its publication in 1935, this periodical was based in Hà Nội, but it moved to Sài Gòn in 1954 due to Vietnam War (see footnote 66, 67). Several important articles about OLLV were published in this periodical. Third, *Mission* was published under the care of the apostolic vicar Joannes Cassaigne and aimed to empower a wide audience to participate in the mission of the Church. It printed several significant articles about the devotion to OLLV. However, not many records exist about this periodical's history.

Along with these periodicals, several books were published that addressed the story of OLLV, the history of the development of the cult of OLLV, and her abundant favors for both Christians and non-Christians. Their authors included Dominic Cẩn Ngọc Hồ, Joseph Trang Văn Trần, J.B. Hướng, Mathew Thành Văn Lê, Peter Nghĩa, and Huôn Phát Phan, who all made significant contributions to the development of the cult of OLLV.[79] For example, as we have seen, Dominic Cẩn Ngọc Hồ collected and published two editions of *The Legend Poem of La Vang*. His commentary was initially published as three articles in *NKDP* in 1929, then republished as a complete book in 1932.[80] In addition to preaching about OLLV at mass and conferences, Hồ wrote several articles about the

---

79. Joseph Trần, *Historical Narrative*; Ho, *The Legend Poem of La Vang*; V. Lê, *Our Lady of La Vang*; Kinh L. Nguyễn, *Tuần Cửu Nhật Kính Đức Mẹ La Vang*; P. Phan, "The Apparition of Our Lady of La Vang," 308–17.

80. Hồ, "The Legend Poem of La Vang," 53–54.

history of the church of OLLV, the solemn pilgrimages, and the healings that were published in that periodical between 1912 and 1923.[81]

Along with the emergence of new publications, the cult of OLLV continued to develop over time. Initially, schedules for processions were laid out by the Bishop Caspar of Huế. The annual Lunar New Year pilgrimage and, at this point, the triennial August pilgrimage were one-day events. While the Lunar New Year procession only took place at La Vang, the August procession began at the Church of Cổ Vưu and ended at La Vang. Known as solemn pilgrimages, this devotion attracted a diverse group of pilgrims. The pilgrimage had become a part of the lives of the members of the diocese of Huế by 1904,[82] and reciting the rosary, singing songs, and praying privately to OLLV were common practices associated with it.

Over time, these practices were enhanced. Soon after his consecration as the Bishop of Huế, Eugène-Marie-Joseph Allys (1852–1936) decided that the great processions should last for three days—"the Tridium de fêtes."[83] This schedule continued to be honored by his successor, Bishop Alexandre Chabanon (1873–1936), after he retired in 1931. The new bishop also paid more attention to the sacred shrine; he decided that the processions should be entirely performed at the shrine of OLLV instead of proceeding from Cổ Vưu to La Vang. He established that the date of the Lunar New Year procession should be flexible and could take place on any of several possible days, depending on the bishop's decision. Under the subsequent care of Bishop François Arsène Lemasle (1874–1946), participation in the procession was strongly encouraged as a form of devotion to OLLV.[84] The schedules developed for the processions built up the tradition of OLLV, as both the annual and triennial pilgrimages became the signature pastoral ministries of the diocese.

Meanwhile, the formal rite of OLLV was also being created. First, the liturgy of Marian titles was celebrated at the sanctuary of OLLV. Soon after 1900, Bonin decided to celebrate the feast of the Blessed Virgin Mary at the Church of OLLV because the faithful loved her. In his report,

---

81. See J. Trần, *Tiểu Sử và Thư Mục Đức Cha Dominic Hồ Ngọc Cẩn*; Roux, "Le Grand Pèlerinage," 837.

82. See Cadière, "Souvenir," 45. Cadière succeeded Bonin as pastor of Cổ Vưu in 1904, the time of the great pilgrimage.

83. For more details, see Cadière, "Souvenir," 45; Roux, "Le Grand Pèlerinage," 834.

84. Stanislas Nguyễn, *Sacred Land of La Vang*, 67–68; AMEP, vol. 761, 154; The Archive of Diocese of Huế, "Directoire du Vicariat Apostolique Huế," 1941, #265.

Bishop Caspar not only acknowledges the growing devotion to OLLV, but also indirectly approves Bonin's decision:

> The sanctuary of OLLV continued to attract pilgrims; [therefore,] Father Bonin decided that all the feasts of the Blessed Virgin would be celebrated in the early morning specifically to satisfy the devout Christians and allow them to receive communion. The mass is often sung, and the pilgrims never fail to come *en masse* to beseech the help of the Holy Mother.[85]

The devotion to OLLV that was being expressed through the Marian feasts that took place at the Church of OLLV represented a significant step forward for the cult of OLLV. Furthermore, in this episcopal report, we see that the cult of OLLV actually developed between 1900–2. Combining these elements with Michael Cadière's "Souvenir" makes it possible to conclude, first, that Bonin created the formal cult of OLLV, and second, that it was clearly approved by his bishop.

We see here also that the name of OLLV, in particular, was elevated and honored. This title had been invoked during the persecutions that took place between 1798 and 1900, and later on, in the context of free religious practice, continued to be honored. During the great pilgrimage that took place in 1910, Patinier encouraged the pilgrims to love and trust in Our Lady of La Vang. His exhortation was quoted in Allys's annual report: "Before the mass with an enthusiastic speech, Father Patinier urges the pilgrims to love OLLV more and more and to trust confidently in Her."[86] Patinier's acknowledgement of the protection of OLLV and her maternal care for all Vietnamese people emerged from his personal experiences at La Vang and had a huge impact on the promotion of the cult of OLLV beyond the local people.

Furthermore, in his annual report in 1913, Allys stated, "The name Our Lady of La Vang is becoming more popular every day among all the missions of the Cochinchine."[87] In a 1919 homily, Dominic Cần Ngọc Hồ preached that, just as the visitation to Elizabeth made her rejoice, OLLV

---

85. AMEP, vol. 761, 101. The original quote is "Le sanctuaire de Notre-Dame de La Vang continue à attirer les pèlerins; M. Bonin a décidé qu'à toutes les fêtes de la sainte Vierge, il y aurait une messe basse pour satisfaire la dévotion des chrétiens et leur permettre de communier. Bien souvent la messe est chantée et les pèlerins ne manquent pas d'accourir en foule pour implorer le secours de la Bonne Mère."

86. AMEP, vol. 761, 154. The original quote is "avant la messe, M. Patinier adresse quelques vibrantes paroles aux pèlerins, pour les exhorter à aimer de plus en plus Notre Dame de La Vang et à ne mettre aucune limite à leur confiance en Elle."

87. Allys, "Annual Report in 1913," AMEP, vol. 761, 179.

visited La Vang and gave it abundant graces which delighted all.[88] In 1932 Roux added, "What is obvious is that the Blessed Virgin chose this small quiet valley for her place in Annam, as she chose other places in various countries of the world. It is she who attracts the crowds and she who delights to grant abundantly spiritual and temporal favors. At first, it was the purely local cult of OLLV, which has continued to grow, and it is now out of the whole of Indochina that crowds flock."[89] And as we saw, in "A Prayer to the Holy Mother La Vang," Joseph-Marie Thích Văn Nguyễn declared OLLV to be the Mother of Jesus Christ, God, and humanity.[90] These records demonstrate the strong belief in OLLV, situate her apparition at La Vang as her visitation, and proclaim her rich theology.

The title of the Church of OLLV, "Our Lady Help of Christians," also helped to elevate the name OLLV. In Vietnamese culture, a person's title can replace their name, especially when they are in a high position. The title Our Lady Help of Christians thus helped reinforce the dignified image of OLLV, who always helps Christians, just as the Church taught. A number of French and Vietnamese scholars mention this title in their work.[91] This title was reinstated during the erection of the new church of OLLV in 1913, per Allys: "The mass of Our Lady Help of Christians, the title of the new Church, was celebrated by Fr. Combourieu, Provincial of the Laos Mission."[92]

The image of OLLV, along with her name and title, played a role in promoting the cult of OLLV. A statue of Notre Dame de Victoire [Our Lady of Victory] was installed during the first diocesan pilgrimage in 1900. No records exist that document the reasons why the church leaders decided to use this statue; however, the fact that French missionaries were in charge

---

88. Dominic Cẩn Ngọc Hồ, homily published with the title "Be Joyful" in *NKDP*, No. 562. (1919), 745–47.

89. Roux, "Le Grand Pèlerinage," 833. This original quote is "Ce qui est de toute évidence c'est que la Ste Vierge a choisi ce vallon solitaire pour son pied à terre en Annam, comme elle en a choisi d'autres en divers pays du monde. C'est elle qui y attire les foules, et Elle se plaît à y distribuer abondamment ses grâces spirituelles et temporelles. Aussi le culte de N. D. de La-vang, d'abord purement local n'a cessé de grandir, et c'est maintenant de toute l'Indochine que les foules y accourent."

90. J-M. Nguyễn, "A Prayer to the Holy Mother La Vang," line 3, 15–16.

91. For example, J. Trân, "Nhà Thờ Đức Mẹ La Vang," 556; Lemasle, "Pèlerinage de Notre Dame de La Vang," 50; Roux, "Le Grand Pèlerinage," 841; Stanislas Nguyễn, *Sacred Land of La Vang*, 54; Q. Trân, *Pilgrimage to Diocese of Huế*, 1:225.

92. Allys, "Annual Report" 1928, 121. The original quote is "La messe de Notre-Dame Auxiliatrice, titulaire de la nouvelle église, a été chantée par M. Combourieu, Provicaire de la Mission du Laos."

at the diocese of Huế and that OLLV had protected the Christians during the long century of the persecutions likely influenced this choice. Also, the statue of Our Lady of Victory depicts the unique relationship between the Holy Mother and Jesus Christ. This image was introduced to the Vietnamese people during the early days of Christianity in the country,[93] and the image of OLLV was subject to ongoing theological interpretations—in this case relating, perhaps, to victory over persecution.

At the same time, favors and healings credited to OLLV became widespread. As we have seen a collection of reports of earlier incidents was published in both French and Vietnamese, and many believed that these gifts signaled approval for the name OLLV. Another witness to the powerful name OLLV was Huy, a seminarian from the Diocese of Quy Nhon, who had been suffering from typhoid fever. All typical treatments failed, and even the French Sisters at the hospital felt that there was nothing else to be done. However, after being advised to pray to OLLV, Huy did so, and began to recover:

> Confined to my bed, in hopelessness, I was waiting to die when I received a visit from Father Perreaux, whom I formerly assisted as catechist. The Father told me about Our Lady of La Vang. He told me that the Holy Virgin had already granted plenty of favors at that place and that she seemed to dedicate lavish favors to our land of Annam. . . . Indeed, it was Our Lady of La Vang who healed me, and I thank her with all my heart. Scholars and saints have declared themselves powerless to celebrate the Holy Mother. I am ignorant; I cannot undertake such a task, but these few lines written by order of my superiors tell everyone that Our Lady of La Vang never abandons those who have recourse to her.[94]

---

93. Joseph Trân, "Kiệu Ảnh Đức Mẹ Nhà Thờ La Vang," 557; Roux, "Pèlerinage à Notre-Dame de Lavang," 788. See also P. Phan, *Mission and Catechesis*, 271–72.

94. Lemasle, "Guerison de Pierre Huy." For information about other healings, see Bulletin de M.E.P (1932), 461–62; 465–66; V. Lê, *Our Lady of La Vang*, 56. Lemasle was an administrator of the church of OLLV from 1911–21. In 1937, he became bishop of Huế. The original quote is "Cloué sur mon lit, désespère, j'attendais la mort quand je reçus la visite de P. Perreaux que j'avais verve jadis comme catéchiste. Le Père me parla de Notre-Dame de Lavang, me dit que la Sainte Vierge avait déjà fait en ce lieu de nombreux miracles, qu'elle semblait vouloir, sous ce vocable, combler de ses faveurs notre terre d'Annam. . . . C'est bien Notre-Dame de Lavang qui m'a guéri, et je la remercie de tout mon cœur. Des savants, des saints se sont déclarés impuissants à célébrer dignement cette bonne Mère. Je ne suis, qu'un ignorant qui entreprendre pareille tâche, mais ces quelques lignes, écrites par ordre de mes supérieurs, dissent ne sait pas s'exprimer; je ne peux pas à tous que Notre-Dame de Lavang n'abandonne jamais ceux qui ont recours à elle."

Even though his recovery took about four months, Huy believed that he was healed after praying a novena to OLLV. Many other favors and incidents of healing credited to OLLV were reported in books and other publications such as *NKDP*.

Furthermore, as the pilgrimages continued to be organized, the number and diversity of the pilgrims increased. Discerning the exact number of pilgrims is a difficult task, but it seems that each year more and more pilgrims were arriving, as Allys wrote: "What is certain is that the number of the pilgrims has increased with each pilgrimage."[95] As with Lourdes, the rise of the railway probably assisted; Cadière made it more convenient and affordable for pilgrims to make the journey to La Vang by negotiating a special fare with senior officials of the Indochina Railways.[96]

Peter Nghĩa (1891–1981), who was born at Cổ Vưu and ordained for the diocese of Huế in 1918, highlighted the growing number of pilgrims and his hometown's strong devotion to OLLV. Nghĩa describes that under the direction of the pastor, the lay faithful of the district decorated the Church and the surrounding sacred land as well as put-up welcoming signs along the pathways. The pastor encouraged his parishioners to guide their children and invite their neighbors to venerate the Holy Mother by going on the pilgrimage to La Vang. But pilgrims also started to come from across the nation as they gained confidence in OLLV.[97] Nghĩa saw the significant roles played by the pastor and the lay faithful of Dinh Cát/Quảng Trị in developing this national thirst for the great pilgrimage. These observations are supported by statistics cited by Bishop Lemasle. In 1900, he wrote, there were twelve thousand participants, and the number of pilgrims went up to thirty thousand in 1938.[98] Indeed, despite the fact that La Vang was located on a deserted mountain, the holy land became like a busy city.

The diversity of the pilgrims who arrived at the site also grew with time. The apostolic vicars noted that these came from many different regions, such as Tonkin, Annam (central Vietnam), Cochinchine,

---

95. AMEP, vol. 761, 179. The original quote is "ce qui est certain, c'est que le nombre des pèlerins augmente à chaque pèlerinage."

96. Cadière, "Souvenir." For more details, see J. Trân, "Procession of the Holy Mother at the Church of La Vang"; Hổ, "Kiệu đại hội tại La Vang."

97. Peter Nghĩa, "Tam Nhụt đại hội tại La Vang," 540.

98. Lemasle, "Huế." The original qupte is "On a évalué à plus de 30.000 les pèlerins qui ont passé à La Vang durant ces trois jours." Bishop Lemasle was a previous pastor of Cổ Vưu and organized several pilgrimages. See Nghia, "Tam Nhut Dai Hoi tai La Vang."

Cambodia, and Laos. They also mentioned specific cities: Sài Gòn, Quy Nhơn, Vinh, Hà Nội, Lạng Sơn, Nong-Seng, and Lao.[99] The gathering was international, as Allys wrote regarding the great pilgrimage of 1928: "I cannot remain silent about the most delightful event for our Mission: the blessing of the church of La Vang and the pilgrimage, which took place on this occasion. It was the Vicar Apostolic who blessed this new sanctuary in the presence of S.G. Mgr. Gouin, the Apostolic Vicar of Laos, and many clergy, whose ranks, as we noticed, were representative of the Missions of Saigon, Quinhon, Vinh, Nong-Seng, and Hanoi."[100] Ten years later Lemasle reported, similarly, "The Catholics and even the non-Christians came there from various regions of Indochina, even from Langson, Hanoi, Laos, and Saigon."[101]

As this last quotation suggests, it was also clear to observers that the crowds of pilgrims included non-Christians, whose numbers also grew as the number of solemn pilgrimages increased. Although J.B. Roux started his mission in 1898 and perhaps went on pilgrimages to OLLV beginning in 1900, he did not write about OLLV until 1932, when he pointed out, "A certain number of the non-Christians were among this crowd (more than one could be seen prostrating themselves from afar towards the sanctuary, their foreheads in the dust), because the pagans, too, have great confidence in OLLV, and, like the Christians, they address requests to her: 'This place, they said, is linh [sacred/spirit],' that is to say, the supernatural divine manifests itself there in an effective way."[102] Roux's article also gives a sense of how many people might have made the journey that year:

---

99. See Allys, "Annual Report" 1928, 119–22; Lemasle, "Huế," 156–60.

100. Allys, "Annual Report" 1928, 121. The original quote is "Je ne puis passer sous silence un événement des plus consolants pour notre Mission: la bénédiction de l'église de Lavang, et le pèlerinage qui eut lieu à cette occasion. C'est le Vicaire Apostolique qui a béni ce nouveau sanctuaire, en présence de S.G. Mgr Gouin Vicaire Apostolique du Laos, et d'un nombreux clergé, dans les rangs duquel on remarquait des représentants des Missions de Saïgon, Quinhon, Vinh, Nong-Seng et Hanoï."

101. Lemasle, "Huế," 156–60. The original quote is "Des catholiques et même des païens y sont venus des diverses parties de l'Indochine, même de Lạng Sơn, de Hà Nội, du Laos et de Saïgon."

102. Roux, "Le Grand Pèlerinage de Notre Dame de La Vang," 840. The original quote is "Un certain nombre de païens se trouvaient parmi cette foule (on en voyait plus d'un se prosterner de loin vers le sanctuaire, le front dans la poussière), car les païens, eux aussi, ont une grande confiance en N.D. de La-Vang, et, comme les chrétiens, ils lui adressent des requêtes: 'ce lieu, dissent-ils, est linh,' c'est-à-dire, le surnaturel, le divin s'y manifeste d'une manière efficace."

> What was the number of pilgrims during these three days? It is very difficult to say, even approximately; but according to the estimation of several reliable people, it seems that the following figures are not exaggerated. Nearly seven thousand people took part in the inaugural procession of the first day. In the evening, this number was almost doubled. Then the number rose to about twenty thousand and held there until the end. But during the procession of the Blessed Sacrament, it surely exceeded twenty-five thousand.[103]

For Roux the increasing number of the pilgrims mattered, but their acts of worship and veneration were even more important. In the phrase of *Sacrosanctum Concilium*, the pilgrims exhibited "full, active, conscious" participation in worship and devotion.

The great pilgrimages were major sources of pastoral and religious formation. At La Vang, pilgrims prayed unceasingly, day and night by reciting the rosary, chanting, and saying other prayers. Roux quoted one participant: "'We only heard the sound of songs and prayers,' noted a pilgrim from Hanoi who wrote his impressions in a beautiful article published by the *Avenir de Tonkin*."[104] The continuous prayer took place at the sanctuary. Bishop Lemasle also noted this practice: "With what piety, what truly touching devotion, the Christians recited prayers day and night! And not only inside of the Church of OLLV, but also outside."[105] The pilgrims also participated in the Sacrament of Confession and received the Eucharist. In 1914, Lemasle reported, there were six thousand penitents and ten thousand communicants.[106] This period was indeed marked by an ongoing formation of the faithful.

---

103. Roux, "Le Grand Pèlerinage de Notre Dame de La Vang," 840. The original quote is "Quel fut le nombre des pèlerins pendant ces trois jours? Il est bien difficile de dire, même approximativement: mais d'après l'estimation de plusieurs personnes dignes de foi il semble que les chiffres suivants ne seraient pas exagérés. A la procession inaugurale du premier jour prirent part près de sept mille personnes. Le soir, ce nombre était presque doublé. Puis le chiffre monta jusqu'à environ vingt mille et s'y maintint jusqu'à la fin. Mais pendant la procession de St-Sacrement il dépassa surement vingt-cinq mille."

104. Roux, "Le Grand Pèlerinage de Notre Dame de La Vang," 840. The original quote is "'On entendait seulement le bruit des chants et des prières,' note un pèlerin de Hanoi qui a consigné ses impressions dans un bel article publié par l' Avenir de Tonkin."

105. Lemasle, "Hué," 159. The original quote is "avec quelle piété, qu'elle dévotion vraiment touchante les chrétiens récitaient jour et nuit des prières, non seulement dans la vaste église de N.-D. de La Vang, mais aussi en dehors!"

106. See Lemasle, "Pèlerinage de Notre Dame de La Vang," 51; Roux, "Le Grand Pèlerinage de Notre Dame de La Vang," 841.

The History of the Devotion to Our Lady of La Vang

Pilgrims also learned about OLLV through conferences, sermons, and homilies that described the Marian apparition and the history of the devotion. Roux, for example, reported many sermons and conferences in his 1932 article that explored the relationships between OLLV or the Holy Mother and the Church, the Eucharist, and evangelization.

> In the afternoon around three o'clock, Father Can gave a lecture on the origin and development of the cult of the Blessed Virgin at La Vang. This conference is the greatest interest to the Christians. In fact, many, even those who are very devoted to OLLV, are completely unaware of the history of this venerable sanctuary. . . . They are above all in honor of the Blessed Virgin, OLLV, whose name never ceased to be exalted and invoked by thousands of voices and thousands of hearts during these blessed days.[107]

This formation was important because in Vietnam basic Catholicism was often taught by helping people memorize the Creed and several prayers. Sermons and conferences thus played an important role in the ongoing formation of the lay faithful. In addition to acquiring knowledge about the story of OLLV, the pilgrims honored and invoked the name OLLV continuously and concretely. Allys wrote in 1910 that "one of the great advantages of such a demonstration is, says Father Cadière, that the Christians, who gathered in such large numbers, encourage each other, become aware of their strength, and feel their faith and their attachment to the religion enlarged."[108] Both the bishop and the clergy realized that because they gathered huge numbers of pilgrims, the great pilgrimages offered a good opportunity to provide deeper faith formation.

During this time, finally, the construction on the grounds surrounding the church of OLLV was undertaken collaboratively. Construction was continuous, and the lay faithful freely participated under the care of

---

107. Roux, "Le Grand Pèlerinage," 837, 840. The original quote is "L'après-midi, vers trois heures, conférence par le P. Cẩn sur l'origine et le développement du culte de la Ste Vierge à La-Vang. Cette conférence intéresse au plus haut point les chrétiens: beaucoup, en effet, très dévots à N. D. de La-Vang, ignorent complètement l'historique de ce vénérable sanctuaire. . . Elles sont surtout à l'honneur de la Sainte Vierge, Notre Dame de La-Vang, dont le nom, durant ces jours bénis, ne cessa d'être exalté, invoqué par des milliers de voix, par des milliers de cœurs."

108. Allys, "Annual Report" 1910, 154. The original quote is "Un des grands avantages d'une telle manifestation, c'est, dit M. Cadière, que les chrétiens, réunis en si grand nombre, s'affirment, prennent conscience de leurs forces et sentent grandir par là leur foi et leur attachement à la Religion."

the clergy both by donating and by volunteering time and labor. While discussing this type of work, Cadière writes that "The Church was the work of my predecessors. Or, better, everyone had a hand in it. Fr. Bonnard had ordered the timber for the framework. However, Fr. Patinier had done the work and raised the Church."[109] Other building was done in accordance with the need of the pilgrims. A well was dug in 1903, and several buildings designed to serve the clergy and the pilgrims were constructed over time. By 1924, the Church of OLLV had been degraded by flood and tropical storms, so Bishop Allys called for donations to rebuild. A diverse group of donors from around the nation ensured that the construction was complete after around four years.[110] Unlike the first brick church, built on the sacred land where the oral tradition said that OLLV stood when she appeared, the new church was rebuilt a distance away because the bishop wanted to preserve the old church for the sake of history. Unfortunately, it was eventually demolished because it became too dangerous. After it was torn down, however, a *Linh Đài Đức Mẹ La Vang* [A Sacred Shrine of OLLV] was built on the old church's floor; it was blessed during the thirteenth great pilgrimage in 1955 (fig. 6).[111]

---

109. Cadière, "Souvenirs," 47. The original quote is "L'église était l'œuvre de plusieurs de mes prédécesseurs. Ou mieux, tous y avaient mis la main. Le Père Bonnard avait commandé le bois de la charpente. Mais c'est le Père Patinier qui l'avait fait œuvre et qui avait élevé l'glissé."

110. Morineau, "Thu Cam On," 534.

111. See Stanislas Nguyễn, *Sacred Land of La Vang*, 51; Q. Trân, *Pilgrimage to Diocese of Huế*, 3:152–54. AMEP holds the image of the sacred sanctuary.

The History of the Devotion to Our Lady of La Vang

Fig. 6: The Shrine of Our Lady of La Vang was built in 1955, IRFA, bt. Vietnam 29 (© France-Asia Research Institute/MEP with document reference).

The architecture of the Church and its grounds combined Western and Eastern styles. J.B. Huong described the first brick church of OLLV, built around the turn of the century: "The inside of the Church is designed in accordance with Annamese architecture.... The outside of the Church looks like the European style.... There are two towers in front of two sides of the Church."[112] Apparently, Western and Eastern styles fused in the construction of the church and served as an early example of architectural inculturation. The new church erected in 1928 was also designed in a way that combined the styles of Western churches and ancient Vietnamese buildings. As Roux described, "Father Parmentier, the director of the French School of the Far East, designed the Church in a new style, which combined the classic architecture of the Western churches with the architecture of the ancient people of Indochina."[113] The harmony between West and East made the church even more beautiful because it

---

112. Hướng, "Going to Visit the Sanctuary of Our Lady of La Vang," 268. The original quote is "bề trong nhà thờ theo cách kiểu annam, vừa chứa đặng vài trăm người. Mặt tiền có hơi theo kiểu tây.... mà trước có hai tháp làm dang ra hai bên."

113. Roux, "Le Grand Pèlerinage de Notre Dame de La-Vang," 834. The original quote is "M. Parmentier, alors Directeur de l'Ecole Française d'Extrême-Orient, en traça le plan. Il est conçu dans un style nouveau: aux formes classiques des églises d'Occident s'unissent des réminiscences de l'architecture des anciens peuples de l'Indochine."

was unifying. This type of stylistic balance would continue into the third period of OLLV's history (1961–2021).

The sanctuary of OLLV became an even more significant refuge during stages of political chaos. In a 1960 report, a missionary of MEP in the diocese of Huế named Louis Valour (1895–1979) said that "La Vang, a center of pilgrimage, was chosen for Father Etchrren [to visit] as an entirely Vietnamese environment where he had the opportunity to meet many Vietnamese Fathers passing through, which will benefit his future ministry."[114] Evidently, then, the sanctuary was understood as a spiritual center for many people before it was chosen as Trung Tâm Thánh Mẫu Toàn Quốc La Vang [The National Center of the Holy Mother La Vang] in April of 1961 by the Bishops of South Vietnam.[115] Moreover, the history of devotion to OLLV, as presented above, displays that pilgrims came from many different territories. Just as they did when the BVM appeared in 1798 to offer protection and strengthen their faith, the Vietnamese people, especially the Vietnamese Catholics, trusted OLLV to keep them resilient and help promote peace across the nation.

The great pilgrimages were suspended after 1938 and did not resume until 1955, when one occurred from August 17–19. In *Mission*, Fr. Peter Viên provided descriptions of the event that echoed details about previous great pilgrimages, such as the huge and diverse number of pilgrims, processions of OLLV and the Eucharist, recitation of the rosary, and chants. One of the most important dimensions of the event was prayer for mothers and family life. For example, Viên noted, "A mass was celebrated on the 18th to pray for mothers, and after the mass there was a ritual for the mothers to dedicate their children and their families to the Holy Mother."[116] This ministry honored the vocation of married women and reflected the way that Marian devotion empowered women's vocations.

As we have seen, the socio-political chaos that stemmed from the French colonial administration, World War II, the First Indochina War,

---

114. Louis Valour, "Report in 1960," https://irfa.paris/en/ancienne_publication/rapport-annuel-1960/region-sud-indochine. The original quote is "Lavang, centre de pèlerinage, a été choisi pour le P. Etcharren, en un milieu entièrement vietnamien où il a eu l'occasion de rencontrer de nombreux Pères Vietnamiens de passage, ce qui lui sera profitable pour son ministère futur."

115. The Bishops of the South of Vietnam, Conference (DaLat: April 13, 1961); Stanislas Nguyễn, *Sacred Land of La Vang*, 103.

116. Viên, "Đại Hội Kính Đức Mẹ La Vang," 380. The original quote is: "Ngày 18, có lễ riêng cho các Bà Mẹ gia đình. Sau lễ có nghi thức cho các Bà Mẹ dâng con và gia đình cho Đức Mẹ."

and the beginning of the Vietnam War were key factors that affected and shaped the second period of the history of devotion to OLLV (1900–61). In the midst of struggle and division, Vietnamese people continued to believe that OLLV was there for them. This period was marked by tremendous growth, and the devotion of OLLV developed far beyond what it had in the first period. Just as OLLV arrived during a time of persecution and accompanied an earlier generation of Vietnamese Christians, so too did she continue mothering the Church in Vietnam during the ups and downs of this second period.

3

The History of Devotion to Our Lady of La Vang Continues

The Third Period (1961–2022): Robust National Devotion to OLLV

THE THIRD PERIOD OF the history of devotion to OLLV is a fascinating mix of success and struggle. These six decades of devotion reflect the history of Vietnam, including the Vietnam War, the tensions of a political transition, and an improving relationship between the Church and the government after the 1980s. At the beginning of the third period, devotion to OLLV moved from the local to national as the Vietnamese bishops designated the shrine of OLLV as Trung Tâm Thánh Mẫu Toàn Quốc La Vang [The National Center/Shrine of the Holy Mother La Vang], and at the same time Pope John XXIII approved their request to elevate the church of OLLV to the rank of a minor basilica. These two ecclesiastical decisions, along with further actions of later church leaders (especially Pope John Paul II), assisted in expanding devotion to OLLV despite periods of suffering. The efforts of the local church, especially the involvement of the Catholic Bishops' Conference of Vietnam, aided the recovery of devotion to OLLV as the tense relationship with the government eased over time.

This chapter is structured into three sections that examine the devotion to OLLV in the context of the socio-political situation of Vietnam. The first section, on 1961–72, examines the continuing initial growth

The History of Devotion to Our Lady of La Vang Continues 101

of national devotion to OLLV; the period from 1972–88 represents the restricted but still resolute devotion to OLLV; and the third, from 1988–2022 delineates the robust national, even international devotion to OLLV.

Sources for Study of Devotion to OLLV from 1961 to 2022

The sources for this history of devotion to OLLV are diverse. Many of them come from the local church, namely, the Archive of the Archdiocese of Huế, from periodicals, and from scholars who study OLLV. I also use material from the teaching of the universal Church. The Archive of the Archdiocese of Huế holds its history, episcopal teaching about OLLV, the biographies of the ordained, and documents written by the clergy of the Archdiocese. The archives also have a variety of periodicals, such as the surviving issues of the important magazine *Đức Mẹ La Vang* [*Our Lady of La Vang*].[1] This magazine covered the history of OLLV, updates on the construction of the National Center/Shrine of the Holy Mother of La Vang, schedules of worship and of pilgrimages, articles on Catholicism in general, and other related topics. Although *Đức Mẹ La Vang* encompassed thirty-five issues from 1961 to 1964, many were permanently lost due to the Vietnam War. What remains in the archive, however, provides significant evidence about activity during the early 1960s.[2] Later, I will also draw on the periodical *Công Giáo và Dân Tộc* [Catholic and Nation]. Founded after 1975, this periodical published several important articles about OLLV, on topics such as national pilgrimages and inculturation. For diaspora publications, I will draw on several websites of federations of Vietnamese Catholics in the USA and Dân Chúa Châu Âu to demonstrate the devotion to OLLV beyond the Vietnamese border. Since the hierarchy of the Catholic Church in Vietnam was established in its present

---

1. Because Matthew Lê's account has the same title, *Đức Mẹ La Vang* [Our Lady of La Vang], I keep the title of this periodical in Vietnamese: *Đức Mẹ La Vang*.

2. Later *La Vang Nội San* [Journal of La Vang] filled the gap it left; however, it is for insiders, not the general public. *Tông Đồ* [Mission] also provided several articles about national pilgrimages during the 1960s. Another periodical, *Đức Mẹ Hằng Cứu Giúp* [Our Lady of Perpetual Help] was a monthly magazine under care of the members of the Redemptorist Province in Vietnam. Founded in Hanoi in 1935, this periodical was relocated to Saigon in 1954, where it ended by the middle of 1975, but it was restored in 1985 in Long Beach, CA. This magazine provided several historical accounts of the devotion to OLLV before 1975. Several periodicals, such as *Bản Tin La Vang, Nguồn Sống, Sống Tin Mừng*, and *Vì Chúa* also published articles about pilgrimages to and/or poems about OLLV before being shut down after 1975.

form in 1960, in the story of the third period of the history of devotion to OLLV, the terms for several titles are also updated accordingly. In this chapter I refer to the Church in Vietnam, the Archdiocese of Huế, the Archbishop of Huế, the National Shrine/Center of the Holy Mother La Vang, the Basilica of Our Lady of La Vang, and the National Pilgrimages (every third August).

The First Period: 1961–1972

Socio-Religious-Political Factors

As previously discussed, events following World War II led to two simultaneous Vietnamese governments with the 17th Parallel as a border (see fig. 4). In the 1960s, internal conflict escalated with the Buddhist protests against the policies of President Diệm Đình Ngô in Sài Gòn in 1963, followed by his assassination the same year.[3] His death indirectly affected devotion to OLLV, as I will discuss later. Along with the Tet Offensive in 1968, the Easter Offensive demolished Quảng Trị province in 1972, leaving the Basilica of OLLV and its surrounding buildings a mass of rubble. Only the shrine and the belltower of the basilica survived (see fig. 9).

---

3. See Hammer, *A Death in November*. President Ngô was born into a devout Catholic family, whose family members included both military officers and martyrs. He is a blood brother of Archbishop Martin-Peter Thục Đình Ngô. Investigating the Buddhist crisis in 1963 is beyond my study in this project, which focuses on history and theology of Vietnamese devotion to OLLV. In fact, the Vietnam War remains a complicated topic. The year 1963 was chaotic in South Vietnam with several critical events, such as the Buddhist protests and movement in Huế and Sài Gòn , the immolation of the monk Thich Quang Duc, and the assassinations of Mr. Diem Dinh Ngo, President of South Vietnam, and his brother, a Vietnamese archivist and politician. The first two events probably lead to the third one that caused Archbishop Thuc Dinh Ngo, a blood brother of the late President, to be "exiled;" after the second session of the Vatican Council ending in Rome in 1963, the Archbishop remained outside Vietnam and resigned his office in 1967. However, international observers view the immolation of Thich Quang Duc in 1963 as evidence that Buddhists were persecuted under the regime of President Diem Dinh Ngo,. In reality, the Buddhist protests and movements continued happening after his death. See Robert J. Topmiller, *The Lotus Unleashed: The Buddhist Peace Movement in South Vietnam, 1964–1966* (University Press of Kentucky, 2002); David L. Anderson and John Ernst. *The War that Never Ends* (Lexington: The University Press of Kentucky, 2014); Geoffrey Shaw, *The Lost Mandate of Heaven: The American Betrayal of Ngo Dinh Diem, President of Vietnam* (San Francisco: Ignatius Press, 2015); Mitchell K. Hall, *The Vietnam War*, 3rd Ed. (New York: Routledge, 2018); Christopher E. Goscha, *Vietnam: A New History* (New York: Basic Books, 2016; *Liberator of Asia: The True Story of Ngo Dinh Diem*, DVD, produced by Ignatius Press (San Francisco: Ignatius Press, 2022).

In addition, because communist soldiers occupied Quảng Trị province, many local Catholics and others fled further into southern Vietnam.

The Dawn of National Devotion to OLLV: Hope and Struggle

It is fascinating to observe the devotion to OLLV in this calamitous period which saw both hope and struggle. The Bishops of South Vietnam designated the grounds of OLLV as the National Center/Shrine of the Holy Mother La Vang (hereafter NC-OLLV) on April 13, 1961. Pope John XXIII elevated the church of OLLV to the rank of a minor basilica on August 22, 1961. These ecclesial promotions meant the beginning of a stronger devotion to OLLV recognized at the national level and an enthusiastic national and international commitment to the construction of the NC-OLLV. After this the triennial great pilgrimage began to be considered a national pilgrimage, beginning with the 15th pilgrimage in 1961; however, national pilgrimages were suspended or shortened after that due to the Vietnam War and the subsequent political transition.

As the Archbishop of Huế, President Diệm Đình Ngô's oldest brother, Peter-Martin Thục Đình Ngô (1897–1984), was very important for both the NC-OLLV's construction and the devotion to OLLV.[4] The archbishop was both the director of the construction of the NC-OLLV and the host of the great pilgrimages. He also actively promoted national devotion to OLLV by establishing periodicals and encouraging the use of other media, such as radio, video, and TV. It was he who invited collaborators and provided goals for the magazine *Đức Mẹ La Vang*, by which he hoped to communicate with the Vietnamese laity about the construction of the NC-OLLV and all things related to OLLV. On the first page of the first issue, the archbishop reported:

> [The bishops] chose the Shrine of OLLV as the national shrine to dedicate to the Sacred Heart of the Immaculate Conception of the Holy Mother. They instructed that the grounds surrounding the Basilica should be constructed in such a way as to become the center of perpetual adoration of the Eucharist and the center of veneration of the Vietnamese martyrs. . . . [A place] to pray

---

4. See Bích Ngọc Lê, *Figures of Diocese of Huế*, 2:263–69. Born into a devout Catholic family in Huế, Archbishop Ngô inherited a strong devotion to OLLV and an interest in his ancestor martyrs.

for peace, the unification of the nation, and religious freedom through the intercession of OLLV.[5]

Peace, reunion of the nation, and religious freedom were the urgent needs not just of Catholics but of all the Vietnamese people. As the archbishop reminded readers, "La Vang is the house of all Vietnamese people, both Christians and non-Christians."[6] Just as OLLV was a mother of all, La Vang became the common house. This was why it was important that the magazine communicate the status of the construction of the NC-OLLV.

Đức Mẹ La Vang also provided space for studies about OLLV and other topics, such as parenting, Catholic education, Marian devotion around the world, and theologies of specific celebrations at the National Marian Center. For example, in an article titled "Đây, La Vang của Chúng Ta" [Here, Our La Vang], A. Th, the author, presented the story and the history of development of the Shrine of OLLV. He concluded that "We have enough reasons to believe that La Vang will unite the north, the middle, and the south. La Vang is the center of unity of faith of the Viet nation."[7] Though the magazine lasted only three years, it was the first periodical dedicated to OLLV and intended for all the Vietnamese people. It also encouraged study of many aspects of the devotion to OLLV.

Simultaneously, Archbishop Ngô put major effort into organizing the fifteenth great pilgrimage. He was active in inviting all Vietnamese people, both Catholics and non-Catholics, to participate; his letters and radio speeches expressed the hope that everyone would receive his warm invitation and his call for peace, union, and religious freedom. The archbishop also spoke of the purposes for participating in this great pilgrimage in an invitation letter published in the first issue of *Đức Mẹ La Vang*: "To encourage the devotion to OLLV, to pray for the hierarchy of the Church in Vietnam in a new mission, to pray for the Church in Vietnam in a new situation, to beg the Holy Mother to protect us from communist systems, the great pilgrimage to OLLV will take place from the 17th to 22nd of August 1961."[8]

The urgent need of the Church was to serve the urgent need of the nation. To call for devotion to OLLV, who had protected Christians

---

5. Archbishop Ngô, "Mấy Lời Phi Lộ," 3.
6. Archbishop Ngô, "Mấy Lời Phi Lộ," 4.
7. A. Th, "Đây, La Vang của Chúng Ta."
8. Archbishop Ngô, "Lời Hiệu Triệu," 19.

during the past centuries of persecutions, was to entrust to her the Vietnamese people. Also, as representative of all the Vietnamese church leaders, the archbishop invited all Vietnamese to participate in the fifteenth triennial pilgrimage.

> Our dream is to see peace and national union. . . . We would like to invite you, everyone throughout the nation, whatever religions, whatever political perspectives, to] participate in the great pilgrimage to venerate the Holy Mother at her Shrine, which was built due to the donations of Christians and non-Christians of the north, the middle, and the south.[9]

At the NC-OLLV, everyone was included in the invitation to pray together for the crucial need of peace and unity for the Vietnamese. The archbishop's invitation was also broadcast on the radio across the south of Vietnam; he hoped to gather the People of God to entreat OLLV for peace, unification, and religious freedom.

He also invited many members of the Church to be co-organizers of the pilgrimage. Bishops, clergy, and laity collaborated by taking up various responsibilities, such as preparing a dais on which to celebrate mass, confession, conferences, and processions. This preparation manifested one of the most heartfelt moments of devotion in the history of the cult of OLLV. Although those in North Vietnam could not come, an estimated three hundred thousand pilgrims from South Vietnam took part.[10] A video titled *Đại hội La Vang 1961* [Marian Congress of La Vang 1961] shows the delighted pilgrims: Christians and non-Christians, bishops, clergy, religious men and women, laity, young people, civilians, students, soldiers, officers, and even the President of South Vietnam.[11] Answering the invitation, they went on pilgrimage to OLLV to pray for the peace and unity of the nation. One pilgrim, the American Catholic priest Raymond J. DeJaegher, described the pilgrimage in his article "Our Lady of the 17th Parallel." He observed the dangerous location of La Vang at the crossing point during the Vietnam War, stating:

> The free Vietnamese countryside is terrorized by guerrilla packs, which have infiltrated from the north or which have been

9. Archbishop Ngô, "Invitation," VTVN Radio Huế and Sài Gòn on August 9, 1961.

10. From 1954–75, there was no communication between the Archdiocese of Hanoi in the north and two other Archdioceses in the south of Vietnam, and no travel was possible.

11. A part of this video can be found at https://www.youtube.com/watch?v=aFQhCKoytIE. See also Viên, "Đại hội kính Đức Mẹ La Vang."

recruited locally by Communist cadres. These perpetrate their murders by night and vanish into the jungle or thin air with the coming of daylight. And sometimes they operate by day. A pilgrimage in Vietnam, especially if one comes from a distance, involves an element of the heroic.[12]

In addition, La Vang was still a wild mountain region, so accommodations were rugged even by Asian standards, as DeJaegher observed. Despite these obstacles, he estimated more than two hundred thousand pilgrims were at the closing event.

Taking place from August 17–22, 1961, the fifteenth pilgrimage became the longest on record. Each day was dedicated to prayer for specific groups: the first day for mothers of families, the second for the sick, the third for the military, the fourth for the suffering church in the north, the fifth for members of Catholic Associations, and the last day for the nation of Vietnam and for the erection of the basilica.[13] At the end of each day, there was a solemn procession, and following that a solemn mass for all participants. The pilgrims felt growth in connectedness and in responsibility for the peace of the nation. Despite lacking accommodations, they felt comfort, protection, and care not only from being at the Shrine of OLLV but also from the program of the pilgrimage.

Moreover, pilgrimage is a major tool of faith formation, and the national pilgrimage of 1961 might be considered among the strongest experiences of faith formation in Vietnam up to this period (fig. 7). Each day, masses were celebrated with beautiful homilies; the pilgrims prayed endlessly; clergy delivered sermons at conferences; and processions took place to praise the Eucharist, OLLV, or the relics of the martyrs. Many pilgrims went to confession indoors and outdoors, with "forty priests at a time hearing the unending lines. Hundreds of thousands of hosts were consecrated."[14] Furthermore, it was a part of the tradition of La Vang that recitation of the rosary, hymnody, and chants were uninterrupted day and night. The pilgrims expressed to OLLV their hopes for the end of the war, for national unity, and for religious freedom. Just like the pilgrims in 1900, these pilgrims were reminded that OLLV had protected their

---

12. DeJaegher, "Unsere Liebe Vom 17 Breitengrad." From 1954–64, Fr. DeJaegher was in Vietnam serving as a special adviser to the President Diệm Đình Ngô, along with other positions. For his further biography, see http://www.weihsien-paintings.org/NormanCliff/people/individuals/deJaegher/txt-Raymond%20DeJaegher.htm.

13. Archbishop Ngô, "Đại Hội La Vang."

14. DeJaegher, "Our Lady of the 17th Parallel."

ancestors from succumbing to persecutions, so they too were called to trust confidently in OLLV in their present moment. In addition to its evangelization benefits, this pilgrimage was a significant occasion of faith, strengthening the Vietnamese as they faced new struggles.

Fig. 7: The 15th Great Pilgrimage/the National Pilgrimage in 1961, IRFA, bt. Vietnam 29 (© France-Asia Research Institute/MEP with document reference).

On the last day of the national pilgrimage, August 22, 1961, Pope John XXIII gave his approval for elevating the Church of OLLV to a basilica.[15] The purpose of the new minor basilica would be to be a place of Marian devotion to pray for the Church to overcome enemies, and for faith to be protected, for a nation united, and for religious freedom. In addition, the Pope repeated the bishops' words that the Shrine of OLLV is the house of prayer where perpetual adoration should take place along with devotion to OLLV. The Pope also noted the strong faith of the ancestors of the pilgrims during the past centuries and encouraged the Vietnamese faithful of the present day to grow strong in faith, hope, and love, imitating their martyr ancestors. In doing so, the Pope not only reinforced the unity of the Church, but also advocated for the dawn of robust and widespread devotion to OLLV—a new move in the history of devotion to OLLV as "true piety." Indeed, the papal and episcopal promotions alike were like endorsements of the story of OLLV, affirming the oral traditions as worthy of belief and thereby strengthening devotion to OLLV.

15. John XXIII, "Magno nos solatio."

With the papal approval of the basilica, devotion to OLLV inspired hope that she would bring peace and unification to the nation. After anointing and censing the altar and all parts of the basilica, the Archbishop of Huế, as the representative of the larger Church in Vietnam, declared: "From now on, the Basilica and all the surrounding grounds of the sacred Shrine of OLLV are the house, the land of the Blessed Virgin Mary, and the National Pilgrimage Center of all the Vietnamese people."[16] This announcement at the end of the first national pilgrimage signified the hope that the NC-OLLV would be a common home for the children of OLLV—that is, all the Vietnamese. Because of these new episcopal and papal recognitions, not only did the cult of OLLV flourish spiritually, but also, she attracted more devotees and material support.

Archbishop Ngô accordingly developed the NC-OLLV by expanding its sacred grounds and inviting architects to design a new church in harmony with the bishops' goals. The construction plans called for a facility that would serve pilgrims at all seasons, especially during the national pilgrimages, and provide space for conferences. In addition to designing and supervising the project, the archbishop invited many people, such as experts in graphic design, construction engineers, and donors of both labor and artifacts, to get involved in the construction project, which began in July 1961. The archbishop went to the site almost every day to supervise construction. Many of the large number of attendees of the fifteenth pilgrimage committed themselves to help build the House of Prayer for all the Vietnamese, providing money, labor, and other services. The completed construction included a retreat building for clergy, a rectory, a building for pilgrims, a rosary square, the Stations of the Cross, and three monuments to memorize martyrs of the north, middle, and south of Vietnam.[17]

Under the direction of Archbishop Ngô, the project was carried out well. However, other construction remained unfinished when the archbishop suffered a kind of exile after his brothers, President Diệm Đình Ngô and Chief Advisor Thuc Đình Ngô, were assassinated in 1963.[18]

16. Quoted in Ngọc Văn Nguyễn, *Sacred Land of La Vang*, 104.
17. B.L.B., "Đức Tổng Giám Mục Huế với Đức Mẹ La Vang."
18. See Hammer, *A Death in November*. Investigating the Buddhist crisis in 1963 is beyond the scope of this project. The year 1963 did have several critical events, such as the Buddhist movement in Hue and Sai Gon and the assassinations of Mr. Diem Dinh Ngo, President of South Vietnam, and his brother, a Vietnamese archivist and politician. The first two events led to Archbishop Thuc Dinh Ngo's exile. International observers view the self-immolation of Thich Quang Duc in 1963 as evidence that Buddhists were persecuted

The History of Devotion to Our Lady of La Vang Continues

Archbishop Ngô was in Rome at the Second Vatican Council and was advised to remain outside Vietnam. After staying in Rome for a while, he moved to the United States, where he died in 1984.

Fig. 8: The shrine of Our Lady of La Vang was rebuilt in 1963 (AAOH).

under the regime of President Diem Dinh Ngo. See. Topmiller, *The Lotus Unleashed*; Anderson and Ernst, *The War that Never Ends*; Shaw, *The Lost Mandate of Heaven*; Hall, *The Vietnam War*; Goscha, *Vietnam*; *Liberator of Asia*.

The new shrine was built on the site of the former shrine of OLLV but featured three artificial cement banyan trees instead of the octagonal shape of the original (fig. 8). Also, a dais was included for a statue of OLLV and an altar. Because there is no record about the intention of this new design of the shrine, it may be interpreted as representing the story of OLLV, the Trinity, and/or the three archdioceses of the Church in Vietnam. When OLLV appeared, she stood next to a banyan tree; the three banyan trees of the design may be symbolic of the post-1960 Catholic hierarchy of the Church in Vietnam. Though incomplete, a statue of Our Lady of Grace was installed with a temporary podium. Along with the urgent needs met by divine grace, devotion to OLLV furthered the unification of the members of the Church in Vietnam, as the church leaders intended.

The hope for peace and unification prayed for at the fifteenth pilgrimage was also expressed through art and literature. For example, the Vietnamese artist Phi Hung was inspired to paint OLLV as Our Lady of Grace.[19] His painting was used for the cover of the first issue of Đức Mẹ La Vang in 1961. Father Joseph-Marie Thích Văn Nguyễn described this painting:

> Here the Holy Mother wears 12 stars, her feet on the Moon, her eyes look down the nation of Vietnam, her hands extend as if she protects the nation. In front of her is the Pacific Ocean, behind her is the snowy Himalaya, the ocean is the deepest and the largest, the mountain is highest, of the world. Our Lady of La Vang is the BVM of Southeast Asia.[20]

OLLV herself was depicted as a gentle, kind, and beautiful Vietnamese woman in a simple traditional dress, *áo dài*. In the context of the 1960s, Phi Hùng's message was that to venerate OLLV was to pray for divine help that brought peace, unity, and religious freedom not only for the Vietnamese people but also for the people in this corner of the continent.[21] Without necessarily fully intending it, Phi Hùng composed the image of OLLV to support her identity: a Vietnamese Mary, a mother of mercy to protect the Vietnamese and the people in southeast Asia. OLLV

---

19. Phi Hùng, "Đức Mẹ La Vang."

20. J-M Nguyễn, "La Vang và Đức Mẹ Việt Nam."

21. The "domino theory" proposed that a communist government of one nation in Southeast Asia would quickly spread over its neighbors; on the other hand, if devotion to OLLV would protect Vietnam from communist triumph, she would also protect its neighbor nations.

would reconcile division not only among the Vietnamese people but also among southeast Asians more broadly speaking.

Also in 1961, Khiêm Đình Phạm published his *Our Lady of La Vang is the Queen of Victory*. He chose an image of a statue of Our Lady of Victories, installed during the first diocesan pilgrimage in 1900, to be the cover of his book. In the context of the ongoing war, he argued, it was important to venerate OLLV directly because she has helped her supplicants overcome strife many times in many other places. We have seen through those two avatars, Our Lady of Victories and Our Lady of Grace, devotees expressed their trust in OLLV's maternal mercy and powerful help. These double images of OLLV reflect Mariology in the Vietnamese context, taking into account social, cultural, and political circumstances. Vietnamese people look to OLLV for grace and victory, and for her mercy and power to overcome obstacles caused by the Vietnam War. Fr. DeJaegher's "Our Lady at the 17th Parallel" argued something similar. "It is not the deliberation of statesmen or the efforts of governments that will save Southeast Asia and the world," he wrote. "It was the supplications and sacrifices of the faithful, beseeching the Mother of God who still commands the Heart of her all-powerful Son."[22]

Many others helped spread the story of and the history of devotion to OLLV by writing in both French and in Vietnamese. For example, French missionary M. Bernard wrote "La Vierge Marie au Viet Nam" in 1969, and Ngọc Văn Nguyễn authored *Sacred Land of La Vang*, published in 1970.[23] In the increased political chaos and after the Tet Offensive of 1968,[24] national pilgrimage to OLLV was impossible; therefore, publications such as these reinforced the traditions of OLLV and thereby helped to uphold the resilience of the members of the Archdiocese of Huế despite the barriers to further triennial pilgrimages. This is what OLLV had done throughout the nineteenth century, as we have seen. To recall the joyful and suffering history of OLLV was to strengthen faith in God and confidence in OLLV during this new tragedy.

Despite suffering after the Tet Offensive, devotion to OLLV kept going. Because Archbishop Ngô could not return, he resigned his office. His successor, Archbishop Philip Điền Kim Nguyễn, continued to shepherd God's people of the Archdiocese of Huế and fostered the traditions of

22. DeJaegher, "Our Lady of the 17th Parallel."

23. Bernard, "La Vierge Marie au Viet Nam"; Stanilas Nguyễn, *Sacred Land of La Vang*.

24. Wirtz, *The Tet Offensive*; Mangold and Penycate, *The Tunnels of Cu Chi*.

La Vang until his death. Archbishop Nguyễn organized the seventeenth national pilgrimage in 1970. Though it lasted only one day, it showed extraordinary devotion to OLLV. The number of the pilgrims was small, and unlike in 1961 most came from the Archdiocese of Huế. Despite a short and simple pilgrimage, the pilgrims prayed with all their hearts and placed their trust in OLLV.

The next national pilgrimage, however, could not be organized at all because of the Easter Offensive in 1972. While the faithful migrated further into southern Vietnam, many were killed on the highway in Quảng Trị, which became known, grimly, as *Đại lộ kinh hoàng* [the horrific highway]. Many buildings of the NC-OLLV were smashed. A few lay faithful and Sisters of Lovers of the Holy Cross, however, still remained and with their pastor kept the traditions of La Vang going. They were, indeed, worthy descendants of the Vietnamese martyrs, as demonstrated by their trust in God and devotion to OLLV.

In summary, the period of 1961–72 was defined in large part by the Vietnam War and the hierarchy's response. On the one hand, the devotion to OLLV became robust with the events that transpired during the fifteenth national pilgrimage in 1961, the construction of the NC-OLLV, and its elevation to basilica status. The beginning of this third period of the history of devotion to OLLV could be seen as the start of the "golden age" of OLLV. But soon, all those achievements were destroyed, and the national pilgrimages were interrupted due to the war. However, even though things seemed hopeless, OLLV's promise stayed alive in the hearts of Vietnamese Catholics, especially the faithful of the Archdiocese of Huế.

The Second Period: 1972–1988

Socio-Political Factors

Unlike the Christians executed in nineteenth-century Vietnam, often known as the red martyrs, Church members in Vietnam during 1972–1988 could be called the "white martyrs," because Christians were persecuted for their faith without any direct bloodshed. During this period, the relationship between the Catholic Church and the communist regime was extremely tense. Most migrants from North to South Vietnam in 1954 were Catholics, and the purpose of the devotion to OLLV at the fifteenth national pilgrimage in 1961, as discussed previously, had been in part to express the church leaders' reactions to the communist system. The migration and the pilgrimage might be seen as responses by the Catholic Church against the communist system at the beginning of the Vietnam War. Although the Church expressed that her pastoral ministry was to live at the heart of the nation, the communist regime applied restrictive rules after gaining control of the entire country. Many Vietnamese people, including soldiers, military clergy, and those related to the political leaders of South Vietnam were imprisoned soon after April 30, 1975. The imprisonment of Bishop Francis Xavier Thuận Văn Nguyễn was one such example.[25] All missionaries were also expelled from Vietnam. In this tense environment, the Church could not put energy into organized devotion to OLLV.

The cult of OLLV was also slowed because most religious activities, including ordinations, worship, and devotions, were made subject to governmental approval. Life was difficult for most people, but even more difficult for Catholics because of the restrictions placed on their activity. Even after a new policy, Đổi mới, known as the Renovation of 1986, which developed the free market, religious restrictions only slowly improved over time.[26] The bishops could not even meet together until 1980. Along with forming the Catholic Bishops' Conference, however, the bishops at that time reaffirmed the National Center/Shrine of the Holy Mother La Vang.[27]

At the same time, the Archdiocese of Huế, which includes Quảng Trị and Huế provinces, underwent trials due to conflicts among the provincial governments. According to the records in its archives, many members, including priests and the lay faithful, migrated to the south of Vietnam and overseas. Several priests of the archdiocese were imprisoned after 1975.[28] The conflict escalated due to violations against human rights and religious freedom. One observer of the history of OLLV during 1972–1988 states, "khó khăn và tế nhị."[29] It was a situation of "khó

---

25. See FX Nguyễn, *Testimony of Hope*.

26. See Paul Nguyễn, *Việt Nam Dấu Yêu, Quê Hương & Giáo Hội*; Peter Sâm Nguyễn, "Vietnamese Immigration Family," 69–86. Also see ACBCV Pastoral Letters; John Paul II, "Meeting with the Vietnamese Catholic Community of the United States."

27. ACBCV, "A Record of the Meeting 1980." Also see ACBCV, "Letter Calling for Donation." In this letter, along with mentioning the decisions of the Church in 1961, the bishops reiterated their decision in 1980 and called for donation to rebuild the Basilica of OLLV.

28. See Archives of the Archdiocese of Hue, Biographies of Clergy of Huế.

29. Q. Trần, *Pilgrimage to the Diocese of Huế*, 3:270. For related notes, see H. Nguyễn, "Our Lady of La Vang and Tra Kieu in Vietnam," 71. "Khó khăn và tế nhị" is challenging to translate.

khăn" [difficulty] because the restrictive rules applied not only to the church leaders but also the faithful. Given further obstacles like expensive transportation and the lack of communications, it was hard to go on pilgrimage to OLLV. There was "tế nhị" [tension about speaking up] because it was dangerous to speak about religious restrictions and the violation of human rights.

Moreover, the Quảng Trị governors occupied the property of the archdiocese, including the extensive grounds of the NC-OLLV.[30] The government of the two provinces prevented people from going on pilgrimage to OLLV by not allowing them to go toward La Vang.[31] At this point, only the Shrine of OLLV and the belltower of the basilica survived, and the shrine was often defiled by anonymous perpetrators during the night. During this difficult time of poverty and threat, Fr. Emmanuel Gioang Vinh Nguyễn, the administrator of the shrine from 1975–95, together with the local laity and religious women, protected the Shrine of OLLV by building fences and taking turns sleeping in the shrine in order to protect it from vandals.[32]

To observe devotion to OLLV during 1972–88, therefore, is to pay attention to two things. First, despite the brevity of their statement, when the bishops of the CBCV approved the shrine as the NC-OLLV in 1980, their decision played an important role in promoting the unity of the whole Church, both in Vietnam and the world. Second, it is important to remember that the Archdiocese of Huế and its members had been, and even in this period continued to be, witnesses to the presence of OLLV. During this time these witnesses included figures already mentioned, such as Archbishop Phillip Điền Kim Nguyễn and Father Emmanuel Gioang Vinh Nguyễn, as well as Sister Agatha Sinh Thị Lê with her seven sisters who remained at a convent next to the NC-OLLV, and the local laity who also remained there and gave their love to OLLV. These figures are important links who kept the history of devotion to OLLV going, as is explored in the following pages.

30. See AAOH, "Archbishop Philip Điền Kim Nguyễn," "Religious Men and Women," and "The National Pilgrimage Center of La Vang." Also, at the Ad Limina 2018, Archbishop Joseph Linh C. Nguyễn, the President of CBCV, gave a report to Pope Francis, "Diễn từ triều yết Đức Thánh Cha Phanxicô."

31. Q. Trần, *Pilgrimage to Diocese of Huế*, 3:272–73.

32. Emmanuel Nguyễn, "Hồi ký mục vụ" ["pastoral diary"]. See also Paul Trần, *Pilgrimage to Diocese of Huế*, 3:271.

Devotion to OLLV among the Persevering Members of the Archdiocese of Huế

Local devotion to OLLV during these challenging years was humble but earnest. Although all the bishops approved the NC-OLLV in 1980, as previously stated, pilgrims during this time were primarily from the Archdiocese of Huế, and mainly the local parishes in Quảng Trị province. During this decade, the members of the Archdiocese of Huế proved themselves to be resilient Christians and robust devotees of OLLV. As one example, Philip Nguyễn was courageous enough during this period to defend religious freedom, human rights, and civil rights publicly. Through speeches and letters, he expressed the beliefs of the Catholic Church, emphasizing that the Church in Vietnam served to ensure the abundant life of everyone, including their true freedom, rights, and equality. The Archbishop encouraged his people to grow in faith, hope, and love, as well as to advocate for devotion to OLLV.[33]

Trusting in OLLV despite the tense relationship with the government, the Archbishop gathered his people at the shrine to worship God and entrust their struggles to OLLV. He often went to the shrine during the Lunar New Year to celebrate mass with clergy, religious men and women, and the lay faithful. When he was unable to join them, he sent a letter with his blessings. For example, on February 14, 1983, the archbishop encouraged the members of the archdiocese to offer their challenges to OLLV and invited them to pray for all needs at individual and communal levels. He exhorted the faithful to pray for stronger faith and for a gift of fidelity like that of their martyr-ancestors:

> Amid the persecution of Christians in 1798, the Holy Mother came at La Vang, comforting and encouraging our ancestors.... They persevered during the trials of faith.... From that time until now going on pilgrimage to OLLV has become a tradition of the Church in Vietnam, and it serves a spiritual need of Vietnamese laity.[34]

---

33. See the AAOH, "Archbishop Philip Điền Kim Nguyễn." Letters dated February 28, 1976; April 15, 1977; October 27, 1977; July 15, 1979; October 19, 1983; and October 17, 1984, primarily addressed religious freedom, human rights, and equal civil rights and were sent to the governors of Huế and of Quảng Trị provinces. See also Archbishop Phillip Nguyễn, "Thư Chung gởi Tổng Giáo phận Huế" ["A General Letter to the Archdiocese of Huế"] (AAOH, April 1, 1975); Bích Ngọc Lê, *Figures of Diocese of Huế*, 2:270–82.

34. Philip Điền Kim Nguyễn, "Letter to Pilgrims on Lunar New Year 1983," AAOH.

During the time of "khó khăn và tế nhị," remembrance of the continued protection, care, and help that OLLV promised was necessary to strengthen hope in God. The association of OLLV with endurance of persecution is one indication of a deeply inculturated devotion to Mary that was now understood to be explicitly Vietnamese.

In those circumstances, the Archbishop decided to organize the eighteenth national pilgrimage in 1978. The Archbishop's letter of invitation not only encouraged his flock to participate in the pilgrimage but also encouraged them to imitate the BVM in her obedience to and trust in God, who is forever faithful. Even though, in the time of "khó khăn và tế nhị," most of the participants still came from the Archdiocese of Huế, around ten thousand pilgrims overcame all hindrances to join in worship of God and devotion to OLLV. Though it was designated a national pilgrimage, there were no expensive decorations, flowers, or palanquin processions, and it only took place for one day, on the morning of Sunday August 20, 1978. At the same time, it was still necessary formation for all the pilgrims. For Paul Trần, "The 18th National Pilgrimage is the poorest one in the history of pilgrimages to OLLV. . . . [However,] it is the most meaningful, beautiful, and strongest devotion to OLLV in the history of the devotion to her."[35]

Devotion to OLLV was promoted on other occasions as well. The Archbishop often taught his "lambs [and] sheep" to trust in OLLV and to visit her at the NC-OLLV. For example, during a diocesan clergy retreat in 1983, he reminded them to "Always believe that La Vang is the place the Holy Mother appeared. The Holy Mother granted La Vang to the Church in Vietnam, specially to the Archdiocese of Huế."[36] Before passing away, Archbishop Philip implored his flock to remember what had been done at the Shrine of OLLV. He emphasized the multiple levels of papal and episcopal approval for the Shrine, but the most important reality, the Archbishop underscored, was the promise of OLLV herself: "Henceforth all those who come to pray to me in this spot will see their wishes fulfilled."[37] The remembrance of the promise of OLLV and of all the recent decisions about the shrine, the Archbishop emphasized, were

---

35. Q. Trần, *Pilgrimage to Diocese of Huế*, 3:272.

36. Archbishop Philip Điền Kim Nguyễn, "Sermon to Priests on August 8, 1983," AAOH.

37. Archbishop Peter Nhơn V. Nguyễn, "Letter to the People of God" (ACBCV, October 12, 2012), https://hdgmvietnam.com/tin-tuc/tu-lieu-viet-nam-muc-vu; Philip Điền Kim Nguyễn, "Letter to the People of God," 1987, AAOH.

sufficient reasons to keep devotion to OLLV alive, along with essential faith formation.

In addition, like his archbishop, Fr. Emmanuel Gioang Vinh Nguyễn, the pastor of Diêm Sanh and the administrator of the NC-OLLV from 1975–95, persisted in keeping the cult of OLLV going. Due to the complete destruction of the basilica, he facilitated building a temporary church with an iron roof. Together with the faithful and the religious Sisters, Father Emmanuel Nguyễn protected and continued to build the NC-OLLV, although in an ad hoc manner. In addition to the protective fences around the Shrine of OLLV, the lay faithful also built simple shelters so that pilgrims could rest while they were at the NC-OLLV.[38] Fr. Nguyễn himself often came to the shrine to preside over mass, host pilgrimages, and guide prayer and/or meditation, even with few participants, especially on Marian memorials and solemn feasts. Despite being interrogated by the local government, he provided meditations to lead the faithful to grow in faith and hope. Although every religious activity at the NC-OLLV had to receive permission from the local government, Nguyễn said, "Those years were the most beautiful of my life. I, too, grew in stronger faith and hope as well as perseverance to become a better shepherd. Another thing was to gain belief in OLLV: she keeps her promise. She is there, always!"[39]

The religious sisters who carried on the cult of OLLV also remained close by the NC-OLLV, reciting the rosary at the shrine, participating in the liturgy, and performing other works like guardian angels of the NC-OLLV. Along with her seven Sisters of Lovers of the Cross of Huế, Sister Agatha Sinh Thị Lê had been living near by the NC-OLLV since 1975. Collaborating with the pastor and the lay faithful, the sisters protected the NC-OLLV by faithfully praying at the Shrine, volunteering to guard it day and night, and remaining there even when threatened by the local governors. Sister Agathe Lê recalls, "We did not think about the future of the NC-OLLV; we only built it and protected it day by day. We could not imagine the NC-OLLV as you see today. We only kept encouraging one another. . . . We do believe that OLLV keeps her promise."[40]

---

38. Q. Trần, *Pilgrimage to Diocese of Huế*, 3:268–72.

39. Sr. Mary Kim Anh Thi Tran, interview with Fr. Emmanuel Gioang Vinh Nguyễn (Huế, May 20, 2019).

40. Sr. Mary Tran, interview with Sr. Agatha Sinh Thị Lê (The NC-OLLV, May 18, 2019).

Life in Vietnam, especially in Quảng Trị, was not only tense but also generally difficult in these years. This is what caused Paul Trần to invoke the phrase "khó khăn và tế nhị" to describe the period. In his homily at the twenty-first national pilgrimage, Father Peter Kính Hoàng preached: "To go on pilgrimage to La Vang is to go back to our Mother's house. To our Mother's house, we go back. Do not be afraid! No one has power to prevent us. Even though we are stopped from going, we still go to [La Vang]. To our Mother's House, we go back."[41] With these beautiful and courageous words, Father Peter represented the resilient community of faith of the Archdiocese. No longer was La Vang a wild jungle; it was the house of Mary, the house of faith and hope, as the community of faith upheld.

In summary, the years 1972–88 can be an example of an ever-ancient-ever-new global issue: a power struggle between religious and secular spheres. The history of OLLV during those years is a record of suffering and earnest struggle. During those difficult years of bitter relationships, the devotion to OLLV shone like the morning star, empowering believers to persevere. Although the annual and national pilgrimages only took place sometimes and then on a single day, the story of OLLV was retold, her history was recapped, and her cult was kept alive. These realities remind us of the important role of shepherds of the church, and of the honored role of all the faithful of the Archdiocese of Huế.[42] This is evidence of an organically developed, deeply ingrained inculturation of the faith in the form of Marian devotion. The following section will explore devotion to OLLV after the Pope told the story of OLLV in 1988.

The Third Period: 1988–2022

The last section of this chapter, covering 1988–2022, demonstrates devotion to OLLV growing increasingly on a national and even international level. It discusses the role in this growth of the Pope as the head of the universal Church and of the Catholic Bishops' Conference of Vietnam as the heads of the local Church. I focus especially on the years 1998–99, the 200th anniversary of the apparitions of OLLV.

---

41. Q. Trần, *Pilgrimage to Diocese of Huế*, 3:272.
42. See John Paul II, "Homily on the Canonization of 117 Martyrs in Vietnam."

The History of Devotion to Our Lady of La Vang Continues

Social-Political-Religious Factors

The years 1988–2022 saw many rapid changes in the society of Vietnam, both positive and negative. After the Renovation of 1986, as previously mentioned, the lives of ordinary people began improving. For example, many young people could obtain higher education and master other languages, and more people started to open their own businesses. Later still people gained access to the internet, allowing more cultural exchange to take place across the world. At the same time, there was an increase in social problems, including inequality, unjust wages, and corruption. Individualism, relativism, and consumerism were also on the rise within the population.[43] Despite this mix of negative and positive, many Catholics and even non-Christians were motivated to go on pilgrimages to OLLV in these years.

Moreover, the world was changed by the fall of communism in the Soviet Union and Eastern Europe in 1989. That forced the Vietnamese government to discern how to lead Vietnam in a new context. They wanted to secure diplomatic relations with other nations.[44] The government, for example, agreed to assist the United States to "determine the fate of Americans missing in action" in three areas, including Quảng Bình, Quảng Trị, and Kon-tum, during the Vietnam War. This action led to the embargo of 1994 and then the establishment of diplomatic relations in 1995 between the two countries. In the same year, the Vietnamese government made further steps to join the global network by applying to become a member of the World Trade Organization. However, the request was not approved until January 11, 2007.[45] The twelve-year process contributed to a reform that allowed religions to enjoy more freedom, though this occurred only slowly, over time. Finally, the government admitted indirectly that the NC-OLLV was a religious territory for the worship of God and veneration of OLLV, and no longer hindered pilgrims from visiting OLLV. It could be said that the governors read "the signs of the time" for the protection of their own authority.

---

43. Taylor, *Social Inequality in Vietnam*; CBCV, "Pastoral Letters" of 1998, 2007, 2013, ACBCV. See also "Vietnamese Family Today"; Pham, Vu, and Nguyen, "The Court System"; Burr, *Vietnam's Children in a Changing World*.

44. See Vietnamese Government, "18 Years of Renovation: 1986–2003," August 28, 2010. http://www.chinhphu.vn/portal/page/portal/chinhphu/noidungchinhsachthanhtuu?categoryId=799&articleId=2957; Beresford, *Vietnam*.

45. World Trade Organization, "Vietnam," https://www.wto.org/english/thewto_e/acc_e/a1_vietnam_e.htm.

Three additional factors contributed momentum to the devotion to OLLV. First, the canonization of the 117 martyrs in Vietnam in 1988 had a great impact on the devotion to OLLV. Second, though the government did not allow religious bodies to establish private schools from K-12,[46] it allowed the first Catholic university to be re-opened in 2015.[47] This has played a role of formation as well as education. Indeed, the establishment of this Catholic university was promising for the future of research in Mariology in the context of Vietnam, including research on OLLV. Her story and the cult are considered a resource for studying the theology of inculturation, of evangelization, of pilgrimages, of the mission of the lay faithful, and of vocation. Lastly, the many Vietnamese Catholics who became residents in other countries began to establish the cult of OLLV in their new homes, too.[48]

The Significant Impacts of the Popes on Devotion to OLLV

The Popes, and especially Pope John Paul II, have greatly influenced the members of the Church in Vietnam to increase devotion to OLLV. Despite making no ecclesial decisions about the NC-OLLV, Pope John Paul II was the first pope to tell the story of OLLV to the world. A new hope for robust devotion to OLLV was awakened again because of the canonization of the martyrs of Vietnam in 1988. Just a couple hours after he canonized the 117 martyrs in Vietnam, the Pope used his *Angelus* on June 19, 1988, to describe the apparition of OLLV and the history of her cult. He also highlighted earlier ecclesial decisions promoting the shrine, which, the Pope added, were worthy reasons to rebuild the destroyed basilica. He called for the basilica to be under construction as soon as possible in pursuit of peace and freedom. To be devoted to OLLV, the Queen of Martyrs, was, for the Pope, to lead the Vietnamese Catholics

---

46. See Dang, "Leadership Preparation in Higher Education."

47. Học Viện Công Giáo Việt Nam [Catholic Institute of Vietnam] was established in 2015; it awards bachelor's and master's degrees only in theology at the time it is established. See http://hocvienconggiao.edu.vn/gioi-thieu.

48. Despite having been established in 1975, the leaders of the Vietnamese Catholic Federation in Germany did not name a patron saint until 2013, when they declared the Blessed Virgin Mary under the title Our Lady of La Vang (https://ldcg.de). A shrine of OLLV was erected in the Holy Land in 2018. Many churches and shrines of OLLV have been erected in the United States, such as in Houston, Dallas, Las Vegas, Orange County, San Jose, and at the National Basilica of the Immaculate Conception in Washington DC; see http://vietcatholic.net/News/Html/54557.htm.

to God, and in doing so, to foster harmony and true civil rights.[49] On the one hand, the Pope's teaching and exhortation played a significant role in establishing a better dialogue between the Church and the Vietnamese state. On the other hand, his teaching to the whole Church about OLLV influenced Vietnamese Catholics positively.

Through visits *ad limina apostolorum*,[50] regular canonically required visitations of local bishops to the Holy See, Pope John Paul II strengthened the unity among the bishops of CBCV. He encouraged devotion to OLLV as one expression of unity. In 1990, in addition to meeting the bishops as a whole group, the Pope had a short conversation with each. In his final words at the eucharist they concelebrated, the Pope praised OLLV and entrusted them to her.[51] Unification and collaboration among them, the Pope believed, would be enhanced if OLLV was held closer in their hearts along with Jesus Christ, her divine Son.

In his conversations and blessings, the Pope often entrusted the Church in Vietnam to OLLV. Again in the 1996 *ad limina apostolorum* visitation, the Pope commended the bishops to the protection of OLLV, saying, "I entrust you to the protection of the Mother of Jesus Christ, Our Lady of La Vang, whom you are going to celebrate on the 200th year of her appearance on August 15, 1998."[52] The Pope emphasized OLLV as the Mother of the Lord, and therefore, the Mother of the Church and of all the Vietnamese. For him, therefore, OLLV is integral to the story of the Church in Vietnam. He affirmed that it was important to venerate OLLV through truly national pilgrimages. Church leaders at all levels would then grow in collaboration, facilitating unity among themselves and their people, and, we can add, further consolidating a truly inculturated Vietnamese Catholicism.

Through diverse encounters on different occasions, John Paul II kept working to strengthen the unity of all members of the Church. Even those who lived in diaspora, he noted, were connected in OLLV. Knowing the Vietnamese were a part of his general audience in Rome, on November

---

49. John Paul II, "Angelus."

50. "*Ad limina apostolorum*" means "the thresholds of the apostles"; Catholic bishops are bound to go on pilgrimage to Rome every five years to pray at the tombs of Saints Peter and Paul and meet with the Pope and other pontifical officers to report about their diocese and/or the local church. See *The Code of Canon Law 1983*, 399–400.

51. See Joseph Trần, *Thoáng nhìn 60 Năm Giao Hảo Tòa Thánh Vatican và Nhà Nước Việt Nam*, 373–75.

52. John Paul II, "Speech to the Vietnamese Bishops."

25, 1992, the Pope said: "I am aware of the difficulties and sacrifices that the Catholics of Vietnam have to face in everyday life. I want to assure you and them that I am close to you in thought, with affection and with prayer. Your fidelity to Christ and to the person of the Successor of Peter is a reason for honor for the whole Church and a reason for great joy for me."[53] The Pope understood the struggles of his Vietnamese children. He connected their suffering to their martyr ancestors and led them to discover divine providence. In that moment, the Pope praised the history of the Church in Vietnam, saying: "Your presence, dear brothers and sisters of Vietnam, is particularly significant, since just yesterday we celebrated the liturgical memorial of the Vietnamese martyrs; one hundred and seventeen martyrs, including eight bishops, fifty priests, fifty-nine lay people, and among them a woman, Agnès Thành Thị Lê, mother of six children. These Christians witnessed their fidelity to Christ to the point of the supreme sacrifice of their own life, in the period between 1745 and 1862."[54]

The Pope reminded them that OLLV came to ensure, protect, and be present in the midst of that heroic history. He revived stories that heartened the Vietnamese in their suffering and reconnected the diaspora to their history. Going on, the Pope reminded them that the Marian Shrine at La Vang—OLLV—was dedicated to the Queen of Martyrs. The Pope entrusted to her the entire Vietnamese Catholic community and encouraged them to develop freedom, peace, and moral progression.[55] This was a powerful message because the Pope framed the teaching to affect diverse people around the world. An inculturated Vietnamese devotion was now being "universalized," recognized as part of the heritage of the universal church and in continuity with her faith. The faithful in diaspora had a special role to play in this "universalization."

Not only did the Pope strengthen the Church in Vietnam to unite and be devoted to OLLV, but he also, on other occasions, specifically spoke to those who lived in diaspora. During his apostolic journey in Denver, CO in 1993, the Pope taught the city's extensive Vietnamese Catholic diasporic community: "Do not forget the Church in Vietnam. . . . Perhaps the greatest challenge of the present is to heal any ill-feeling or divisions. . . . Too much suffering has left profound wounds. Reconstruction

53. John Paul II, "General Audience."
54. John Paul II, "General Audience."
55. John Paul II, "Angelus," Nov. 25, 1992 and Oct. 26, 1994; John Paul II, "Address to Vietnamese in the US"; John Paul II, and "Speech" to bishops on their Ad Limina, December 14, 1996.

The History of Devotion to Our Lady of La Vang Continues

will only be possible with the cooperation of everyone, and this in turn calls for mutual respect, forgiveness and unity of purpose.... I commend the whole Vietnamese Catholic community to the intercession of Our Lady of La Vang."[56]

The divisions and the woundedness in the hearts of the Vietnamese coming out of the Vietnamese War would be healed, the Pope said, if they were presented to OLLV. Although it was still several years away, the Pope reminded Vietnamese Catholics around the world to prepare for the 200th year of the Marian apparitions at La Vang. On October 26, 1994, for example, the Pope stated, "While the Church in Vietnam prepares to celebrate the 200th Jubilee of the apparition of the Holy Mother at La Vang, I invite you to deepen your faith and unity with one another in your native country in order to build a better future for your offspring."[57] OLLV is thus the mother of all Vietnamese Catholics, and in her they become one flock of Christ. This is, in effect, a statement about a distinctively Vietnamese Catholic identity, one that Pope John Paul II did not create on the spot, but that had developed over the centuries and could be celebrated on the upcoming anniversary.

To mark the holy year of the 200th anniversary of OLLV, the Pope sent a letter to the whole Church in Vietnam, providing impetus to the theology of OLLV, which included her message of hope, her maternal protection, and her role as a unifier among diverse Vietnamese people. As I described in the first chapter, the Pope laid out a theology of OLLV by repeating her words in order to point out her message of hope. The message of hope, the Pope taught, is what encouraged believers to go on pilgrimage to OLLV throughout the past two hundred years, and it should continue to encourage them to go on pilgrimage. The Pope re-emphasized that her message of hope was always kept alive at the shrine through the tradition of pilgrimages. It is a theology of hope rooted in faith, most significant in our human journey. It is a theology of hope rooted in a particular Marian devotion. In other words, the theology of OLLV is Mariology—the theology of Mary who is "our life, our sweetness and our *hope*"—rooted in the context of Vietnam.[58] OLLV, as the Pope taught, is the story of the Mother of Jesus Christ with the Vietnamese people. OLLV is therefore not just another story of a Marian apparition,

56. John Paul II, "Speech," Denver, 1993.
57. John Paul II, "Angelus," October 26, 1994.
58. John Paul II, "Letter to the Cardinal Paul Joseph Phạm Đình Tụng." The 200th Jubilees of the apparitions of the BVM at La Vang ran January 1, 1998 to August 15, 1999.

of a miracle regardless of context. She becomes the subject of a Mariology, and through Mariology, a theology fully located in the Vietnamese culture, her cult helped to solidify a Vietnamese Catholic identity. As a result, the Church in Vietnam rises in its significance, *as* Vietnamese, to the universal Church as a whole.

In the same letter, basing his statements on the apparition, the Pope explained the threefold structure of the pilgrimage to OLLV, paralleling the three theological virtues of faith, hope, and love: "May she make them pilgrims of steadfast faith in the person of Christ, the one Saviour of humanity, pilgrims of hope, waiting anxiously for the hour of God, for the harvest of the seed already scattered on the ground, pilgrims of charity living their vocation of unity, fraternity and service amidst their brothers and sisters whose life they share!"[59] Here the Pope expressed his view that going on pilgrimage to OLLV is an act of prayer to OLLV, enabling pilgrims to strengthen their vocations so as to become more steadfast in faith, stronger in hope, and more devout in charity. At the NC-OLLV, the pilgrims learned from OLLV, a perfect disciple of Jesus Christ through her trust in God: "Advocate, Auxiliatrix, Adjutrix, and Mediatrix."[60]

In the same context of the 200th Jubilee, the Pope further taught Mariology in the Vietnamese context. He urged the Catholics of Vietnam to learn from Mary because "In intense and deep union with God, she obeyed his call with total fidelity. . . . Never letting difficulties discourage her, she gave full expression to the longing of the Lord's poor, a radiant model for those who put all their trust in God's promises."[61] The Pope, in his letter, joined with the pilgrims in spirit to invoke ardently "the Mother of Christ, the Mother of men, for the entire people of Vietnam and for Christian communities, originally from here, who now live abroad." Thus, the Pope also in this context acknowledged the reality of the migration of Vietnamese people: no matter where they live, in OLLV they are united and connected to their roots. It seems that OLLV has united Vietnamese near and far in the worship of God.[62]

At the same time the last three popes, beginning with John Paul II, had a positive influence on the nation of Vietnam itself, politically

---

59. Pope John Paul II, "Letter to the Cardinal Paul Joseph Phạm Đình Tụng."
60. *Lumen gentium*, 62.
61. Pope John Paul II, "Letter to the Cardinal Paul Joseph Phạm Đình Tụng."
62. In "Letter to the Cardinal Paul Joseph Phạm Đình Tụng," the Pope appointed him a special papal envoy to the celebrations of the second centennial of apparitions of OLLV on August 13–15, 1998.

speaking. He worked to improve the relationship between church and state. Initially, he facilitated a diplomatic relationship between the Vatican and Vietnam soon after his election. After informal dialogues, the Pope sent his representative, Cardinal Roger Etchegaray, to Vietnam in 1989. Subsequently, the Pope continued to negotiate with the Vietnamese leaders about religious freedom, which included appointing bishops, establishing seminaries, and administrating the candidacy of religious communities of consecrated men and women. He promoted Catholic schools, church properties, and charitable organizations. That all bishops of the Catholic Bishops' Conference of Vietnam could go to the *ad limina apostolorum* visitations during the 1980s into 1990s was one outcome of the influence of the Pope. Although it has been slow, the life of the Church has indeed revived and progressed gradually. For example, four seminaries were allowed to reopen in 1989, and the government allowed a limited number of students to be accepted into seminary formation.

The Pope continued to send his delegates to Vietnam, which created a better relationship. Pope John Paul II sent fourteen delegations from the Holy See to Vietnam beginning in 1989, and several times he welcomed the Vietnamese delegation to Rome.[63] All his work to initiate and make progress in diplomatic relations helped ease the relationship between the Church and Vietnamese state as well as to strengthen the Church in Vietnam. All that helped to indirectly promote devotion to OLLV, in whose care and protection, as the Pope believed, all Vietnamese were included. Further, the teaching of the Pope provides sufficient inspiration to explore the theology of OLLV, which was then and remains now a starting point for facilitating the mission of the Church in Vietnam.

The ministry of Pope John Paul II brought further results through his successors. Pope Benedict XVI continued the work of his predecessor to foster a harmony between the Church and Vietnamese state by keeping up diplomatic relations. In addition, the aforementioned process of application to the WTO probably enabled the 2008 opening of two other seminaries, which were allowed to accept students in accordance with their capacity.[64] In 2010 the Quảng Trị governors also returned the land that belonged to the NC-OLLV. This allowed the bishops to take steps

---

63. A. Trần, Thoáng nhìn 60 Năm Giao Hảo Tòa Thánh Vatican và Nhà Nước Việt Nam, 1960–2020.

64. For more details, see CBCV, "General Letter," 1989 and 2008, ACBCV; Affatato, "Bishops of Vietnam."

towards rebuilding the Basilica of OLLV.[65] The Pope continued to establish diplomatic relations and promote religious freedom in Vietnam. The Church's effort eventually brought a new step in diplomatic relations: a non-residential pontifical representative for Vietnam in 2011.[66] The Church continues to work toward the highest level of diplomatic relations.

The Impacts of the Catholic Bishops' Conference of Vietnam to Devotion to OLLV

Though it was established in 1960, the hierarchy of the Church in Vietnam did not have its first meeting as a whole until 1980. During the meeting, the bishops established the Catholic Bishops' Conference of Vietnam (hereafter CBCV) and approved the NC-OLLV. They meet annually, and at the end of each meeting, they deliver either a general letter or a pastoral letter to all the members of the Church. However, their letters did not mention devotion to OLLV until the pastoral letter of 1997. They also did not make a public statement of their reapproval of the NC-OLLV until 2012, when they called for donations to reconstruct the new building of the basilica. However, since the popes' support and the 200th year of Jubilee, they have further engaged devotion to OLLV in their teachings, pastoral guidance, and especially participation in the national pilgrimages to OLLV.

1997 was special for both the universal and local Church: preparation for the Great Jubilee of 2,000 years of the Mystery of the Incarnation and the dawn of the 200th jubilee of OLLV. In their letter, the bishops re-emphasized the teachings of the Pope, who encouraged all the members of the Church in Vietnam to be devoted to OLLV.[67] In unity with the

---

65. Dang, "Government Announces Intention."
66. CBCV, "Diplomatic Relations," 2020, ACBCV.
67. CBCV, "General Letter" (ACBCV, 1997). In their letter, the bishops stated, "Năm 1998 sắp tới là năm đặc biệt đối với tất cả chúng ta. Giáo Hội Việt Nam sẽ mừng kỷ niệm 200 năm Đức Mẹ hiện ra tại La Vang (1798–1998), an ủi phù hộ các giáo hữu trong cơn thử thách. Đức Thánh Cha Gioan Phaolô II đã nhiều lần nhắc đến biến cố trọng đại này và phó dâng Giáo Hội Việt Nam cho Đức Mẹ La Vang. Hiệp với vị Cha chung, chúng tôi tha thiết mời gọi anh chị em đi vào năm ân sủng này, với tất cả lòng hiếu thảo mến yêu Mẹ Maria, và hân hoan bước theo Mẹ trong cuộc lữ hành đức tin chan hòa yêu thương và hy vọng. Xin Mẹ dẫn đưa chúng ta đến cùng Chúa Giêsu là Đấng Cứu Độ hôm qua, hôm nay và mãi muôn đời." (CBCV, "General Letter" (ACBCV, 1997), 6.

The History of Devotion to Our Lady of La Vang Continues

Pope, the letter of the CBCV stated, the bishops invited their people to go on pilgrimage to OLLV for the jubilee year, particularly to attend its opening mass and to learn from the BVM. They further taught that the 200th anniversary of the Marian apparition at La Vang celebrated years of robust devotion to OLLV. At La Vang, they noted, OLLV has played a role of unity, as is her maternal vocation, among the members of the Church in Vietnam.[68] OLLV was the mother of unity by whom the members of the Church were gathered to worship God and to strengthen their faith.

Now and then, the bishops have spoken in support of devotion to OLLV in their teachings through their letters. At the end of their general letter in October 1998, the bishops reminded their people that they have been celebrating a holy year of the 200th jubilee of the apparition and referenced devotion to OLLV under the title Our Lady of Help of Christians,[69] which had been recognized since 1900. Most of the bishops themselves participated at the opening mass of the 200th Jubilee of the apparition of OLLV.[70] Through their letters, the bishops taught that OLLV has become mother of the Church in Vietnam, to whom they had entrusted their mission and people.[71] OLLV was an important figure before, during, and after the meeting of the bishops in the CBCV.[72] For example, during the year 2003, which was dedicated to evangelization, the bishops asked OLLV to guide them in discussion, decisions, and pastoral projects.[73] Moreover, during the Year of the Eucharist, 2004–2005, they prayed to OLLV to teach them how to contemplate Jesus in the Eucharist. To close that year, the Church gathered the People of God at the

---

68. Pope Paul VI announced that the BVM is the Mother of the Church at the closing of the Second Vatican Council. See more Pope Paul VI, "Address during the Last General Meeting of the Second Vatican Council." https://www.vatican.va/content/paul-vi/en/speeches/1965/documents/hf_p-vi_spe_19651207_epilogo-concilio.html.

69. CBCV, "General Letter" (ACBCV, 1997), 21. The bishops stated, "Chúng ta cùng nhau hướng về Đức Mẹ La Vang, Mẹ phù hộ các giáo hữu mà Giáo Hội Việt Nam chúng ta đang cử hành kỷ niệm 200 năm Người hiện ra. Xin Mẹ đào tạo chúng ta trở nên những con người yêu thương và phục vụ như Chúa Kitô, những con người tràn đầy niềm hy vọng trong Chúa Thánh Thần, hân hoan sống Tin Mừng và nhiệt thành loan báo Tin Mừng."

70. Q. Trần, *Pilgrimage to Diocese of Huế*, 3:304–5. Note that the Jubilee marked significant devotion in the history of OLLV due to diverse participants, which included all the bishops, a number of clerics, consecrated women and men, and a huge number of the lay faithful of 25 dioceses of the Church in Vietnam.

71. CBCV, "General Letter," 2001, ACBCV.

72. CBCV, "General Letter," 2006 and 2011, ACBCV.

73. CBCV, "General Letter," 2003, ACBCV.

NC-OLLV to worship and to give energetic devotion to OLLV.[74] In general, we can see that the bishops gradually included OLLV in their teaching and practice.

Additionally, the more supportive the Pope's teaching was, the more the CBCV became closer to OLLV. One powerful example was their pastoral letter in 2011, sent after the holy year 2009–10, as the Church gave thanks to God for the 350th anniversary of the establishment of the first two dioceses in Vietnam (1659–2009) and for fifty years of the establishment of the hierarchy of the Church (1960–2012). Their letter's title was quoted from "The Prayer to Our Lady of La Vang": "Together [We] Build a Culture of Love and Life." On the one hand, the bishops recognized the value of working together. They had become more aware of the value of collaboration in taking care of God's sheep and lambs. On other hand, they were taking a positive path by building a culture of love and life based on the universal truth about the dignity of the human person. They used "The Prayer to Our Lady La Vang" to facilitate their pastoral guidance. In doing so, they demonstrated their faith in OLLV as the Mother of the Church in Vietnam.

In that pastoral letter, the bishops proposed important liturgical and formation strategies. Regarding worship of God, each archdiocese opened the holy year by celebrating a solemn liturgy at the sacred lands dedicated to the Vietnamese martyrs. Together they closed the holy year with a solemn liturgy at the NC-OLLV. Regarding formation, they reviewed circumstances in society and the life of the ordinary people by pointing out both opportunities and positive improvements as well as addressing social and moral problems. They also praised Vietnamese culture, including the values of family, charity, and gratitude, as well as acknowledging multiple Asian religions. After affirming the Church's mission, the bishops re-emphasized unity in the life of the Church in Vietnam, evangelization, and comprehension of the teachings of the Church about social issues. They provided pastoral strategies including participation in the life of the Church with conscious awareness, formation, work for integral human development, and charity. At the end of their letter, the bishops dedicated their pastoral proposals to OLLV. They also exhorted their people to unite with OLLV to worship God, to imitate Mary in order to strengthen their faith and perseverance, and to accompany her to commit themselves to evangelization.

---

74. CBCV, "General Letter," 2004, ACBCV.

Through their letters, the bishops not only showed their unity with the Pope, but they also expressed their wisdom through their teaching and devotion to OLLV. It may seem that it took a long time for CBCV to commit to OLLV. However, from the content reviewed above witnessing to the bishops' gradual recognition of OLLV, readers may appreciate the bishops' care toward fostering complementarity of Western and Eastern wisdoms in their own circumstances. If theology values context, OLLV is an excellent example of how cultural and historical context interacts with devotion. At the same time, in society, politics, and religions during the past sixty years with the multiple political transitions in Vietnam, the bishops of the CBCV have been growing in dialogue, unity, and collaboration with one another.

Alongside their engagement with OLLV in their teachings, the bishops have themselves participated in national pilgrimages to OLLV. According to Paul Trần, the pilgrims to OLLV during the period 1975–90 consisted primarily of the faithful of local parishes. That meant most of the pilgrims came from the Archdiocese of Huế.[75] Trần observed that in 1996, the national pilgrimage involved more members of the Church in Vietnam, including several bishops, clergy, and their flocks. By the jubilee of the 200th anniversary of the apparitions of OLLV, it was clear that participation in the national pilgrimages had become a part of the bishops' national agenda.

The reconstruction of the basilica became the first work to involve the whole church in Vietnam under the care of the CBCV. The President of the CBCV facilitated a construction project that included committees for funding, construction, sacred arts, and communication. Along with members from the clergy, religious, the lay faithful, and non-Christians, a bishop was appointed head of each committee. OLLV brought collaboration. For example, after receiving back the land of the NC-OLLV in 2010, the CBCV opened a competition for architectural design proposals for the Basilica of Our Lady of La Vang. They hoped to choose the best proposal for reconstruction of the basilica.[76] In 2012, they also announced a layered construction project that planned first to rebuild the Basilica and then other necessary buildings to serve the pilgrims and the national pilgrimages. Keeping the surviving belltower of the damaged Basilica,

---

75. Q. Trần, *Pilgrimage to Diocese of Huế*, 3:270–72, 292–93.

76. CBCV, "Thông báo của dự án La Vang" ["Announcement of La Vang Project"], 2011, ACBCV.

they constructed the new one behind it (fig. 9).⁷⁷ They called for donations from a variety of Vietnamese people at home and abroad.⁷⁸ The CBCV fostered communication throughout committees established in 2013.⁷⁹ After eight years of construction, the basilica was supposed to be dedicated at the thirty-second national pilgrimage, August 13–15, 2020. This year also marked the sixtieth anniversary of the establishment of the hierarchy of the Church, 1960–2020. However, the COVID-19 pandemic outbreak prevented the ceremonies from being celebrated. The CBCV had to cancel until further notice.⁸⁰

Fig. 9: The surviving belltower of the old basilica blessed in 1928.

Along with the CBCV, the Archbishop of Huế, Étienne Thể Như Nguyễn (1935–present), has made a great impact on devotion to OLLV. One of his contributions was to facilitate continuing inculturation, beginning with a new statue of OLLV. At the annual meeting of the CBCV in 1997, he introduced a new statue to the bishops that shows the support

77. Matthew Nguyễn, *Đồ án thiết kế Trung tâm hành hương Đức Mẹ La Vang*.
78. CBCV, "Thư Kêu Gọi" ["A Call for (donation)"], 2012, ACBCV.
79. CBCV, "General Letter," October 10, 2013, ACBCV; "Funding Committee for the National Center of the Holy Mother La Vang," October 15, 2013, https://hdgmvietnam.com/chi-tiet/thong-bao-ve-viec-thanh-lap-ban-van-dong-quy-kien-thiet-den-thanh-la-vang-25898.
80. CBCV, "Thông Báo đình hoãn Đại hội Đức Mẹ La Vang" [Announcement of Postponement National Pilgrimage to OLLV], 2020, ACBCV.

for OLLV in the Vietnamese culture. At the beginning of the 200th Jubilee of the apparition of OLLV, the new statue was installed at the NC-OLLV. Archbishop Nguyễn was also active in adapting liturgy into Vietnamese culture, including veneration of ancestor martyrs, sacred arts, architecture, liturgy, and devotional practices.[81]

As discussed above, the Popes and the CBCV have worked to advance religious freedom in Vietnam, and in so doing they promoted devotion to OLLV. Even though a bishop must still go through the government process regarding episcopal appointments, the worship of God and pious devotion can be freely practiced. In particular, the worship of God and the devotion to OLLV at the NC-OLLV are now considered ordinary religious ceremonies, so there is no need for permission to gather the People of God at the NC-OLLV. The local governors themselves are often present at the opening and/or closing of the national pilgrimages.[82]

The 200th Year of the Jubilee of the Apparition of OLLV, 1998–99

An increase in popular devotion to OLLV occurred during the period of 1988–2022, with a major surge at the opening of the 200th Jubilee year in 1998. This was in the bigger context of the 1998 Synod of Asian Bishops in preparation for the Great Jubilee of the Universal Church in 2000. The opening of the jubilee pilgrimage lasted three days, from August 13–15, 1998. This section focuses on the devotion to OLLV at the opening of the jubilee because it renewed the cult of OLLV in the new context created by the message of the Pope, the focus of the Catholic Bishops' Conference of Vietnam, and the jubilee itself. Scholars, especially theologians, were invited to study OLLV because of a belief that Vietnamese culture had been inculturated into liturgy and Marian devotion during this jubilee.

In a letter opening the jubilee year, Pope John Paul II taught a theology of hope connected with OLLV. The Pope quoted the words of OLLV: "Have trust, be willing to suffer hardship and sorrow. I have already granted your prayers. Henceforth all those who come to pray to me in this spot will see their wishes fulfilled." Her words, the Pope taught, became an

---

81. Étienne Thế Như Nguyễn was the first priest ordained at the Basilica of Our Lady of La Vang in 1962. His biography implies that he inherited strong devotion to OLLV by birth. See AAOH, "Archbishop Étienne Thế Như Nguyễn;" Bích Ngọc Lê, *Figures of Diocese of Huế*, 2:283–94.

82. Archbishop Joseph Linh Chí Nguyễn, "Welcoming Speech" and "Sending and Closing" at the 30th National Pilgrimage to OLLV, Aug. 13 and 15, 2017, AAOH.

enduring message of hope. Although her message has been handed down for two hundred years, it remains relevant today. The Pope continued that because of her message, the shrine "has been able to keep alive the tradition of pilgrimages."[83] By summing up "the tradition of pilgrimages," the Pope reminded the pilgrims not only about the history of OLLV, but also of their own strong devotion to OLLV through misery and struggle, and the way it expressed and nourished their hope. The Pope taught that through devotion to OLLV, people refresh their vocations, for they "receive comfort and strength, to face life's trials"[84] and regain connection to their traditions and roots. This applies not only to those on pilgrimage to OLLV, but also to the faithful who place their trust in OLLV. OLLV, the Pope taught, made "them pilgrims of steadfast faith . . . pilgrims of hope . . . [and] pilgrims of charity living their vocation of unity, fraternity and service."[85] It was OLLV, claimed the Pope, who helped strengthen the faith, hope, and love of those who trust in her. He was not only the first Pope to tell the story of OLLV, but also the first Pope to emphasize her words as a "message of hope" that everyone, especially Vietnamese Catholics, can relate to. In effect, if not in words, the Pope called attention to the cult of OLLV as a deeply inculturated Vietnamese devotion and to a theology of hope intertwined with her devotion.

In addition, the Pope involved himself further in promoting communion among the Vietnamese people. He granted a golden chalice featuring his own coat of arms to the Basilica of OLLV. He also appointed Cardinal Paul-Joseph Tụng Đình Phạm (1919–2009), the Archbishop of Hanoi, to be his papal envoy at the Jubilee. Through this act, the Pope expressed not only his care and love for the pilgrims, but also participated in the Jubilee by proxy. Moreover, the Pope granted a plenary indulgence to all those who were able to go on the pilgrimage and to those who could not go physically but nevertheless united in prayer and embodied the spirit of the Jubilee. In that way, the Pope facilitated unification among the members of the Church in Vietnam and those who had departed from Vietnam into the diaspora: "I send you, Your Eminence, my affectionate Apostolic Blessing which I willingly extend to the bishops, to the priests and to those preparing for the priesthood, to the religious and to all the faithful of Vietnam and the diaspora."[86] The Pope suggested that

83. John Paul II, "Letter to Cardinal Paul Joseph Phạm Đình Tụng."
84. John Paul II, "Letter to Cardinal Paul Joseph Phạm Đình Tụng"
85. John Paul II, "Letter to Cardinal Paul Joseph Phạm Đình Tụng."
86. John Paul II, "Letter to Cardinal Paul Joseph Phạm Đình Tụng"; Vệ Đức Nguyễn,

The History of Devotion to Our Lady of La Vang Continues

everyone could receive God's grace through OLLV. His heart and prayer, the Pope further stated, were united with all the pilgrims in a spirit of devotion to her.

Along with this support from the Pope, the Catholic Bishops' Conference of Vietnam facilitated solemn devotion to OLLV beginning at the opening of the Jubilee. They proposed as the theme of the Jubilee: "With OLLV, [We] Journey together toward the Great Jubilee 2000 of Salvation."[87] They offered a new statue of OLLV to the shrine. Likewise, all the homilies emphasized the deep connection between Marian devotion and salvation by prioritizing the story of OLLV, her title Our Lady of Help of Christians, and the two hundred years of Marian rituals at La Vang. Also, these homilies empowered pilgrims to grow in faith, hope, and love. For example, Bishop Paul Hòa Văn Nguyễn began with the title of OLLV, Our Lady Help of Christians, walked through the story and the rituals, and then concluded by encouraging the pilgrims to contemplate her message of hope, as the Pope had called it. From there, the bishop further explored the hope grounded in God that led to devotion to OLLV under the Marian title Our Lady of Help of Christians. He preached that her promise offered her protection to strengthen their faith, hope, and love.[88]

Moreover, as a member of the CBCV, the Archbishop of Huế, enthusiastically hosted the opening of the Jubilee in 1998. Born in Quảng Trị in 1935, he was ordained a coadjutor bishop in 1975 but resigned in 1983 due to his health. Having been appointed as a member of the Congregation of Interreligious Dialogue in 1992, he was later appointed Archbishop of Huế in 1998. Throughout his life, especially during his time as the archbishop, he welcomed pilgrims and presided over the meditation at La Vang. At the Jubilee, he preached that throughout the history of two hundred years since her appearance at La Vang, the BVM had always interceded for all Vietnamese people. The Archbishop further observed, "We enter the year of grace; the long year of prayer will praise God for entrusting us to the Holy Mother who is dwelling among us in the very Vietnamese culture."[89] At the vigil meditation, the archbishop also contemplated her title "Our Lady of Help of Christians." His prayer included "May the Mother of La

"Lời chào mừng" ["Welcoming speech"], in *La Vang 200 Năm*, 22.

87. Paul-Joseph Phạm, "General Letter," in *The Sanctuary of Our Lady of La Vang*, 53. Also see CBCV, "General Letter" 1997, ACBCV.

88. P-H Nguyễn, "Homily," in *La Vang the 200th Year*, 34–36. He was the bishop of the diocese of Nha Trang from 1975–2009.

89. Étienne Nguyễn, "Welcoming," in *La Vang the 200th Year*, 22.

Vang be the Morning Star. . . . May the Holy Mother of La Vang, Our Lady Help of Christians, pray for us."[90] These titles taken together show that an ancient devotional title, one that ultimately traces its history back to the third century, was inculturated fully in Vietnam in the devotion to OLLV. It also shows that this inculturated faith was recognized as, simply, the faith of the universal Catholic church.

Additionally, as the host of the Jubilee, Archbishop Étienne Nguyễn commissioned the composition of "The Prayer to Our Lady of La Vang" (hereafter "The Prayer") which has become the official prayer to OLLV. "The Prayer" echoes the Joseph-Marie Thích Văn Nguyễn's "A Prayer to the Holy Mother La Vang," as reviewed in chapter 1, and the famous poetic prayer of Hàm Mặc Tử, as well as expressing the tradition of OLLV (see page 203). This prayer also cultivates the teaching of Pope John Paul II regarding a culture of love and of life. It displays the belief in OLLV—the Mother of God—so it contains petitions from the congregation and/or those who use it to pray to her. "The Prayer" can be translated:

O [I bow to] Mother Mary, Our Lady of La Vang, full of grace, radiant with
thousands of rays, incomparable saints and angels
God lovingly chose you, Mother, pure and holy,
To give a birth to save all creation.
You, Mother, chose La Vang to appear [in order to]
help our ancestors, non-Christians and Christians
amid their persecution and hardships
Since then, Mother still forever give abundant grace, grace for soul and body,
for the sick, the distressed, and let no one request that OLLV does not answer.

O [I bow to] Mother Mary, Our Lady of La Vang,
The Holy Mother of God, and the Mother of humanity,
grant abundant grace to your loving the children, we earnestly implore, and
transform us , so [that may we] cultivate kindness and compassion hearts and
to foster a civil culture of love and life together.

Bless us always to live a holy life with devout hope
and at the end of life, may we attain the joy of eternal life with you, Mother,
and enjoy glory in the Trinity. Amen.[91]

90. Étienne Nguyễn, "Meditation," in *La Vang the 200*[th] *Year*, 88.
91. "Kinh Thánh Mẫu La Vang" ["The Prayer to Our Lady of La Vang," 1997, ACBCV. I choose "The Prayer" to distinguish this from JMT's 1938 "A Prayer to the Holy Mother La Vang" in 1938. Also, "the Holy Mother" can be translated "Đức Mẹ" or "Thánh Mẫu;" therefore, I translate "Kinh Thánh Mẫu La Vang" into "The Prayer to Our Lady of La Vang" and "Lời cầu cùng Đức Mẹ La Vang" into "A Prayer to the Holy

"The Prayer" sounds poetic strains interweaving Mariology with its Vietnamese context and culture. The text of the prayer recalls the history of the Church in Vietnam during the persecutions and the strong faith of the Vietnamese ancestors. Precisely as their Mother, OLLV—the Mother of God—becomes the Mother of all Vietnamese, who journeys with and transforms them to become holier through the virtues of kindness and compassion in order to foster a culture of love and life toward the Kingdom of God.

Along with the spirit of the Synod of Asia 1998, the solemn opening of the Jubilee was structured as an explicit practice of inculturation, applied to everything from decoration to liturgy.[92] One of the most important rituals was to inaugurate the new statue of OLLV. At the first pilgrimage in 1900, as we saw, a statue of Notre Dame de Victoire was installed at the Church and then at the Shrine of OLLV. At the beginning of the Jubilee, the new statue of OLLV, donated and approved by the CBCV, was installed, depicting her as a Vietnamese woman and holding the Baby Jesus depicted as a Vietnamese baby child (fig. 10).

Mother La Vang."

92. Huyền Vi, writing in *Catholic and Nation*, pointed out that inculturation was applied "maximally"; see "Suy tư về Hội nhập văn hoá khởi đi từ La Vang" ["Thinking about inculturation starting from La Vang"], 4.

Fig. 10: A new statue of Our Lady of La Vang holding the Baby Jesus, c. 1998 (AAOH).

The archbishop explained these and other aspects of the new statue:

> The Blessed Mother was lovingly dressed in a [Vietnamese] queen's outfit, ivory-white long cloth, blue-green mantle with gold trim, corresponding to pale yellow shoes. Her crown depicts Mary as both a benevolent Mother and a mighty Queen. She held the Child Jesus in her arms, her head leaned slightly towards the Son, and the Son leaned slightly towards her, expressing the two, Mother and Child, with a mindful eye looking down on the children below. The majestic Child Jesus, in a pink robe, has a golden circle in front of his chest in the words ALPHA and OMEGA ("I am the beginning and the end"). In the posture of the perfect Divine Mercy, the Lord's left-hand points to His merciful Sacred Heart. Because Mother La Vang heard [whomever cries to her], the Lord blessed the children of Vietnam and those who trusted in him by extending his right hand toward the believers.[93]

OLLV did not leave a specific image, as in the story of Our Lady of Guadalupe, but this ended up providing an opportunity for the church leaders over the years to interpret her appearance. The history of the new statue of OLLV began when Archbishop Étienne saw a statue of *Duc Me Vietnam* [A Vietnamese Mother] in California sculpted by Văn Nhân, a Vietnamese American artist in the United States. The Archbishop invited Văn Nhân to sculpt a statue that would be assimilated to Vietnamese cultural elements just as her story already was—for example, the Holy Mother and the Baby Jesus were to wear Vietnamese traditional dresses, áo dài khăn đống. The CBCV grant its approval for the new statue to replace the older one at the shrine in 1997.

The new statue of OLLV marked a significant step in Marian inculturation at the NC-OLLV, and even in the history of the theology of inculturation in Vietnam. It was not the first inculturated image of Mary or Jesus to be made.[94] But as the first such inculturated statue to be in-

93. Archbishop Étienne Nguyễn, "Ý nghĩa bức tượng Thánh Mẫu La Vang" [Meanings of a statue of the Holy Mother La Vang"] in Paul Trần, *Pilgrimage to the Diocese of Huế*, vol. III, 28–29. Sister Mary Fiat, interview with Archbishop Étienne (Huế, May 2019). The archbishop says that the statue's development was a process of collaboration among the People of God. A new statue was also a result of the effort to interpret the apparition in the context of Vietnamese culture. This new image inspired Thao Nguyen, SJ, "Inculturation for Mission."

94. Martin Ấn Ngọc Lê's dissertation, for example, includes a collection of portrayals of the BVM with the Baby Jesus with Vietnamese features; see "La dévotion Mariale au Việt Nam," 225–54.

stalled at the NC-OLLV by the CBCV, it made an impact on those who follow this very popular devotion. When I asked about the history of this new image of OLLV, Archbishop Étienne, now emeritus, was excited to tell me that the image was a result of many people's ideas and reflection. Since 1998 there have been several iterations of the statue because additions or changes were made after consulting theologians.[95] For example, twelve stars were added to a bandanna of the statue of OLLV, a reference to Revelation 12:1. The current statue is made of marble, which carries deep meaning in the Vietnamese culture. The Archbishop noted that the statue has been developed in the aftermath of the Asian Synod in 1998, which encouraged liturgical inculturation.[96] In addition, devotion to OLLV would become a sign of unification, as the new statue has been installed in many regions in Vietnam and the Vietnamese diaspora.

During the opening of the Jubilee pilgrimage, the liturgy, devotion, sacraments, and performances reflected Vietnamese culture. Every liturgy was solemn, with a procession devoted to either the Eucharist, OLLV, or the Vietnamese martyrs. The last day included solemn processions of all three palanquins. Large-scale performances displayed the story of the lay faithful and the Marian apparition in 1798. There were meditations on the rosary, music, light dancing, and other performances, all of which facilitated faith formation. Paul Chu Q. Trần, analyzing these events, saw them evidence of beautiful and successful inculturation in which the Vietnamese arts had been adapted into religious rituals.[97]

During the 200th Jubilee homilies generally expanded on Marian characteristics and reflected on the story of OLLV. The beginning of this jubilee in 1998 marked the sacred land of the NC-OLLV as "a school of Mary." The NC-OLLV was again reemphasized as the Mother House of all Vietnamese. As the host of the opening the jubilee, Archbishop Étienne said that "La Vang is the land of the Holy Mother [and] her house, [and] she is our Mother. Mother's house is our house, which always is opening to welcome all children of the Mother."[98] Furthermore, at the vigil mass for the feast of the Assumption, the Archbishop gave a remarkable homily. He described two centuries of continuous prayer at La Vang to the Mother La Vang, repeating her words: "Children, have trust, be willing to

---

95. Sr. Mary Kim Anh Thi, interview with Archbishop Étienne (Huế, May 2019).

96. See Joseph Dũng A. Trần, *Hội Đồng Giám Mục Việt Nam*, 465–500.

97. Q. Trần, *Pilgrimage to Diocese of Huế*, 3:327. Inculturation has been a constant question among Catholic scholars in Vietnam; see for example Ket Chinh Nguyen, "Hội nhập văn hóa tại Việt Nam."

98. Archbishop Étienne Nguyễn, "Welcome Speech," 70.

The History of Devotion to Our Lady of La Vang Continues 139

endure suffering.... All those who come to pray to Mother [me] in this spot Mother [I] will listen and grant them according to their wishes." The two centuries, he said, had one history of love. He further stated:

> Our Lady of La Vang, the Holy Mother of Nazareth, is an ordinary woman . . . but in her soul were incredible wonders, marvelous. The height of faith, hope, and love. . . . She said Fiat . . . danced, singing Magnificat . . . [and] stood at the foot of the Cross. . . . [So] Be steadfast of faith, hope, love to read the history of the Church. . . . to forgive . . . to read 'the signs of the times.' With Our Lady of La Vang, [we] journey together toward the Great Jubilee 2000 of salvation. With Our Lady of La Vang, [we] enter the third millennium with joy and hope. Amen.[99]

The archbishop preached that pilgrimage to OLLV as important to formation in faith, hope, and love, reinforcing the theology of OLLV preached by John Paul II.

Indeed, the 200th anniversary of the Marian apparition of OLLV significantly energized the faithful's devotion to OLLV, not only on pilgrimage but also at home, as church leaders encouraged their people to venerate OLLV in their daily lives. Before dismissing the pilgrims at the end of the solemn mass, Cardinal Paul-Joseph Tụng Đình Phạm, the papal envoy, spoke: "As we go back home, may Our Lady of La Vang continue following us and may she always grant help to us so that we may practice what the Archbishop preached to us at the mass yesterday."[100] The cardinal's message was that OLLV would go home with the pilgrims, and through devotion to her, the pilgrims would continue growing in faith, hope, and love. Participants likely numbered around 200,000, including 16 bishops and around

---

99. Archbishop Étienne Nguyễn, "Bài giảng" ["Homily"] in *La Vang 200 Years*, 79–83. A part of his homily in the Vietnamese language: "Hai trăm năm La Vang: Lời kinh dài hai thế kỷ...Hai trăm năm Mẹ La Vang: 'Các con hãy tin tưởng, cam lòng chịu khổ. Mẹ đã nhậm lời các con kêu xin. Từ nay về sau, hễ ai chạy đến cầu khẩn cùng Mẹ tại chốn này, Mẹ sẽ nhậm lời ban ơn theo ý nguyện.'Hai trăm năm La Vang: Một lịch sử tình yêu, lịch sử đá vàng, . . .Đức Mẹ La Vang, Đức Mẹ Nazareth là một phụ nữ bình thường của đời thường, . . . nhưng bên trong Mẹ là những kỳ diệu khôn tả, là những chiều cao nhiệm mầu. Đó là chiều cao của Đức Tin, Đức Cậy, Đức Mến nơi Mẹ. Tin, Cậy, Mến. . . lời thưa Fiat. Tin, Cậy, Mến . . . nhảy mừng trong bài Magnificat. Tin, Cậy, Mến . . . đứng dưới chân Thập giá. . . . Hãy đứng ở đỉnh cao Tin, Cậy, Mến để thấy được trong dòng lịch sử Giáo hội pha lẫn ánh sáng và bóng tối, . . .Hãy đứng ở đỉnh cao Tin, Cậy, Mến . . .Cùng Mẹ La Vang tiến về Năm Đại Toàn Xá 2000. Cùng Mẹ La Vang bước vào thiên niên kỷ thứ ba trong vui mừng và hy vọng. Amen".

100. Cardinal Phạm, "Huấn từ bế mạc" [Sermon of Closing], in *La Vang 200 Years*, 122. The original quote is "Chúng ta ra về xin Đức Mẹ tiếp tục theo chúng ta về địa phương và luôn luôn ban ơn phù trợ để chúng ta thực hiện những lời mà Đức Tổng đã căn dặn chúng ta trong Thánh lễ hôm qua."

330 clergy.[101] Indeed, after the 200th anniversary the history of devotion to OLLV has spread out and begun a new era, not only across the whole territory of Vietnam but also in diaspora across Asia, Europe, Australia, and North America, and especially in the United States.

Devotion to Our Lady of La Vang in the Third Millennium

The cult of OLLV has been built up continually across the last two decades. In 2002, the Congregation for Divine Worship and the Discipline of the Sacraments approved a liturgical rite of memory of OLLV to be used at the NC-OLLV.[102] This rite reflects the history of OLLV, including the martyrs and the loving Holy Mother. As Pope Paul VI taught, there are many ways of veneration of the BVM, and the highest one takes place at the liturgy.[103] With the liturgical rite approved, devotion to OLLV can now take place at that level, suggesting an approval that her apparition is worthy of belief. The rituals of OLLV have been augmented since, for example with the addition of the first Saturday devotions by Archbishop FX Hồng Văn Lê (2012–16). All members of the Archdiocese of Huế participate in this ritual and cultivate a culture of shared responsibility and collaboration.[104]

One of the most solemn experiences of devotion to OLLV since the opening of the third millennium was the 31st great pilgrimage in 2017. This section illustrates four reasons for the pilgrimage's success: a) the number of participants; b) theologies of maternity of OLLV and Our Lady of Fatima; c) inculturated liturgy and rituals; and d) accommodation.

First, the number of pilgrims was huge and diverse. At the opening mass, the participants numbered up to fifty thousand. Because the pilgrimage organizers only have records of the opening mass attendees, this number would likely be larger when including participants throughout the entire event.[105] The participants included Vietnamese people from

101. Tống, *Hai trăm năm-Một cảm tưởng*, 34.

102. The Congregation for Divine Worship and the Discipline of the Sacraments, *Textus Missae et Lectionarii de Beata Marie Virgine ad usum Sanctuarii Nationalis de La Vang lingua latina et vietnamensi exaratus* [*Masses and Lectionary of the Blessed Virgin Mary at the Use of National Marian Shrine of La Vang in Latin and Vietnamese Languages*]. Prot. 1439/02/L., approved August 2, 2002.

103. Paul VI, *Marialis Cultus*.

104. AAOH, 2012.

105. Quốc Chung et. al., "Những ngày sum vầy bên Mẹ la vang" ["Dates of Union with Mother La Vang"] in Catholic and Nation, no. 2119 (HochiMinh City: Le Quang Loc, 2017), 9.

Vietnam and from the diaspora across the United States, Europe, and Australia. People from Laos, Cambodia, and Thailand also attended. Along with most of the church leaders in Vietnam, Archbishop Leopoldo Girelli—non-residential pontifical representative for Vietnam—and Cardinal Fernando Filoni—prefect of the Congregation of Evangelization of People—participated in this pilgrimage. A huge number of musicians and choir members also served during the pilgrimages. The two bands of trumpets and drums comprised 1,550 players from the dioceses of Bùi Chu and of Thái Bình (northern Vietnam).[106] There was also an orchestra—with many national instruments—serving during the liturgy. Though the number is not on record, an array of choir members came from churches across Vietnam, including lay faithful and religious sisters and brothers. Similarly, as performers retold the stories of the Marian apparitions at Fatima and at La Vang as well as meditating on the Glorious Mystery of the Rosary, the media captured thousands of people participating in the performances and praising the Mother of God with floral crowns and wreaths. More than two hundred volunteers cleaned up, while many doctors and nurses served the pilgrims.[107] The People of God gathered at La Vang to worship God together through devotion to OLLV—and to serve each other.

Secondly, the pilgrims became more aware of Mary's maternal love due to this pilgrimage. The theme was "Living the Message of Fatima: Repentance and Conversion; Devotion to the Heart of the Holy Mother; Recitation of the Rosary" because this triennial pilgrimage also took place during the 100th anniversary year of the Marian apparitions at Fatima. This theme shaped all events of the pilgrimage, including homilies, sermons, and performances. A sermon on Fatima, for example, emphasized the merciful maternity of the Mother of God to those physically and spiritually poor, connecting those at La Vang in 1798 with those at Fatima in 1917. Another homily explored how both Marian apparitions proclaimed a common message of hope by exploring their contexts and describing the presence of the Holy Mother as "Star of the Sea" to comfort, guide, and grow in faith for the vulnerable then, and now also for the pilgrims today. Those two stories of the Marian apparitions were

---

106. Maria Tuyệt Thị Nguyễn, *I Bow to the Holy Mother La Vang, I Love You*, 221–42.

107. For more detail see the AAOH, 2017; Maria Tuyệt Thị Nguyễn, *I Bow to the Holy Mother La Vang*, 221–42. The two presentations included Sister Hồng Quế, "With Mary, the Young are Confident to Enter Married Life," and Bishop Dominic Mạnh Văn Nguyễn, "The Anniversary of 100th Jubilee of the Marian Apparition in Fatima" (AAOH, 2017).

intertwined to stress the love of the Holy Mother for her poor children. An important component of devotion to OLLV, also made clear in the devotion to Fatima, is the exploration of the loving care of the Mother of God for the vulnerable in all aspects of life.

Thirdly, the Masses, rituals, processions, and performances were nearly all inflected by Vietnamese culture, except for one performative recounting of the Marian apparitions at Fatima. More than 600 youth performed a dedication of flowers to OLLV. They addressed multiple diverse cultural ethnicities in Vietnam. More than 200 Sisters of Lovers of the Holy Cross of Huế and of St. Paul de Chartres performed as well.[108] The first part of the evening included a representation of Fatima using Portuguese costumes and music. This was followed by a recitation of the Glorious Mysteries, beginning with a reading of a Gospel passage and including a hymn with dancing. This performance closed with a culturally Vietnamese play of the Marian apparition at La Vang. For example, colorful lanterns, a unique cultural practice of Huế, were formed into a large rosary in front of the Shrine of OLLV. This performance reinvigorated the reception of the historical Marian apparitions at La Vang and Fatima, asking people to move towards repentance, conversion, and courage to live the Gospel by reciting the rosary. Indeed, devotion to OLLV provides space and time to cultivate Vietnamese practices in the liturgy, devotion, and other rituals. The juxtaposition of the celebration of Our Lady of La Vang with one of the most famous authorized apparitions of Mary surely was, in part, meant to imply that the apparitions at La Vang were just as authentic.

Last, but not least, difficult conditions never prevent pilgrims from going to La Vang. In the third millennium, accommodation still remains a big issue during national pilgrimages. The local hotels only met the need of around 10% of the pilgrims. Restaurants were overwhelmed, and water and sanitation remained big issues due to very hot weather in August in central Vietnam.[109] Therefore, simple tents were raised on the campus of the NP-OLLV, and the pilgrims slept on the ground. Most had to bring

---

108. "Đêm Diễn Nguyện" ["A Night of Performance"] appears to be becoming a standard practice for the pilgrimage. For example, it has been added to a ritual of First Saturday Devotion (AAOH, 2017).

109. Quốc Chung et. al., "Dates of Union with Mother La Vang," 11. The original quote is "Ba ngày trước mặt hứa hẹn sẽ rất khó khăn về nơi ăn chốn ngủ, cũng như mọi điều kiện sinh hoạt khác." When I myself went on a six-day pilgrimage in June of 2022, although I had a hotel, there was not sufficient food locally. Mentioning this reality is merely to say that the pilgrims are wholeheartedly devoted to OLLV.

food and water with them. The lack of accommodations was an issue at the fifteenth pilgrimage in 1961, as mentioned above. After sixty years, it remains an urgent issue. Despite such difficult conditions, the number of pilgrims has still increased over time.

Devotion to OLLV has absolutely become the biggest gathering of the Church in Vietnam. This review of the thirty-first National Pilgrimage demonstrates a big step in devotion to OLLV. The global and local churches were present. Most of the Bishops of Vietnam, clergy, religious Sisters and Brothers, seminarians, and laity went on the pilgrimage, took part in its rituals, and volunteered to help out. In Vietnam, it appears that the Church's devotion to OLLV proves that devotion to Mary is indeed an "intrinsic element of Christian worship."

Since 2017, further rituals have become significant for the pilgrims. To mark the 170th anniversary of the establishment of the Archdiocese of Huế in 1850, Archbishop Joseph Linh Chí Nguyễn decided to venerate OLLV as the patron of the Archdiocese in 2019. Each parish now uses the Prayer to the Holy Mother La Vang on the first Saturday of each month. In his homily, the Archbishop stated that all the land of the archdiocese had now become the sacred land of La Vang.[110] The CBCV had also planned to erect a new building of the Basilica of OLLV in 2020, when the thirty-second great pilgrimage was to have taken place.[111] In June of 2022, the Archbishop of Huế further approved an extended monthly ritual for the first Saturday that begins on the previous Friday evening. The parishes of the archdiocese volunteer in rotation to take charge the ritual, which includes a procession of OLLV, a performance, and a recitation of the rosary. Following this evening devotion, the Archbishop of Huế presides over a solemn mass on the next Saturday morning.[112]

Nowadays, devotion to OLLV facilitates the teaching of the Church and celebrates the diverse subcultures in Vietnam. For example, the annual pilgrimage took place from August 14-15, 2022. The theme was "Mother Mary: a Model of Communion," anticipating the 2021–2024 synod theme, "Communion, Participation, and Mission."[113] Although it was only an

110. Archbishop Joseph Linh Chí Nguyễn, "Quyết định" ["Decree"] (AAOH, Dec. 26, 2019).

111. See http://www.asianews.it/news-en/Some-80,000-Catholics-visited-La-Vang-shrine-to-celebrate-the-Assumption-of-Mary-(photos)-47805.html.

112. Rev. Michael Hải Ngọc Phạm, announcement (The NC-OLLV, Jun. 4, 2022).

113. The AOH, "Giới thiệu hành hương thường niên Đức Mẹ La Vang 2022" ["Introduction of the Annual Pilgrimage in 2022"], https://www.youtube.com/watch?v=-wxPieMyojU.

August annual pilgrimage, several dioceses and diverse ethnic groups participated, bringing their own subcultures into performances.[114] The "Night Performance," for example, combined a concert, a choir performance, a recitation of the rosary, and a musical play (fig. 11). Each decade of the recitation of the Joyful Mysteries began with a meditation of the Word, then the recitation of the decade, and then a musical play, including those drawn from the subcultures of Bắc Ninh and of Huế.[115] The Night Performance ended with "The Merciful Father," based on the parable of the lost son in the Gospel of Luke 15:11–32. This musical play echoed "chèo," a type of ancient northern Vietnamese music.[116] The performance created a space for both brothers in the parable to recognize their own failings and express their conversion. It reminded pilgrims that family life is a fundamental force for each family member, and the members of the diverse subcultures are all members of one Vietnamese family (fig. 12). This annual pilgrimage closed the history of devotion to OLLV during the period of 1988–2022.

Fig. 11: The Night Performance at the Annual 2022 Pilgrimage (AAOH).

114. See the Archdiocese of Huế, "Dâng hoa và Cầu nguyện" ["Offering flower and Prayer"], https://www.youtube.com/watch?v=mxWltj523pM.

115. The AOH, "La Vang 2022- Đêm Diễn Nguyện bên Mẹ La Vang" ["La Vang 2022: A Night Performance at Mother La Vang"], https://www.youtube.com/watch?v=cn4oNQJtTZA. See also AAOH, 2022.

116. The Diocese of Thái Bình, "Người Cha Nhân Hậu" ["The Merciful Father"], https://www.youtube.com/watch?v=cn4oNQJtTZA. See also AAOH (2022).

The History of Devotion to Our Lady of La Vang Continues

These chapters have sought to demonstrate that devotion to OLLV began after the Marian apparitions at La Vang in 1798, that devotion to OLLV has been continual at La Vang, and that it has spread across the nation and then across the diaspora in Asia, North America, Europe, and Australia. The history of devotion to OLLV is the history of resilient Christians who persisted in hope throughout the ups and downs of their nation and their church. Such devotion inculturates and becomes its own identity. A summary of the rituals of veneration of OLLV shows that they have become significant engines of faith formation for the Vietnamese Catholics and those immigrants in diaspora. Truly, OLLV is the Ecclesial Mother of Vietnam, the fruit of a practice that has been developing as an inculturation of Marian devotion for the past 225 years.

Fig. 12: The Closing Mass of the 2022 August Annual Pilgrimage to OLLV was taken in front of the Basilica of OLLV (AAOH).

4

Our Lady of La Vang

The Ecclesial Mother

AT THE END OF the third session of the Second Vatican Council, Pope Paul VI proclaimed that Mary was "Most Holy Mother of the Church, that is, of all the Christian people and pastors."[1] In the universal context of worldwide conflicts and different Marian approaches, the Pope's proclamation solemnly recognized her spiritual maternity. The chaotic global context of the mid-twentieth century included World War II, the Cold War (1947–91), the Korean War (1950–53), and the Vietnam War (1958–75). During the first half of the twentieth century, there were two primary Catholic approaches to Mariology.[2] While maximalist Mariology focuses on Mary's unique role in the history of salvation as Mother of God, as the source for her maternal relationship to Christ, a more minimalist Mariology emphasizes Mary's role within the divine economy of salvation in connection to the Church. Both of these approaches directly and indirectly impacted the papal declaration about Mary, Mother of the Church.

On December 18, 1960, around a month after the hierarchy of the Catholic Church in Vietnam was established, the bishops of South Vietnam entrusted their new mission to the BVM under her title of "the Immaculate Conception." They chose the grounds of the Sacred Shrine of OLLV as the National Center/Shrine of the Holy Mother La Vang

---

1. Paul VI, "Discourse of 21 November 1964," and "Address during the Last General Meeting of the Second Vatican Council." John Paul II quotes it, see Redemptoris Mater, §47.

2. See Schillebeeckx and Halkes, *Mary: Yesterday, Today, Tomorrow*.

(NC-OLLV) on April 13, 1961 and, as we have seen, requested the elevation of her church to a basilica rank.³ They also invoked OLLV as the Holy Mother of all Vietnamese people and prayed to her for peace, unity, and religious freedom. In the context of these events, this chapter shows how Vietnamese Catholics' devotion to OLLV is a story of how she came to be viewed as their Holy Mother and the Holy Mother of the Church in Vietnam. Considering this history, the recent ecclesial teaching in support of the Marian title "Mother of the Church" is appreciated. as it has become a culturally embedded reality in the devotion to OLLV.

This chapter begins with an exploration of the recent history of the title Mother of the Church. Then, I show how earlier historical Marian titles found a unique home in the story of and devotion to OLLV soon after her apparition up through the present date. Finally, this chapter analyzes several essential documents by the bishops of Vietnam to illustrate how in the twenty-first century they continue developing the tradition of OLLV in connection with the title, Mary Mother of the Church.

Theology of Mary, Mother of The Church

This first section explores the theology of Mary Mother of the Church, with attention to two of her titles. Although the Marian titles "Our Lady Help of Christians" and "Our Lady of Grace" have non-Vietnamese backgrounds, they were available to help express the maternal love of the Blessed Virgin Mary, the Mother of the Church, in particular circumstances, including those of the Church in Vietnam.

The Blessed Virgin Mary: Mother of the Church

The Magisterium teaches devotion to the BVM as the Mother of the Church. On February 11, 2018, Pope Francis placed the memorial celebration of Mary, Mother of the Church, into the General Roman calendar. His decree recalls Paul VI's proclamation of the BVM as Mother of the Church at a closing section of the Second Vatican Council in 1964 and when closing the council in 1965. Paul VI deepened our understanding of this Marian title during his papal reign through his teachings and popular devotion. However, this Marian title has long biblical and traditional roots.

---

3. Stanislas Ngọc Văn Nguyễn, *Sacred Land of La Vang*, 103–6.

Regarding these roots, Paul VI stated that "What Christ wanted, we too want. What the Church has taught over the centuries, we too teach: Mary is the Mother of Christ, Head [of] his mystical Body, that is the Church."[4] He said also that as BVM was the Mother of the Church, she was the Mother, "that is, of all Christian people, both the faithful and of the Pastors."[5] On the Cross, Jesus said to his mother, "Woman, behold, your son, [and to his beloved disciple] Behold, your mother" (Jn. 19:26–27). She accepted this "beloved disciple" as her son,[6] who has been interpreted as the Church, which is the mystical Body of Christ.[7] The Book of Acts also mentions the BVM was present among the early Church in prayer. This, too, is biblical evidence cited by the Pope in support of her maternity of the Church. Indeed, if Jesus Christ is the Head of the Church, the Mystical Body of Christ, then the BVM, the Mother of the Head, is also the Mother of this Mystical Body. Also, she is the ecclesial mother because Jesus entrusted the Church to her.

In his 1967 *Signum Magnum*, Pope Paul VI repeated the title "Mary, the Mother of the Church" often: "Mary is the Mother of the Church not only because she is the Mother of Christ . . . but also because 'she shines forth to the whole community of the elect as a model of the virtues . . . [moreover,] the Church benefits from the maternal presence of God's Mother, because she is tied by an enduring and indissoluble bond to the mystery of the Mystical Body."[8] John Paul II summarized the history of this title in his encyclical *Redemptoris Mater* in 1987 and in his speech at the General Audience on September 17, 1997. The Pope began with the Annunciation: the mystery of the "fullness of time" and as "full of grace" in which the BVM is perfectly united with Christ.[9] She bears the Word of God in her womb, intercedes at the wedding in Cana, stands firm at the foot of the Cross, and is present at the Upper Room;[10] she be-

---

4. Paul VI, "Conclusion of the Third Session of the Second Vatican Council," §7, §32.

5. Paul VI, Conclusion of the Third Session of the Second Vatican Council," §30.

6. John Paul II, *Redemptoris Mater*, §30.

7. Paul VI, "Conclusion of the Third Session of the Second Vatican Council II," §3, §32; Paul VI, *Signum Magnum*; Francis, *Lumen Fidei*, §59; Second Vatican Council, *Lumen Gentium*, §8, §11, §32–33. See also Sarah, "Decree on the Celebration of the Blessed Virgin Mary." Biblical references include Col 1: 18, 2:10; 1 Cor 11:3, 12: 12–27; Eph 1:21–23, 4: 4–5 and 11–16, 5:23; Rom 12: 4–5.

8. Paul VI, *Signum Magnum*, §1; §34.

9. John Paul II, *Redemptoris Mater*, §1. For "fullness of time," see notes 2, 7. For "full of grace," see note 3; 7–11, especially 8–9.

10. John Paul II, *Redemptoris Mater*, §26.

comes a prototype, model and mother of the Church.[11] Just as Pope Paul VI did, Pope John Paul II pointed out that the tradition of proclaiming the BVM as Mother of the Church has its roots in the New Testament,[12] in the teaching of the Fathers,[13] and throughout the teaching of the Church. Returning to Mary's presence with the young Church in the Upper Room, the Pope said, "In the Upper Room Mary's journey meets the Church's journey of faith. . . . [Mary] was in the upper Room, where the Apostles were preparing to take up this mission with the coming of the Spirit of Truth: she was present with them."[14] Being present "from the beginning [of the Church's birth]" the BVM, "as an exceptional witness to the mystery of Christ,"[15] nursed the nascent Church, strengthening the pilgrim Church. In other words, the BVM was and still is present to help the Church grow and carry out its mission.

In the same sources, the Pope continued to provide citations of patristic teaching. He stated, following Irenaeus, that: "Mary 'became a cause of salvation for the whole human race.' (Haer. 3, 22, 4; PG 7, 959), and the pure womb of the Virgin 'regenerates men in God' (Haer. 4, 33, 11; PG 7, 1080)." He quoted from Saint Ambrose: "'A Virgin has begotten the salvation of the world, a Virgin has given life to all things' (Ep. 63, 33; PL 16, 1198), and by other Fathers who call Mary the 'Mother of salvation.'"[16]

John Paul II's argument is that the early Church recognized the significant role of the BVM in salvation history. The Pope continued by referring to figures in the Middle Ages. For example, Saint Anselm addressed the BVM as a mother in all significant aspects, saying: "You are the mother of justification and of the justified, the Mother of reconciliation and of the reconciled, the mother of salvation and of the saved."[17]

11. John Paul II, *Redemptoris Mater*, §2, citing *Lumen Gentium*.

12. Paul VI, *Signum Magnum*, citing *Lumen Gentium*, §55; Sarah, "Decree on the Celebration of the Blessed Virgin Mary," citing Galatians, Gospel of John, and Acts.

13. Paul VI, *Signum Magnum*; see also citations in Sarah, "Decree on the Celebration of the Blessed Virgin Mary."

14. John Paul II, *Redemptoris Mater*, §26.

15. John Paul II, *Redemptoris Mater*, §27. See also Acts 1:13–14.

16. See also Irenaeus, *Adversus Haereses (Against the Heresies)*, book 3, chapter 22, section 4 (Haer. 3, 22, 4) and book 4, chapter 33, section 11 (Haer.4, 33, 11); *Patrologia Graeca*, volume 7, column 959 (PG 7, 959) and volume 7, column 1080 (PG 7, 1080); *Patrologia Latina*, volume 16, column 1198 (PL 16, 1198). See John Paul II, "General Audience."

17. John Paul II, "General Audience." The Pope also cited *Patrologia Latina*, volume 158, column 957 (*Or.* 52, 8; PL 158, 957).

Pope Leo XIII taught that the BVM "was, in very truth, the Mother of the Church, the teacher and Queen of the Apostles."[18] In the modern era, too, Pope John XXIII spoke of Mary as "Mother of the Church and our most loving Mother."[19] Thus Pope John Paul II concluded that all of that evidence led the Council Fathers of the Second Vatican to declare the BVM "Mother of the Church."[20]

The Pope affirmed the teaching of the Church through chapter eight of *Lumen Gentium* about Mary as Mother of the Church,[21] emphasized her heroic faith, and further explored her as an exemplar for the Church.[22] Being chosen by and freely being obedient to God, the Pope confirmed, the BVM became the Mother of Church by grace and by her own virtues. He concluded that, in the Holy Spirit, she "embraces each and every one in and through the Church. She is and has been actively present in the life of the Church ... throughout the Church's history, ... at the center of the pilgrim Church."[23] It is clear for the Pope that "mother" means, or involves, presence. In addition to promoting the recitation of the rosary, the Pope stated, "Mary is the perfect icon of the motherhood of the Church."[24]

At the highest level of the Magisterium, then, the Church has officially taught that the BVM is the Mother of the Church, namely at, and since, the Second Vatican Council. This Marian title, the Council Fathers acknowledged, is grounded in her being "full of grace," the Mother of Christ, of God, of all believers, and even of all humanity—she is the New Eve.[25] Indeed, her motherhood is rooted in grace: "In this singular way she cooperated by her obedience, faith, hope and burning charity in the

18. Leo XIII, *Adjutricem Populi*, 6. See John Paul II, "General Audience," §2.

19. John XXIII, *AAS* 53, 1961, 35; see John Paul II, "General Audience," §2.

20. See John Paul II, "General Audience," §1, §2, §5. The Pope also cited *Lumen Gentium*, §53.

21. John Paul II, "General Audience," §5.

22. John Paul II, *Redemptoris Mater*, §43–44. In these passages, the Pope said, "It can be said that from Mary, the Church learns her own motherhood.... For, just as Mary is at the service of the mystery of the Incarnation, so the Church is always at the service of the mystery of adoption to sonship through grace.... Given Mary's relationship to the Church as an exemplar, the Church is close to her and seeks to become like her: 'Imitating the Mother of her Lord, and by the power of the Holy Spirit, she preserves with virginal purity an integral faith, a firm hope, and a sincere charity.'" He also cited *Lumen Gentium*, §64.

23. See John Paul II, *Redemptoris Mater*.

24. John Paul II, *Rosarium Virginis Mariae*, §15.

25. *Lumen gentium*, §56.

work of the Savior in giving back supernatural life to souls. Wherefore she is our mother in the order of grace."[26] In other words, through Jesus Christ, the BVM becomes the mother of all, in and through being Mother of the Church.

In addition, the structure of *Lumen gentium* demonstrates the Council's view of the significant role of the BVM in the life of the Church. In the eighth chapter, the Council Fathers taught about the BVM after defining the nature, the mission, and the diverse members of the Church in the first seven chapters. This structure means that they entrust the whole Church to the BVM. Her motherhood is declared at the beginning of the eighth chapter: "The Catholic Church, inspired by the Holy Spirit, honors her with filial affection and piety as a most beloved mother," and indeed, "she is clearly the mother of the members of Christ," the Church.[27] Still more, she is "mother of humankind"[28] because her motherhood extends, through the Church, to all. Just as the BVM is virgin and mother, so is the Church.[29] Like the BVM, the Church must keep the faith pure and entire, to be faithful to Jesus Christ,[30] and so the Church's motherhood, like Mary's, reaches to everyone in some way. At the closing of the Council, the Pope declared: "We also earnestly implore the protection of the most Blessed Mary, the Mother of Christ and therefore called by us also Mother of the Church."[31] In the history of salvation, God needed a mother like the BVM; so now worldwide chaos, both Church and world greatly need that mother. She is the mother of the pilgrim church: "she shines forth on earth, until the day of the Lord shall come, a sign of certain hope and comfort to the pilgrim people of God."[32]

After the Second Vatican Council closed in 1965, the Church continued to honor the BVM as its ecclesial mother. We have already seen the contributions of Popes Paul VI and John Paul II. In the new millennium, in preparation for the Great Jubilee in 2000, John Paul II emphasized once again that the BVM is Mother of the Church. For him, the Marian title Mother of the Church is grounded in the sources of revelation as

26. *Lumen gentium*, §61.
27. *Lumen gentium*, §53.
28. *Lumen gentium*, §60.
29. *Lumen gentium*, §63.
30. *Lumen gentium*, §64.
31. Paul VI, "Conclusion of the Third Session of the Second Vatican Council"; *Lumen gentium*, §53.
32. *Lumen gentium*, §68. See 2 Pet 3:10.

interpreted over time in the tradition.[33] In his letter to the closing of the 200th Jubilee of the apparition of OLLV, Pope John Paul II also addressed this title, saying: "I join through prayer the Vietnamese faithful and pilgrims who have entrusted themselves to the motherly intercession of the Virgin Mary, asking *this most Holy Mother to guide the Catholic Church in Việt Nam* on her journey to the Lord, and to help her in the witness she must bear on the threshold of the third millennium. . . . *She is the mother of the pilgrim Church.*"[34]

The Marian title Mother of the Church was also taught during the papacy of Benedict XVI. In *Deus Caritas Est*, the Pope taught that "Mary has truly become the Mother of all believers . . . to her, we entrust the Church and her mission in the service of love."[35] As the Mother of the Church, the Pope declared, the BVM is also a teacher of the Church, being present always, giving courage, and showing the way. The Pope addressed the BVM: "You remain amidst the disciples as their Mother, as the Mother of hope. . . . teach us to believe, to hope, to love with [her]. Show us the way of [Christ's] Kingdom! Star of the Sea, shine upon us and guide us on our way."[36] In other words, Mary, Mother of the Church, was entrusted by the Risen Lord to help the Church to faithfully carry out her mission.

As mentioned above, in placing Mary, Mother of the Church in the universal calendar, Pope Francis demonstrated the important role of the BVM in the life of the Church. Quoting the book of Acts, the Pope taught that the BVM, with the Holy Spirit, is actively present in the Church. She prays with us, walks side by side with us, and prepares the Church's members for the mission. Specifically, the Mother of the Church helps her children recognize what matters for successful evangelization. The Pope stated: "With the Holy Spirit, Mary is always present in the midst of the people. She joined the disciples in praying . . . She is the Mother of the Church which evangelizes, and without her we could never truly understand the spirit of the new evangelization."[37] This title, for Pope Francis,

---

33. John Paul II, "General Audience," 1, 3. See also John Paul II, *Theotókos: Woman, Mother, Disciple*, 233–35; *Catechism of the Catholic Church*, 65–66.

34. John Paul II, "Message of John Paul II for the Conclusion of The Marian Year in La Vang."

35. Benedict XVI, *Deus Caritas Est*, §42.

36. Benedict XVI, *Spe Salvi*, §50.

37. Francis, *Evangelii Gaudium*, §284.

is specifically associated with the evangelizing mission of the Church.[38] Thus in the post-Conciliar period, this title gained prominence and was associated with the maternity of the Church and her mission of evangelization. Further, as a prototype of the Church, the BVM is the Mother of the Church and as such a sign of the hope of the Church. She is the "Hope of Christians."[39]

"Our Lady of Help of Christians," "Our Lady of Victory," and "Our Lady of the Rosary"

As we have seen, the devotion to OLLV developed under the title Our Lady of Help of Christians (hereafter OLHC). This section unpacks the history of this and other associated Marian titles, such as Our Lady of the Rosary and Our Lady of Victory, which all relate to the story of OLLV. Historically, the three titles share a similar background. However, only OLHC and Our Lady of the Rosary remain in the liturgical calendar today.

The Church has invoked the BVM under the title Help of Christians since the earliest centuries of Christianity in association with asking for the protection and the "extraordinary help of the Mother of God."[40] Hilda Graef points out that the title Mother of God was invoked in an early third-century hymn.[41] The text reads in part: "Mother of God [hear] my supplication: suffer us not [to be] in adversity but deliver us from danger."[42] In accordance with this invocation, the BVM under her title Mother of God protects the Church and the believers in times of danger—especially in times of persecution of Christians, as in the mid-third century.[43]

This hymn to the Theotokos is evidence that when in urgent need, the early Christians asked the BVM for her help precisely as "Mother." As part of his lessons on Catholic doctrine, Chinaka Justin Mbaeri, OSJ, provides a series of October devotions to understand the Marian titles through the Litany of Loreto. To present the Marian title "Help of

---

38. Francis, *Evangelii Gaudium*, §286, §288.
39. Paul VI, *Marialis Cultus*, §32.
40. US Bishops' Committee on the Liturgy, *Collection of Masses*, 251.
41. *Traite*, 112, n. 27. Reference in Graef, *Mary*, n. 37. The original quote is "Sub tuum praesidium confugimus, Sancta Dei Genetrix. Nostras deprecationes ne despicias in necessitatibus, sed a periculis cunctis libera nos semper, Virgo gloriosa et benedicta. Amen."
42. Graef, *Mary*, 37–38.
43. US Bishops' Committee on the Liturgy, *Collection of Masses*, 251.

Christians," Mbaeri notes that "The early Christians in Greece and Egypt invoked the Mother of God with the Greek name 'Boeteia,' that is, 'the one who brings help from heaven.'"[44] He further states that "Mary is truly the one who brings us the necessary help from heaven, as recorded in the words of St. John Chrysostom (345 A.D.): 'You, Mary, are the most powerful help of God.'"[45] It seems that the early Church believed in the Mother of God, under that title, as a helper. The highest Marian title, Mother of God, thus laid down the roots for the title OLHC.

The specific title OLHC was strongly endorsed, most famously, by Pope Pius V. During the battle of Lepanto, Pius called for a rosary crusade on October 7, 1571.[46] After Christians triumphed against the odds over the Turks, this title was added into the Litany of Loreto, which at that time was widely recited. The Pope also instituted a new feast of the BVM of Victory on October 7.[47] Because this feast related to a papal call to the recitation of the rosary, Pope Pius V's successor, Pope Gregory XIII, changed the name of the feast to Our Lady of the Holy Rosary and moved it to the first Sunday of October. OLHC, then, is the title that gave rise to the two later titles Our Lady of Victory and Our Lady of the Holy Rosary.

Pope Pius VII further decreed that a feast dedicated to OLHC should be liturgically celebrated on May 24. Leading the Church in one of the most difficult periods in the history of the Catholic Church, which included the aftermath of the French Revolution and political and subsequent social chaos in Europe, Pope Pius VII himself suffered at the hands of Napoleon, as we have noted earlier. First, he was confined at the Quirinale Palace in 1808, then he was taken as prisoner to France from 1809–1814.[48] Returning to Rome, the Pope established a feast of OLHC on May 24—the day he arrived at Rome from exile—to honor the BVM.[49] Since then this feast has been celebrated in many churches. During his captivity in Savona, the Pope prayed wholeheartedly, as Robin Anderson recounts: "Pius VII's first request on arriving at the episcopal palace in exile was to be able to pray daily before the Blessed Sacrament. This was

---

44. Mbaeri, "October Devotion."
45. Mbaeri, "October Devotion."
46. Cipolla, "Sermon for Our Lady of the Rosary."
47. Roten, "Our Lady of Victory" and "Our Lady of the Rosary, Origins."
48. See Anderson, *Pope Pius VII*; Benedict XIV, *Bullarii Romani continuatio*, t.7, pt.1.; Pope Pius IX and Pope Gregory XVI, *Lettres apostoliques*, XXIII-XXXI; Caiani, *To Kidnap a Pope*.
49. Allies, *Pius the Seventh*, 290.

granted.... Here the Pope spent many hours each day in prayer and adoration, asking God's help for the Church and pardon for her persecutors; and here every evening, together with some of his household, he recited the Rosary."[50] Ultimately, Pope Pius X restored the name and the feast to Our Lady of Victory on the original date, October 7.[51] Later, the name was changed to the Blessed Virgin Mary of the Rosary in 1960 and then Our Lady of the Rosary in 1969, while retaining the same day, October 7.[52] Since then, this feast has been a mandatory memorial in the Roman liturgical calendar. While the title Our Lady of Victory no longer has a place in the liturgical calendar, it is still used in popular devotional and theological writings.[53]

In *Marialis Cultus,* Pope Paul VI emphasized the omnipotence in intercession of the BVM. In addition, he noted that the intercession of the BVM leads her devotees to become closer to her Son, Jesus Christ, who transforms hardened hearts: "Through her intercession the dawn of true peace may shine forth to men."[54] In the same encyclical, the Pope appealed to the BVM, saying, "Through your intercession, may God, the avenger of injuries, turn to mercy. May He give back to nations the tranquility they seek and bring them to a lasting age of genuine prosperity."[55] In *Redemptoris Mater,* John Paul II pointed out the intercession of the BVM, saying "With this character of intercession, first manifested at Cana in Galilee, Mary's mediation continues in the history of the Church and the world."[56] Although both Popes may not have intended explicitly to defend her title OLHC, they affirm her omnipotence in intercession. In other words, the title OLHC is implied in their teachings.

As explored above, the Marian title OLHC is associated with the rosary and with victories both spiritual and physical. For example, Pope Leo XIII, in his *On the Rosary,* connected Mary's intercessory help and the Rosary. The Pope taught that the BVM is "the mightiest helper of the Christian people and the most merciful," and that recitation of the rosary

---

50. Anderson, *Pope Pius VII,* 82.

51. Roten, "Our Lady of Victory."

52. See Attwater, *A Dictionary of Mary,* 109, 297, 253. Our Lady of Victories in Paris is the best-known church of the Blessed Virgin in that city after Notre Dame.

53. See Khiêm Đình Phạm, *Our Lady of La Vang is Our Lady of Victory;* Grunow, "Our Lady of the Rosary."

54. Paul VI, *Christi Matri,* §11.

55. Paul VI, *Christi Matri,* §13.

56. John Paul II, *Redemptoris mater,* §40. See more in *Lumen gentium,* §62.

is one of "the most excellent methods of prayer [because it] is a source of great joy to us."[57] These elements illustrate the characteristics of the BVM, OLHC, and the title's association with the rosary. The existence of liturgical celebrations on May 24 (OLHC) and October 7 (Our Lady of the Rosary) is echoed in the nature of the apparition of and devotion to OLLV in Vietnam. Devotion to OLLV under the title of OLHC began very early after the apparition and continues until now. Similarly, the rosary has been associated with OLLV since her apparition.

Mary, "Our Lady of Grace"

The Marian title "Our Lady of Grace" is rooted in the angel's address to Mary at the Annunciation (Lk. 1:28); however, like many other Marian titles, it has developed over time. The feast of Our Lady of Grace is based on the BVM's being "'full of grace' or the mother who brings down graces and benefits on us."[58] Johann Roten, S.M., recounts that the Marian title Our Lady of Grace was used in the fifteenth century, when the Church in France was in urgent need and received help through the intercession of the BVM.[59] As a result, the Shrine of Our Lady of Cambray, also known as Our Lady of Grace, was founded. A famous popular statue was installed at the shrine known as "Notre Dame de Grace et Cambrai," which "depicts Mary standing atop a globe, with her hands down at her sides so that grace can fall from her fingertips upon her children."[60] This title and image have been venerated in many countries throughout the world.

Moreover, devotion to Our Lady of Grace seems to have been strengthened after the Marian apparitions in Paris in 1830 known for the Miraculous Medal. Interestingly, the statue of Our Lady of Grace looks almost like the image on the Miraculous Medal. Designed and revealed to St. Catherine Laboure by the BVM, the medal depicts the BVM standing on the globe, crushing the serpent. Rays fall from her hands and bordering her is an inscription: "O Mary, conceived without sin, pray for us who have recourse to thee."[61] This message is in harmony with the doctrine of Mariology. Indeed, the BVM is "full of grace" to bring hope

---

57. Leo XIII, *Adiutricem*, §1.
58. Attwater, *A Dictionary of Mary*, 99.
59. Roten, "Our Lady of Grace."
60. Lim, "Mary of the Day."
61. See Prévost, , *Catherine Labouré*.

for the rest of humanity. Under the title Our Lady of Grace, devotees are reminded that she is there to intercede for those who are confident or believe in God.[62] Because she is "full of grace," the BVM becomes the mother of the members of Christ, and in turn, she becomes a helpful bridge of salvation for all humans. In this way, the BVM, Mother of the Church, expresses her maternity of grace, a maternity which, through the Church, is extended to all, even those beyond the Church. These Marian titles, associated with each other and all ultimately stemming from Mary's main title as "Mother of God," have developed over time. This began in the Western churches; however, in Vietnam, since 1798, these Marian titles became intertwined in the story of OLLV and thereby received further development in their new context.

OLLV, Mother of the Church Locally and Universally

The recent background of the Marian title Mother of the Church demonstrates its connection to her maternal help, intercession, and Christian hope, echoing the ancient resonance of the title Mother of God. In turn, the titles OLHC, Our Lady of Victory, Our Lady of the Rosary, and Our Lady of Grace emphasize her help and in that way are an expression of her tender maternity. This section shows how devotion to OLLV becomes universalized by its intertwining with the titles studied above, and, at the same time, how these titles become inculturated in Vietnamese faith. That is, it demonstrates how OLLV has become Mother of the Church in Vietnam, and how at the same time, she, the uniquely Vietnamese Mary, is also Mother of the Universal Church.

The context of Vietnam and of the story of OLLV can provide sufficient explanation for widespread devotion to her under the Marian title OLHC. The BVM known as OLLV appeared to Vietnamese Christians in their midst of suffering for their belief in Jesus Christ, and she came to help them. Her story began with Christians running into the jungle (later known as La Vang) to avoid the persecution ordered by King Cảnh Thịnh in 1798. There, they gathered to pray, reciting the rosary. OLLV appeared to give them courage, care for their well-being, and strengthen their hope. Marian devotion under the title OLHC soon developed.[63]

62. *Lumen gentium*, §52–69.
63. Bonnard, "Un procès gagné—Une église à faire," 694.

The first episcopal documentation of this devotion OLHC is from 1806, when Bishop Jean Labartette requested permission to establish the Marian Association of the Perpetual Devotion to the BVM. What actually developed, however, was the Marian Association of Our Lady of Help of Christians, existing at least since 1809. In that year Jean-Joseph Audemar requested holy cards for the many new members of the Marian Association of Our Lady of Help of Christians. These two early sources show that there was extraordinary devotion to the BVM under that title in the region where OLLV encountered the suffering laity in 1798.

The context of the universal Church may provide sufficient explanation about why devotion to the apparition we now know as OLLV first developed under the title OLHC. Perhaps the apparition of OLLV in the time of persecution initially suggested this title as the most appropriate one. But it also was congruent with the devotional preference of Pope Pius VII, as we have seen. Furthermore, the historical situation in France may help to explain why the bishop did not report the Marian apparitions, at least not in the letters that survive. Labartette had to hide in a cave during the persecution in 1798. Although he was the Apostolic Vicar of Cochinchine, he was often at Cổ Vưu parish, demonstrated by many his episcopal letters and reports dated there.[64] But due to the aftermath of the French Revolution and the Napoleonic Wars, MEP could not provide many missionaries to Vietnam to assist him. As a result, Labartette had to build a seminary to train indigenous men to be ordained. It was not an easy task to carry out because of several struggles, such as lack of adequate financing, lack of specialized language knowledge, and lack of rectors. Furthermore, Labartette faced many pastoral challenges. For example, he consulted with Propaganda Fide about the rituals of death and matrimony and its Vietnamese rituals of marriage.[65] These were probably challenges enough to explain without having to try to justify an apparition that no clergy, and indeed no literate person, witnessed. Instead, it seems he decided to do something uncontroversial, namely, establish an official Marian devotion by asking permission to found the Marian Association. Together, this all suggests that Labartette not only knew the story of OLLV but also facilitated communal devotion to OLLV under an already approved Marian title.

---

64. AMEP, vol. 747, 61, 89, 163.

65. Labartette, "69 Questions."

Devotion to OLLV under the title OLHC continued to be taught and practiced in the region. As we have seen, Marian devotion under that title was also promoted by the first bishop of the diocese of Cochinchine septentrionale. Although Bishop Pellerin was personally devoted to the Immaculate Conception, he encouraged the lay faithful to participate in the Marian Association of Our Lady of Help of Christians.[66] This and related titles were in devotional use in France, and the missionaries adapted their own tradition of devotion to their mission's territory in Vietnam. Recall that OLLV appeared to the faithful after they recited the rosary.[67] This reality might have reminded the French missionaries about their own experience under Napoleon. In addition, the image of Our Lady of Grace has appeared on the cover of the periodicals of the MEP since the early twentieth century.[68] However, they still chose the statue of Our Lady of Victory, a title closely related historically to the title OLHC, as the first statue installed in 1900 in devotion to OLLV, marking the end of a long century of persecution. Moreover, the Marian title of OLLV had been recognized in official correspondence as shown above, and under this title, devotional practices and ritual soon developed. That means the French missionaries not only reinforced devotion to OLLV under the more universally recognized titles, but they also found them congruent to the local circumstances, thus helping to inculturate them. At the same time, even without intention, they also lent devotion to OLLV a universal significance for the whole Church.

The early French missionaries of the MEP, including the bishops and clergy, apparently listened carefully to the lay faithful. They witnessed their courage and resilience, even as the missionaries themselves also suffered persecution. They also seemed to realize the history of Christians in Vietnam as part of the history of the universal Church. What they did was inculturate the earlier European title in devotion to OLLV. Their interpretation seemed to imply that OLLV is the story of the BVM coming to help Christians first (Mother of the Church) and through them all the Vietnamese people (Mother of Vietnam), including pagans. This was very different from the French practice back home.

66. AAOH; see also "Tiểu sử Đức Cha Pellerin" ["Bishop Pellerin"] in *Đức Mẹ La Vang*, 88–89.

67. For more on Marian devotion, especially recitation of the rosary, in Vietnam, see Terres, "Le culte de la Sainte Vierge," 141–64; Parreli, "Le cult de Marie au Vietnam," 657–61; Audigou, "Le culte Marial en Indochine," 1003–14.

68. For more details, see the AMEP, "MEP publications (1840–962)."

A statue of "Our Lady of Grace" was installed at the Shrine of OLLV around 1963. This image was venerated in front of the Basilica of OLLV during the fifteenth national pilgrimage in 1961 (see figure 7, page 107). However, the main title of OLLV, OLHC, remained the same. There is no direct document of the episcopal decision about this. But, as an administrator of the NC-OLLV, Joseph Tường Văn Trân installed that statue at the shrine after its foundation was constructed in 1963. In the midst of the Vietnam War, the newly structured Vietnamese Church needed extraordinary grace, and they evidently venerated OLLV for that purpose. If the Vietnamese clergy of the diocese of Cochinchine septentrionale were influenced by French missionaries, it makes sense that in their moments of urgent need, the former devoted themselves to OLLV under the title Our Lady of Grace.[69] They sought OLLV's extraordinary grace to overcome all types of division and violations of freedom caused by the Vietnam War. Indeed, to install the statue of Our Lady of Grace and to dedicate it to OLLV is to signify the belief of the church leaders and the people in OLLV, who in turn keeps her promise by being there and interceding for them. And, even though a new statue was dedicated to OLLV in 1998, depicting her with Vietnamese features, devotion to OLLV has remained under the title OLHC. Despite being replaced several times over the past years, the statue of OLLV expresses the same meanings.[70] Approving the new statue shows that the church leaders in Vietnam came to recognize the significance of inculturation as key for evangelization, both in the past and going forward. The fact is, though, that many Vietnamese pilgrims have paid no attention to this new statue. They go on pilgrimage to OLLV because they believe her presence is there no matter how the art makes her look.[71] Still, devotion to OLLV seems to have increased since that adaptation, as measured by the number of pilgrims to the shrine. Also, many Vietnamese Catholic communities in the diaspora have given the name OLLV to their churches and parish schools, and these often incorporate the new image.

In conclusion, the history of the title OLHC and associated titles, reflects a simultaneous movement both towards inculturation and universalization. Only eight years after the apparition, in 1806, Bishop

69. See Q. Trân, *Pilgrimage to the Diocese of Huế*, 3:194.

70. See Q. Trân, "Lịch sử Thánh Tượng Đức Mẹ La Vang."

71. During my research in Vietnam, I went on pilgrimage to OLLV and had various conversations with diverse pilgrims in 2019 and 2022. Common reasons given for going to OLLV include "to strengthen faith" and "peace."

Labartette wrote from that area to ask to establish a Marian association; this is followed by evidence for the extraordinary devotion in that area under the Marian Association of Our Lady of Help of Christians. This reflects attentiveness to the nature of this particular apparition, who said explicitly that she had come to help. That was an initial moment of inculturation, because though this title was a foreign title, it was brought in and interpreted into the new context. Therefore, despite coming from Europe, the Marian title OLHC reflects responsiveness to the local situation, fit the new setting, and became more and more at home in Vietnam. Further, through devotion to OLLV under this title, OLLV was recognized as having universal significance to the whole rest of the Church. She was the same Mary. These two things show that through devotion to OLLV under this title, OLHC became localized in the Vietnamese context, and at the same time, OLLV became universalized through the worldwide church, over the course of a century and a half after the apparition of OLLV.

The Bishops of Vietnam

It is significant that the CBCV reaffirmed the designation of the grounds of the shrine of OLLV, under the title of OLHC, as the NC-OLLV.[72] It reaffirms that it is indeed OLLV who is and has been venerated under the title OLHC and that it is she, OLLV, who has become the Holy Mother. The expression "Holy Mother" is left unspecified. Surely it implies "Holy Mother of the Church." But it also is open to the resonance of "Holy Mother of all the Vietnamese people," even "of the nation of Vietnam," and these are the developments we will begin to see. The devotion of the local faithful to OLLV over time inspired the whole Church in Vietnam to first honor and then acknowledge OLLV as the ecclesial mother. As the twentieth-century theology of Our Lady, Mother of the Church, developed, it provided language for what was already inculturated in the hearts of the Vietnamese faithful in their devotion to OLLV. It provided language for articulating and cementing this inculturation and developing it further. This section examines five documents of the bishops of Vietnam, showing how they pick up the traditional devotion and develop it in their teachings in relation to the theology of Mary, Mother of the Church.

---

72. The official name is "Trung tâm Thánh Mẫu Toàn quốc La Vang" [The National Center of the Holy Mother La Vang], but "NC-OLLV" is much easier to remember!

The First Archbishop of Huế: Peter-Martin Thục Đình Ngô (1960–68)

The first Archbishop of Huế was Peter-Martin Thục Đình Ngô. During his episcopal installation on April 12, 1961, the archbishop proclaimed publicly, "In this beginning of this new ministry [of mine], my heart cannot help but turn toward La Vang. Our Lady of La Vang is the Holy Mother of our ancestors; OLLV is the Holy Mother of the holy Church during the days of persecutions [and OLLV is] the Holy Mother of all the Vietnamese people."[73] We see here a continuity with the conciliar theological documentation examined just above, which establishes Mary as the mother of humanity because she is Mother of the Church. Here Archbishop Peter-Martin inculturates this more explicitly—*as* Mother of the Church, OLLV is Mother *beyond* the Church—"of all the Vietnamese people." The archbishop's statement invokes the history of OLLV. He mentions her motherhood especially in connection with the persecutions of earlier generations of Christians. Moreover, his statement also mentions his own episcopal mission and his desire to entrust the new hierarchy of the Church in Vietnam, amidst new national difficulties including restrictions on religion, to OLLV. After all, she had been the Holy Mother of comfort, courage, and help since 1798. At his installation, he invoked an inculturated history of devotion in order to inculturate it further.

Archbishop Peter-Martin accordingly began to cultivate solemn devotion to OLLV in 1961, intending to encourage heartfelt devotion among his fellow bishops, all Christians, and in an evangelizing move, all Vietnamese people. First, he sent an invitation letter to the bishops, other diocesan representatives, and national leaders to participate in the 15th great pilgrimage. Then, he called for full participation of all the members of the Church by more broadly circulating his invitation letter. The archbishop addressed all priests and laity, citing the present circumstances, which included the nation experiencing violent conflict, the challenges of transitioning to the newly established hierarchy of the Church, the repression of religion in the north, and the anxiety of the Vietnamese

---

73. Archbishop Peter-Martin Thục Đình Ngô, "Dien Tu" [Instalation Statement] (Huế, April 12, 1961). The original quote is "Trong giây phút này, đứng trước một nhiệm vụ mới, lòng tôi không thể không hướng về La Vang. Đức Mẹ La Vang là Đức Mẹ của tổ tiên, Đức Mẹ La Vang là Đức Mẹ của những ngày đạo thánh bị bách hại, là Đức Mẹ của toàn dân Việt Nam. . ." (B.L.B., "Đức Tổng Giám Mục Huế với Đức Mẹ La Vang" ["The Archbishop of Huế with Our Lady of La Vang"] in Đức Mẹ La Vang, no. 1(Saigon: Gia-Dinh, 1961), 16.

people in response.⁷⁴ That he articulated those realities helped his audience become more aware of the urgent need for OLLV's help and of the benefit of going on pilgrimage.

Archbishop Peter-Martin was passionate about devotion to OLLV throughout the 15th great pilgrimage. He informed his audience of the decision of the bishops that the Shrine of OLLV was chosen to become the National Marian Shrine—the national center of devotion to Mary, of adoration of the Eucharist, and of the veneration of Vietnamese Martyrs.⁷⁵ His reasons for devotion to OLLV were for her help of Church and nation. The archbishop added that all believers should continue to promote devotion to OLLV, to pray for the hierarchy of the Church in this important transition, and to solicit the Holy Mother to save Catholics from communist atheism. He added, "I urgently appeal to all children of the Holy Mother in the land of Vietnam to participate in this great pilgrimage, in great and zealous number, to express our trust, hope, and love of Our Lady of La Vang, the [Holy] Mother of Vietnam."⁷⁶ Thus, OLLV was publicly proclaimed the Holy Mother of Vietnam. Furthermore, devotion to OLLV, as the archbishop had promoted it, for her *help* is another way to continue devotion to OLLV under the title OLHC in these new circumstances of crisis, which, though new, resembled the older situation of persecution.

On August 9, 1961, the Archbishop used Radio Sài Gòn to call for all the Vietnamese people, both Christians and non-Christians, to participate in this pilgrimage. Because of his diverse popular audience of listeners on the radio, the Archbishop introduced OLLV by posing questions and responses: "Who is our Mother? [Our Mother] is the Holy Mother, the Mother of God, the Mother of all humanity, and the Mother of all Vietnamese people, regardless of religion."⁷⁷ The Archbishop seemed to call all Vietnamese people to assemble in the name of "Our Mother." After answering his own question, the archbishop told the story of Mary

74. Archbishop Ngô, "Lời Hiệu Triệu."
75. Archbishop Ngô, "Mấy Lời Phi Lộ," 3-4.
76. Archbishop Ngô, "The Invitation," The original quote is "Ta khẩn khoản kêu gọi toàn thể con cái Đức Mẹ trên đất nước Việt đến tham dự Đại-Hội đông đúcvà sốt sắng để biểu dương một cách sống động lòng tin cậy mến yêu Đức Mẹ La Vang, Mẹ Việt-Nam."
77. Archbishop Ngô, "The Invitation." The original quote is "Mẹ chúng ta là ai? Là Đức Mẹ, Mẹ Thiên Chúa, Mẹ toàn thể nhân loại và Mẹ của tất cả mọi người dân Việt-Nam bất phân tôn giáo. Mẹ cùng ta, theo lời di truyền, đã hiện ra tại La Vang, gần tỉnh Quảng Trị (Trung-Việt) trước đây 160 năm, dưới triều Cảnh-Thịnh."

at La Vang, saying, "Our Mother, in accord with the tradition, appeared at La Vang in Quảng Trị province (in the central Vietnam) [around] 160 years ago, under the reign of King Cảnh Thịnh." Not only did the Holy Mother help Christians in their trials at that time, he said, but also "from that hour," she has constantly helped both Christians and non-Christians, interceding for their needs. By revealing herself as Mother of the Church, she also revealed her maternal care for the Vietnamese people as a whole. As Mother of God and Mother of the Church, she is Mother of humanity, including specifically and especially all Vietnamese people. This is a unique element of the inculturation of Marian devotion in Vietnam.

Archbishop Peter-Martin stated that, during this pilgrimage, the bishops would solemnly proclaim the new name of NC-OLLV. He appealed to her help for the nation, saying "If all the Vietnamese people expressed their trust in the Holy Mother and honestly cry to her, we dare to believe that our nation will be united in brotherhood soon." Consequently, through his invitation on the radio, the archbishop not only handed down the tradition of OLLV, but also invited the whole nation to be united under OLLV as the Holy Mother, the Mother of God, and Mother of all the Vietnamese people.[78]

The Catholic Bishops' Conference of Vietnam—the CBCV (1980–present)

Since its formation in 1980, the CBCV has increasingly impacted devotion to OLLV.[79] Almost twenty years after reaffirming the grounds as the NC-OLLV during their first meeting in Hanoi in 1980, the CBCV called the people to devote themselves to OLLV. They said, "The Church of Vietnam will celebrate the 200th anniversary of the Holy Mother appearing at La Vang (1798–1998), consoling and protecting Christians from trials.... May she lead us to Jesus Christ, the Savior yesterday, today, and forever."[80] In their letter following the Asian Synod of 1998, the CBCV shared the synod's discussion concerning matters such as roles of the lay faithful, women, the youth, the consecrated people, and priests, as well as issues such as how to think about the rituals of ancestors, evangelization,

---

78. See Archbishop Ngô, "The Invitation." The original wording is: "La Vang là của chung của toàn thể quốc dân Việt Nam, cả lương lẫn giáo." Note that there were several Marian shrines in Vietnam; however, the only Marian apparition was at La Vang.

79. The CBCV, "General Letter," 1980.

80. The CBCV, "General Letter," 1997.

interreligious dialogue, and inculturation. At the end of the letter, the CBCV invited all the members of the Church to turn toward OLLV, Mother and Help of Christians, asking her to teach them to live the Gospel and practice evangelization by becoming people of love and service like Jesus Christ, and people of hope and joy in the Holy Spirit.[81] The CBCV entrusted their teaching to OLLV as the Mother of Help of Christians, continuing the tradition of devotion to OLLV under this title. In this way, the CBCV seems to have indirectly approved the apparition.

The CBCV also impacted devotion to OLLV through liturgy. In 2002, the CBCV received pontifical approval for the liturgical rite of OLLV. This rite, used at the NP-OLLV, encourages devotion to OLLV under the title OLHC. The title is expressed in multiple ways in the entrance antiphon, the collect, the prayer over the altar gifts, and the Eucharistic prayer of the mass. The entrance words include, "Hail the Holy Virgin Mary, [who] is the hope of Christians, Mother of help of those who are disappointed and Mother who cares for everyone who comes to her." The entrance antiphon sounds like a development of the request for help beyond just Christians.

2010 was the holy year of the Church in Vietnam, celebrating 350 years since the establishment of the first two dioceses in Vietnam and 50 years since the establishment of the CBCV.[82] After ending this holy year, the CBCV sent a letter to all the people of God, "Together building up a culture of love and life." This is a verse from "The Prayer to the Holy Mother La Vang," which they often cite in their teaching.[83] At the end, they entrusted their pastoral plan to OLLV, saying:

81. The CBCV, "General Letter," 1998. They end their letter, saying "Chúng ta cùng nhau hướng về Đức Mẹ, Mẹ phù hộ các giáo hữu mà Giáo hội Việt Nam chúng ta đang cử hành kỷ niệm 200 năm Người hiện ra. Xin Mẹ đào tạo chúng ta trở nên những con người yêu thương và phục vụ như Chúa Kitô, những con người tràn đầy niềm hy vọng trong Chúa Thánh Thần, hân hoan sống Tin Mừng và nhiệt thành loan báo tin Mừng." Note that the title of the letter is "Together with Mother La Vang [we] move toward 2000—the Great Jubilee of Salvation." See Bishop Paul Hòa Văn Nguyễn, "A homily" on a holy mass of "Our Lady of Help of Christians" using the liturgical rite of Mass's "Our Lady of La Vang," 2002.

82. The CBCV, "General Letter," 2009.

83. Here are several examples. In the letter of 2003, the CBCV facilitated strategies of evangelization, and at the end of the letter, they addressed OLLV, saying, "May the Holy Mother La Vang lead us to evangelization." The original quote is "Nguyện xin Đức Mẹ La Vang dẫn đưa chúng ta trên đường truyền giáo." At the beginning of the annual meeting of 2006, the CBCV addressed OLLV, stating, "We, Cardinal Archbishops [and] Bishops, gather at Pastoral Ministry Centre of the Archdiocese of Huế to participate in our annual meeting, entrust our meeting to the help of Holy Mother La Vang." The

Let us entrust all the pastoral plans of the Vietnamese Church to the Holy Mother La Vang. Together with her, we raise our praises and give thanks to God for all the graces granted to us during the Holy Year. Turning to her, we learn to live in obedience to God's will in all circumstances. Following her example, we are confident and persevering even in the midst of the trials and difficulties that the Church has to face. Together with her, we enthusiastically set out to carry out the mission of evangelization, actively contributing to '[the building of] a culture of life and a civilization of love' in our homeland.[84]

To close the holy year, the CBCV provided pastoral strategies and emphasized the model of OLLV from whom the bishops and all their people learn how to carry out the mission, which they willingly entrusted to OLLV. More recently, in their letter of 2020, the CBCV made use of "The Prayer to the Holy Mother La Vang" to reinforce communion in the life of the Church. The CBCV cited "The Prayer" a couple of times in their letter, stating, "communion in the Church is 'to build up the culture of love and life'. . . [and] 'to build up the culture of love and life,' we call your attention to usage of media."[85] This is an example of how devotion to OLLV inculturates the Church's mission of evangelization in Vietnam.

The Archbishop of Huế: Étienne Thể Như Nguyễn (1998–2012)

Archbishop Étienne Thể Như Nguyễn received and developed the tradition of OLLV, claiming OLLV as Mother of God, the tender mother of every Vietnamese person, a mother, and a model for the Church. In 2006,

---

original quote is "Chúng tôi, Hồng y, Tổng giám mục, Giám mục quy tụ tại Trung tâm Mục vụ thuộc tổng giáo phận Huế, để tham dự hội nghị thường niên, dưới sự phù trợ của Đức Mẹ La Vang." The CBCV invoked OLLV in its 2004 general letter by saying: "May the Holy Mother La Vang teach us to contemplate Jesus Christ in the Eucharist." The original quote is"Nguyện xin Đức Mẹ La Vang dạy chúng ta biết chiêm ngắm Chúa Giêsu Thánh Thể."

84. The CBCV, General Letter, 2011, 48. The original quote is "Chúng ta hãy trao gửi mọi dự định mục vụ của Giáo Hội Việt Nam cho Đức Mẹ La Vang. Hợp với Mẹ, chúng ta cất cao lời ngợi khen và tạ ơn Thiên Chúa về mọi hồng ân Chúa ban trong Năm Thánh (Lc.1,46–55). Hướng lên Mẹ, chúng ta học sống vâng phục Thánh ý Thiên Chúa trong mọi hoàn cảnh (Mc.3,34–35; Lc.11,28; 1,38). Noi gương Mẹ, chúng ta vững tin và kiên trì ngay giữa những thử thách và khó khăn mà Giáo Hội phải đương đầu (2Pr.1,5–8; 1Pr.1, 6–9; Dt.11,32–39; Rm.8,35). Cùng với Mẹ, chúng ta hăng hái lên đường thi hành sứ mệnh loan báo Tin Mừng, góp phần tích cực vào việc xây dựng nền văn hóa sự sống và văn minh tình thương trên quê hương đất nước chúng ta."

85. The CBCV, "Pastoral Letter," 2020.

the Archbishop promulgated a document called "Our Lady of La Vang: Mother of the Vietnamese Catholic Church," addressed to the Vietnamese Catholics in the United States.[86] He retold the tradition of OLLV after briefly discussing the geography and meanings of the name "La Vang." He described the apparition of OLLV, saying:

> One day, while they prayed, the Holy Mother appeared majestically brilliant, immeasurable beauty. Mother is in a robe, holding the Child Jesus in her arms. Mother stood on the grass, near the banyan tree, where they were praying. Mother showed kindness and tenderness, comforted them, endured hardship, and taught them to pick leaves, boiling them to drink to heal diseases.[87]

He also quoted OLLV's words to the lay faithful gathered in prayer, saying, "'Mother also promises: 'Children, believe, endure suffering, Mother has accepted your prayers. From now on, whoever comes to pray to me in this place, I will accept, blessing according to petitions.'"[88] Archbishop Étienne continued, "From that hour, Lá Vằng [area] was to become the Sacred Land of La Vang. People, non-Christians and Christians, go on pilgrimage, praying, asking for help. . . . The Holy Mother keeps her promises, giving grace of physical and spiritual needs. . . . Therefore, the church leaders chose the Shrine of OLLV as the National Marian Center of the Church in Vietnam."[89]

The Archbishop also had discussed in archdiocesan bulletins the impact of the Universal Church, especially of the Popes, on devotion to OLLV through their documents, sermons, speeches, and letters. The last bulletin, as the Archbishop highlighted, announced that the Dicastery for Divine Worship and the Discipline of the Sacraments had approved the transcription of the liturgical text of the Mass of OLLV in Latin and Vietnamese, with permission to use it at the NC-OLLV. The archbishop said that this permission was "the joy and privilege of the Vietnamese people."[90] He did not say the Vietnamese Catholics but "the Vietnamese people." It seems that for him, too, OLLV is the Holy Mother of all of them.

---

86. Étienne Thể Như Nguyễn, "Đức Mẹ La Vang,"in *La Vang Yearbook 2006*, 2–13. Under the care of the Archbishop, "The Prayer to the Holy Mother La Vang" was composed in 1998, the 200th Jubilee of the apparition of OLLV.

87. Étienne Thể Như Nguyễn, "Đức Mẹ La Vang," 4.

88. Étienne Thể Như Nguyễn, "Đức Mẹ La Vang," 4.

89. Étienne Thể Như Nguyễn, "Đức Mẹ La Vang," 4.

90. Étienne Thể Như Nguyễn, "Đức Mẹ La Vang," 5.

Archbishop Étienne also reviewed the brief history of pilgrimages to OLLV, including twenty-five great pilgrimages in the twentieth century. He emphasized the 200th Jubilee of the apparition of OLLV in 1998. He stated:

> Two hundred years of Mother La Vang of the story of the Holy Mother, who appeared in those ancient days. She turned this land into a sacred place, even heaven, because here the eternal heavenly kingdom has come to meet with earthly life, making it pure, meaningful, and extremely valuable. Here the Mother of God came and remained with the children of men to bless and guide their earthly pilgrim along the right path, to meet Jesus, who is the way, the truth, and the life.[91]

These are characteristic emphases of the archbishop's proclamation about of belief in OLLV. She is the Mother of God coming to a wild and dangerous land. In doing so, she transformed La Vang—in a way perhaps symbolic of the whole of Vietnam—into a sacred place, "even heaven," and she remains there to accompany and to be a teacher for her children. He stated:

> The Mother wanted La Vang to become her land, where she expresses her tender maternity to all children [and where] her children express their devotion, trust, and gratitude to the Mother of God. At La Vang, poor and wild, the Mother invited her children to pay attention to prayer, repentance, renewal, and reconciliation. In that spirit of forgiveness and beatitudes, the Mother leads her children to the source of life—Jesus Christ—the world's Savior.[92]

The Archbishop emphasized that the appearance of the BVM at La Vang, or the story of OLLV, had been handed down from generation to generation through families and communities.[93] The sacred land of the NC-OLLV suffered from the Vietnam War and from transitions of

---

91. Étienne Thể Như Nguyễn, "Đức Mẹ La Vang," 6. The original quote is "200 Mẹ La Vang, câu chuyện Đức Mẹ hiện ra những ngày xa xưa ấy đã biến thửa đất này thành một cõi trời, một vùng linh thiêng, vì nơi đây vĩnh hằng thiên quốc đã đến hội ngộ với kiếp phù du long đong, làm cho nó trở nên thanh cao, đầy ý nghĩa và có giá trị vô cùng. Nơi đây Mẹ Chúa Trời đã đến và ở lại với con cái loài người, để thi ân giáng phúc và dẫn dắt người lữ hành trần thế đi trên nẻo chính đường ngay, hầu gặp Chúa Giêsu là đường đi, là sự thực và là sự sống."

92. Étienne Thể Như Nguyễn, "Đức Mẹ La Vang," 8.

93. Étienne Thể Như Nguyễn, "Đức Mẹ La Vang," 6.

Our Lady of La Vang

authority.⁹⁴ This led to his description of La Vang's current infrastructure, including a list of the construction needing completion.⁹⁵

For the Archbishop, the Mother of God has a plan at La Vang, where she leads her children to Jesus Christ. This is what leads the archbishop to proclaim OLLV's ecclesial maternity. Just as the Church must gather the People of God and lead them to Jesus Christ, so to speak, the Mother of God gathers her children at La Vang and guides them to their Savior. Through this analysis, the Archbishop concludes that OLLV is Mother of the Church, and, at the end of his remarks he states, "Our Lady of La Vang is the Mother of the Catholic Church in Vietnam."

On January 6, 2011, Archbishop Étienne praised OLLV as the tender Mother, OLHC, and a model of evangelization for the members of the Church in Vietnam. He gave a speech at the end of the closing solemn Mass of the holy year of the Church in Vietnam.⁹⁶ The participants were diverse. The presider of the Mass was the pontifical envoy, Cardinal Ivan Dias, who was also Prefect of the Congregation for the Evangelization of Peoples from 2006–2012. His co-presiders included the thirty-five archbishops and bishops of the CBCV, the bishops from neighboring countries and further abroad, including the Bishop of Adelaide in Australia, the Bishop of Grenoble in France, the Apostolic Administrator of Paksé in Laos, the Apostolic Administration of Phnom Pênh in Cambodia, a representative of MEP, and the Auxiliary Bishop of Orange County in California in the United States, a major center of the Vietnamese

---

94. The government took most of the sacred land of the NC-OLLV after 1975, and did not return this land until 2009. For more details, see the CBCV, "General Letter," 2012.

95. Étienne Thế Như Nguyễn, "Đức Mẹ La Vang," 7.

96. Archbishop Étienne, "Phát Biểu," 120–24. Archbishop Étienne Nguyễn gave a speech at the end of the holy year at the National Center of the Holy Mother La Vang from Jan. 4–6, 2011. The closing mass of a holy year and the 29th great pilgrimage were combined. The Church in Vietnam celebrated the holy year from November 24, 2009–January 6, 2011). Three major gatherings took place at the three archdioceses. First, the opening Mass took place at Ke So, belonging to the Archdiocese of Hanoi on November 24, 2009. Second, a Congress of the People of God took place at the pastoral center of the Archdiocese of HoChiMinh City from 21–25 November 2010. This gathering included clergy, consecrated people, the lay faithful, and representatives of communities in the diaspora. The CBCV guided the congress to build communion and participation. Finally, the closing of the holy year took place at the National Marian Center of OLLV on Epiphany on January 6, 2011, which was the last day of the twenty-ninth great pilgrimage to OLLV. To close the holy year on the Epiphany the National Center of the Holy Mother La Vang, the CBCV wanted the whole Church in Vietnam to commit to evangelization under the patronage and model of OLLV. For more details see CBCV, "Thư Chung: Công Bố Năm Thánh 2010,"

diaspora. In addition to 1,200 priests, there were around 1,000 consecrated people and more than 5,000 lay faithful from Vietnam and the diaspora. There were also national and local government representatives, such as Vice Prime Minister Nhân Thiện Nguyễn, a delegation of the Hanoi government, the committees of the highest level of the Vietnamese Government, and the local governors of Quảng Trị and Thừa Thiên Huế provinces. There were also other religious leaders, as well as the ambassador from the embassy of the United States in Sài Gòn.[97]

After greeting individual participants and other pilgrims, the Archbishop quoted Psalm 136: "Praise the LORD, for he is good; for his mercy endures forever."[98] On behalf of the Church in Vietnam, the archbishop expressed gratitude to the Universal Church for caring for the Church in Vietnam. He quoted Pope Benedict XVI's letter to the president of the CBCV: "May Our Lady of La Vang, dear to the Christians of your nation [Vietnam], accompany you with her motherly tenderness throughout this holy year."[99] Then the Archbishop affirmed that the Pope's invocation was fulfilled: "Up to now, we have experienced fulfillment of the Pope's wishes through the life of the Church in Vietnam throughout the holy year. Always Mother Mary La Vang has proven to be a tender Mother, OLHC."[100] The Archbishop here emphatically connected OLLV, as a caring mother, to the title OLHC. Then he expressed gratitude toward the pontifical envoy Cardinal Ivan Dias by quoting the Cardinal's words: "[The Envoy at the closing Mass] expressed the communion of the Congregation of Evangelization of the People with the Church in Vietnam, giving thanks to God in the divine providence for guiding this Church miraculously since the establishment [of the first two dioceses in 1659] up to now."[101] Finally, he noted that the Envoy himself had attended the closing Mass precisely in order to express communion between the Universal Church and local Church.

The Archbishop reviewed two important events of the Church during the holy year: the solemn opening Mass of the holy year at Sở Kiện,

97. Archbishop Étienne, "Speech," 120. See Paul Tran, *Pilgrimage to the Diocese of Huế*, 2:337–38.

98. Archbishop Étienne, "Speech," 120; citation of Psalm 136,1.

99. Benedict XVI, Pontifical Message; See also Archbishop Étienne, "Speech," 120.

100. Archbishop Étienne, "Speech," 121. The original quote is "cho đến hôm nay chúng con cảm nhận được lời cầu chúc của Đức Thánh Cha quả thực đã ứng nghiệm trong các sinh hoạt của Giáo Hội Vietnam suốt thời gian Năm Thánh Mẹ Maria La Vang vẫn luôn chứng tỏ là Mẹ hiền, Đức Bà phù hộ các Giáo hữu."

101. Ivan Dias, "Letter," Prot. 4914/10.

which belongs to the Archdiocese of Hà Nội, on November 24, 2009, and the national gathering as known as the Congress of the People of God. In this congress, the participants helped the CBCV develop pastoral strategies. The Archbishop quoted the congress's message, saying that "'During the days of the Congress, we experienced this atmosphere of fraternal communion when all members of the People of God lived together as brothers and sisters in a family.'"[102] This quote is neither the complete statement nor the full results of the whole discussion; however, it expresses a reality that fraternal communion is one of the essential things in the Church in Vietnam: to live as brothers and sisters in the family of God. Perhaps by quoting only this part, the Archbishop wanted to emphasize the success of the Congress in creating a space and time to encounter one another as the Family of God. The Motherhood of OLLV enables the Vietnamese Church to experience unity as the Family of God under the Mother of the Church in Vietnam.

Next, Archbishop Étienne directly concentrated on the current gathering—the great pilgrimage and the solemn closing Mass of the holy year at the NC-OLLV. If earlier gatherings were peaceful and benefited the souls of the participants, in particular, he said, the pilgrimage to end the holy year at La Vang went beyond the church leaders' expectations.[103]

> How can we not think of the very gracious presence of Mother Mary La Vang, the dear Mother of Vietnamese believers who has accompanied us always? Moreover, where there is the Mother of God, there is the Holy Spirit, and the fruits of the Holy Spirit are charity, joy, peace, patience, kindness, goodness, faithfulness, gentleness, and self-control.[104]

102. Archbishop Étienne, "Speech," 121. The CBCV's original quote is "Trong những ngày Đại hội, chúng tôi cảm nghiệm được bầu khí hiệp thông huynh đệ này khi mọi thành phần Dân Chúa sống chung với nhau như anh chị em trong một gia đình."

103. Archbishop Étienne, "Speech," 121.

104. Archbishop Étienne, "Speech," 121–22. The original quote is "Mỗi một biến cố lớn mà Hội Thánh Vietnam cử hành Năm Thánh đều đã được diễn ra cách tốt đẹp, nhịp nhàng. Chính cuộc hành hương kết thúc Năm Thánh tại La Vang này cũng được diễn ra rất êm đềm, ngoài mơ ước. 'Đây sẽ là cuộc hành hương lớn của Dân Chúa về Nhà Mẹ La Vang, để cùng với Đức Mẹ cất cao lời kinh Ngợi Khen và theo gương Mẹ, vội vã lên đường loan báo Tin Mừng Chúa Giêsu cho anh chị em đồng bào của mình.' Làm sao mà không nghĩ tới một sự hiện diện rất ân cần của Mẹ Maria La Vang, người Mẹ thân thương của các tín hữu Vietnam đã đồng hành xuyên suốt. Mà ở đâu có Mẹ Thiên Chúa thì ở đó có Chúa Thánh Thần, và hoa trái của Thánh Thần là bác ái, hoan lạc, bình an, nhẫn nhục, nhân hậu, từ tâm, trung tín, hiền hòa, tiết độ." The Archbishop cited Gl. 5,22.

This theological statement demonstrates that OLLV is the Mother of God and the Vietnamese believers, connecting the ancient title with present reality. After establishing the community of believers in OLLV, the Archbishop recalls the intimate association of the Mother of God, and so OLLV with the Holy Spirit, which allows him to introduce the fruits of the Spirit. His statement also implies that gathering at the NC-OLLV will nourish these fruits. These fruits of the Spirit are the basis of the outreach to those beyond the Church.

Archbishop Étienne stated the closing of the holy year was a time to give thanks to God. At the same time, he said that the Church carried out the mission of evangelization under the patronage of Our Lady of La Vang.[105] He quoted the pontifical envoy: "This is the time to take actions, the time we borrow the word of Peter to speak in the new ear of the history: 'Master, at your command I will lower the nets.'"[106] This quote led Archbishop Étienne to the intimate association of OLLV and the mission of the Church in Vietnam. He said:

> From the Mother La Vang's house, we set out for the mission, [we go with] full of the tenderness of the Holy Mother. With the heart of the Holy Mother, together with the Holy Mother, we are missioning. [Like] the Holy Mother, we mission with kindness and compassionate hearts [to] foster "a civil culture of love and life together."[107]

"With and [like]" OLLV: Archbishop Étienne made the mission of evangelization grounded in her and related it to human flourishing. This flourishing "to foster a civil culture of love and life together," echoed "The Prayer to Our Lady of La Vang." This prayer has thus impacted the episcopal ministry.

Following this, Archbishop Étienne also mentioned the ritual of blessing of the first stone to be used to construct the Basilica of OLLV.

---

105. Archbishop Étienne, "Speech," 122; CBCV, "General Letter," 2010.

106. Archbishop Étienne, "Speech," 122.

107. Archbishop Étienne, "Speech," 122; The original quote is "Năm Thánh 2010 được kết thúc trang trọng tại Trung tâm Hành hương Đức Mẹ La Vang vào dịp lễ Hiển Linh hôm nay.... Cử hành Lễ Bế mạc là cơ hội thúc đẩy chúng ta tạ ơn Chúa về những hồng ân Chúa ban cho Dân Người trong suốt Năm Thánh 2010, đồng thời mở ra cho sứ vụ Loan báo Tin Mừng dưới sự bảo trợ của Đức Mẹ La Vang (The CBCV, Letter Oct. 7, 2010).... Từ nhà Mẹ La Vang, chúng ta lên đường, lòng đầy ắp tâm tư của Mẹ, mặc lấy tâm tình của Mẹ, không chỉ là cùng Mẹ ra khơi, mà còn ra khơi như Mẹ, với 'Tấm lòng từ bi nhân hậu, đại lượng bao dung, cùng nhau bồi đắp nền văn minh tình thương và sự sống' (The Prayer to the Holy Mother of La Vang)."

In the solemn closing Mass, the pontifical envoy blessed twenty-seven stones, representing the dioceses of the Church in Vietnam and all Vietnamese Catholics in the diaspora. The construction of the Basilica thus expresses communion among them. Referencing the Book of Acts, Archbishop Étienne proclaimed that OLLV was present among the Church in Vietnam just like she—the Mother of Jesus Christ—was among the Apostles and the early Church in Jerusalem. The Archbishop reminded his audience that Pope John Paul II had proclaimed OLLV to the universal Church and that he had also expressed his hope that the Basilica of OLLV would soon be rebuilt in peace. Finally, the Archbishop quoted the Pope:

> 'We can think that these very significant acts of the ecclesiastical authority [Pope John XXIII's elevation of the Church of Our Lady of La Vang to become a minor Basilica and the Vietnamese Bishops choosing the Shrine of OLLV to become the National Shrine] serve as a good auspice for the reconstruction of the sanctuary, which we hope will be done as soon as possible in a climate of freedom and peace, and of gratitude to the One whom 'all generations call blessed' (cf. Lk 1, 48). In this way, the sanctuary, through the intercession of the Queen of Martyrs, will be able to develop all its spiritual potentialities in favor not only of Vietnamese Catholics but also of national unity, as well as of the actual civil and moral progress of the country.'[108]

The blessing of the first stone makes the archbishop remember the Pope's desire to rebuild the basilica more than twenty years ago. The basilica was now at the beginning of construction. Archbishop Étienne thanked all the participants and those who had organized the solemn pilgrimage to end the holy year. In addition to apologizing for the lackluster accommodations of the NC-OLLV, he wished everyone a new peaceful year in God and Mother La Vang and ended his speech by repeating the psalm verse, "Praise the LORD, for he is good; for his mercy endures forever."[109]

Archbishop Étienne's speech at the end of the holy year also connected devotion to OLLV and evangelization. Further referencing an abundance of magisterial literature, he shows that the CBCV and he himself regard OLLV as an aid to evangelization in the spirit of reconciliation, unity, and renewal. Through devotion to OLLV, the Vietnamese bishops desire to lead the People of God to the cultivation of the theological

---

108. Archbishop Étienne, "Speech," 123. See John Paul II, General Audience, 1988.
109. Archbishop Étienne, "Speech," 124; Ps. 136, 1.

virtues and the fruits of the Holy Spirit as one of the best means of evangelization. These are the virtues that will help bring about unity of the Church as one family under their one Mother.

The Archbishop of HoChiMinh City: Paul Đọc Văn Bùi (2014–18)

The Archbishop of HoChiMinh City, Paul Đọc Văn Bùi, made a statement on OLLV in his 2015 letter requesting donations for the construction of the Basilica of Our Lady of La Vang. In the opening of his letter, the archbishop established a sense of shared responsibility for the construction of the basilica by addressing his people as a "family."[110] Along with this opening and his conclusion, his letter can be summarized into three major points: a brief story of and history of devotion to OLLV, the CBCV's project of construction of the basilica, and the call for donations.

Archbishop Paul first told the story of devotion to OLLV by explicating the name "La Vang." For the Archbishop, the term La Vang "always evokes [gợi lên] in the hearts of the Vietnamese faithful, in Vietnam and diaspora, the feelings of love, trust, and entrustment in the Holy Mother, who always loves and never rejects her children's petition."[111] He added, "In fact, the Holy Mother has granted grace to many faithful, for both physical and spiritual needs."[112]

After unpacking the transformation of La Vang from a wild and dangerous place to a holy place for worshipping God and devotion to the Mother of God, Archbishop Paul recapped the history of devotion to OLLV. He stated that Bishop Caspar had recognized "Our Lady of Help of Christians" as the official Marian title of OLLV during the Marian Congress in 1900.[113] This historical declaration, the archbishop continued, recalls [gợi lại] the Marian apparition at La Vang in 1798, and he reminded

---

110. Paul Đọc Văn Bùi, "Thư Kêu Gọi đóng Góp Xây Dựng Vương Cung Thánh Đường Đức Mẹ La Vang."

111. Bùi, "Thư Kêu Gọi đóng Góp Xây Dựng Vương Cung Thánh Đường Đức Mẹ La Vang." The original quote is "Địa danh La Vang luôn gợi lên trong tâm hồn của người tín hữu Vietnam, trong trong nước cũng như hải ngoại, tâm tình yêu mến, tin tưởng và phó thác nơi Đức Mẹ, là Người Mẹ luôn yêu thương và không bao giờ từ chối lời cầu xin tha thiết của con cái mình."

112. Bùi, "Thư Kêu Gọi đóng Góp Xây Dựng Vương Cung Thánh Đường Đức Mẹ La Vang."The original quote is "Trong thực tế, biết bao Kitô hữu dad được Mẹ ban cho nhiều ơn lành, ơn phần xác cũng như ơn phần hồn."

113. The Archbishop cited 1901; however, the first diocesan pilgrimage to OLLV took place in 1900, as the second chapter discusses.

them that her apparition strengthened the faith of those who faced challenge and struggle. She brought forth peace and hope for them. The archbishop repeated the familiar words of OLLV, "Children, have trust, be willing to endure suffering. Mother has already granted your prayers. Henceforth, all those who come to pray in this spot Mother will listen and grant them according to their wishes."[114] The archbishop thereby participated, as a representative of the teaching authority of the Church, in handing down the tradition of OLLV. It is especially significant that he was an important church leader of an archdiocese outside the sacred land of La Vang, expanding the reach of her story.

Further, Archbishop Paul remarked that "from that hour" OLLV has continually given comfort and help to pilgrims in their time of need. Since its transformation, he added, La Vang has attracted generations of people, and the bishops have affirmed that through their promotion of the shrine. All in all, the archbishop's historical sketch of devotion to OLLV highlighted four things: the original context of the apparition in persecution; the appearance of OLLV to help the suffering lay faithful; generational responses to OLLV; and episcopal affirmation of the devotion.

Archbishop Paul went on to speak of the urgent need for the reconstruction of the Basilica of Our Lady of La Vang in the aftermath of the Vietnam War and subsequent long term government control of the site. He made it clear that the Church in Vietnam and in the diaspora should make it a priority to rebuild the NC-OLLV and announced that the CBCV had decided to construct the new building in accord with traditional Vietnamese architecture to express inculturated faith. The architecture of the basilica would signify an adaptation of Christianity in the land of Vietnam.[115] The project, which broke ground in 2012, was on a huge scale, requiring a massive mobilization of effort, creativity, and finance.

The archbishop linked donation with ecclesial participation: "Participating in this construction is expressing union in the life of the Church. . . . I earnestly encourage priests, the consecrated women and men, and lay women and men to express your love of the Holy Mother through contribution to the construction of the Basilica of Our Lady of La Vang."[116] The Archbishop suggested that all his archdiocesan family

114. Bùi, "Thư Kêu Gọi đóng Góp Xây Dựng Vương Cung Thánh Đường Đức Mẹ La Vang."

115. Bevan, *Models of Contextual Theology*, 26–27.

116. Bùi, "Thư Kêu Gọi đóng Góp Xây Dựng Vương Cung Thánh Đường Đức Mẹ La Vang," 2. Most of the Catholic churches built during the first several centuries of

members donate on the first Sunday of May 2015, though the collection would remain open during the whole month. His pastoral suggestion carried a double meaning, whereby all the members in his archdiocese matter: while contributing is indeed considered a way to express Marian devotion during the Marian month, it also reinforces a family culture, gathered under their Holy Mother.

In the conclusion of his letter, the Archbishop gave his episcopal blessing as follows: "May God grant grace physically and spiritually to those who participate in the meaningful collections through the intercession of Our Lady of La Vang, the Beloved Mother of all of us."[117] Invoking OLLV as "the Beloved Mother of all of us," his proclamation echoed an element of all of the Marian titles that are connected in some way with her main title, "Mother of God."

The Archbishop of Huế: Joseph Linh Chí Nguyễn (2016-present)

In his opening speech at the annual pilgrimage in August 2022, the current Archbishop of Huế, Joseph Linh Chí Nguyễn, advocated for OLLV as the Holy Mother of the Church in Vietnam and as a model for the Church. His speech took place after the relaxation of the COVID-19 restrictions that had prevented the Church from organizing a pilgrimage to OLLV for two years. Despite some hesitancy to join big gatherings, since the virus still remained a threat, the pilgrimage turnout was around fifty thousand people. Moreover, this pilgrimage occurred after the CBCV released the National Synthesis of the People of God in Vietnam. This synthesis proposed three action points: to meet, to listen, and to discern. It intended these as a way of providing insights into many aspects of the life of the Church in Vietnam, in order to build the Church toward the strategies of the Synod of the Bishops.[118]

Christianity in Vietnam were designed in accord with European architectural styles. As a result, Vietnamese people in general think that a more typical Eastern style belongs to Buddhist culture. The decision to build the new basilica in an Eastern style argued against this common belief.

117. Bùi, "Thư Kêu Gọi đóng Góp Xây Dựng Vương Cung Thánh Đường Đức Mẹ La Vang," 2. The original quote is "nhờ lời chuyển cầu của Đức Mẹ La Vang, là người Mẹ kính yêu của tất cả chúng ta."

118. To carry out the 2021–23 Synodal Church: Communion, Participation, and Mission, the CBCV appointed a team and provided a Documentation Guideline and a Handbook so that all dioceses in Vietnam could use the study and discuss as local synods in 2021. The diocesan study might involve interviews on several topics, such as

Before the pilgrimage, in addition to providing its theme, "The Holy Mother—A Model of Communion," Archbishop Joseph invited all the Vietnamese through their Archbishops and Bishops to join him and the people of the Archdiocese of Huế on the annual pilgrimage. As a result, of the fifty thousand pilgrims who came, most of the dioceses in Vietnam were represented. This active participation made the annual pilgrimage look like more like a triennial national pilgrimage.

Seven of the dioceses had played a role in the program. A drum team of over three hundred came from the Diocese of Bùi Chu, and a teenage trumpet team came from the Archdiocese of HoChiMinh City (Sài Gòn). There were also two groups of Dâng Hoa performers. Dâng Hoa is something like a May Crowning ceremony, only much more elaborate, with dancing and singing amidst the meditating of a community of prayer.[119] A 440-person group came from the Archdiocese of Hà Nội, including people from multiple subcultures with their traditional music. For example, during Dâng Hoa, a group from one ethnic minority played charming gongs. Another performed using traditional Cờ Ngũ Sắc [Five Color Flags]. The other Dâng Hoa came from the diocese of Thanh Hóa and comprised around 60 players. Seven parishes from across Vietnam combined to carry out "*Đêm Diễn Nguyện*" ["An Evening Meditational Performance,"] which included an opening of concert and choir singing, a meditational performance of the Joyful Mysteries, a musical based on "The Parable of the Lost Son," and a closing concert. All teams lent their subcultures as richness to their inculturated performances in honor of OLLV.[120] For example, the Diocese of Bắc Ninh team performed the second Joyful Mystery with the unique traditional music of Bắc Ninh

---

evangelization, expectation, and concerns. Next, the dioceses submitted their reports to the CBCV. Finally, the CBCV discussed all the reports during their annual meeting in April 2022 and released the Synthesis of the People of God in Vietnam at the end of the meeting. It provided the three acting verbs, "Gặp Gỡ—Lắng Nghe—Phân Định" ["to meet, to listen, [and] to discern"]. See the ACBCV, Tài liệu chuẩn bị [Documentation Guideline], and *Cẩm nang* [*Handbook*].

119. See https://www.youtube.com/watch?v=mxWltj523pM. Accessed October 7, 2022. Dâng Hoa lasted two hours and 38 minutes in this pilgrimage. I will detail the rituals of OLLV, including Dâng Hoa and an "Evening Mediating Performance," in a future ethnographic study.

120. Note that "Quan họ Bắc Ninh," a play about the loving relationship between women and men, was adapted into the third decade of the Joyful Mystery in which OLLV is a model to teach us how to love our neighbors. Chèo is an ancient musical theatre form. A composer adapted Chèo into "The Parable of the Lost Son," but it was named "A Merciful Father," as mentioned above.

[Dân ca Quan họ Bắc Ninh]. The Diocese of Thái Bình's team brought its traditional musical of Chèo Thái Bình to sketch "The Parable of the Lost Son." Each act of "Đêm Diễn Nguyện" articulated the theme "The Holy Mother—A Model of Communion" through the participation of these many subcultures. Marian devotion in Vietnam appears to be, as Pope Paul VI said, an "intrinsic element of Christian worship."

In his speech, Archbishop Joseph Nguyễn stated that going on pilgrimage to OLLV was going back to OLLV in order to give thanks to God for OLLV's help, especially during the past two years of COVID restrictions. "We go back to OLLV to thank God. . . . We go back here to say to OLLV that we bow to Mother La Vang, and we love you."[121] The archbishop stated that "We learn from the Holy Mother, a model of communion with God in all circumstances."[122] Just as the Holy Mother was united with God through all her life and put her trust in God, so too, the pilgrims learned to strengthen their communion with God. Recalling how OLLV held the Baby Jesus when encountering the faithful, the archbishop called his listeners to connect with God by holding Jesus Christ in their lives. He also emphasized that pilgrimage to OLLV means going to sacred ground to celebrate communion with one another. Just as OLLV appeared to diverse people in 1798, so too, the pilgrimages often bring together diverse pilgrims. The Archbishop emphasized that devotion to OLLV was a way in which the pilgrims may learn how to participate together in the Church, as they witness the community of pilgrimage as a great family of the Church and of OLLV. He further stated, "We ask OLLV to *help* us communicate with the Church and one another. I wish you all to experience the tenderness, mercy, and care of OLLV, as well as experience friendliness and warmth among one another."[123] The significant contributions of each team coming from the seven dioceses contributed to this sense of communion as something solemn and marvelous. Also, he acknowledged the tremendous efforts of the members of the Archdiocese of Huế to collaborate with other dioceses to organize the pilgrimage, yet another example of communion.

Finally, Archbishop Joseph advocated for going on pilgrimage to the NC-OLLV as a means to learn from OLLV how to carry out the mission of the Church. He mentioned that the annual August pilgrimage had become a significant date for all the children of OLLV across the country and in

---

121. Archbishop Joseph Nguyễn, "Phát biểu khai mạc," at 7:32.

122. Archbishop Joseph Nguyễn, "Phát biểu khai mạc."

123. Archbishop Joseph Nguyễn, "Phát biểu khai mạc." Italics mine.

diaspora, using a well-known subcultural phrase, "đến hẹn lại lên" ["the date comes, [we] gather again"][124] to encourage the pilgrims to return the next year. "OLLV," he said, "cares about gathering her children over the country and in the diaspora.... We transform the sacred land of La Vang—the National Marian Center—to become a space of practice of communion with God, the Church, and one another.... With her, we practice the spirit of synodality [participation and communion.]"[125] The Archbishop exhorted the participants to go back to La Vang in 2023 as part of the thirty-second national pilgrimage. Additionally, he invited them to sing with him the hymn "Cùng Mẹ Ra Khơi" ["Together with the Mother [La Vang, we carry out the] Mission."] The community of pilgrimage is here presented as inspiring the participants to unite and evangelize effectively.

To summarize, Archbishop Joseph Nguyễn praised OLLV as the Holy Mother of the Church in Vietnam, all members of which are part of her family. As the local church leader and the president of the CBCV, Archbishop Joseph led the community of pilgrims to venerate OLLV by fostering participation and inclusion. By publicly acknowledging diverse contributions, the archbishop advocated for a culture of harmony and collaboration that builds up communion and thereby the mission. Through devotion to OLLV, the pilgrim community grows in worshipping God, living in harmony, and becoming more active in evangelization within their own cultural idioms.

As this chapter concludes, we see that the title Mary, Mother of the Church, proclaimed by *Lumen gentium*, has been thoroughly inculturated into the Vietnamese Church, just as, on the other hand, the title is used to signify the importance of OLLV to the universal Church. This is the dynamic we have observed throughout this chapter. Like her highest title, Mother of God, her other titles, including "Our Lady of Help of Christians," "Our Lady of Grace," and "Mary, Mother of the Church," titles of universal ecclesial devotion, have been inculturated in Vietnam through devotion to OLLV. In turn, this very inculturation proclaimed the significance of OLLV to the whole of the Catholic Church. And this, in turn, has helped the various subcultures into which the devotion was inculturated experience themselves as vehicles for the ongoing mission of the whole Church in order to evangelize and build communion.

124. "đến hẹn lại lên" is a famous song about an annual festival in Bac Ninh province. Unmarried men and women exchange reciprocal singing to express their desire to see one another next year. In closing, they sing "đến hẹn lại lên" to date for their next union.

125. Archbishop Joseph Nguyễn, "Phát biểu khai mạc."

5

Vietnamese Theologians and Commentators on Our Lady of La Vang

FOLLOWING THE PREVIOUS CHAPTER's investigation into the history of Marian titles associated with devotion to OLLV and the CBCV's implementation of devotion to OLLV, this chapter traces the work of some contemporary Vietnamese theological commentary on OLLV after the year 2000. The Federation of Asian Bishops' Conference 1999 document *Ecclesia of Asia* emphasized what they called the "triple dialogues" of cultures, religions, and the poor. The CBCV, as we have seen, focused especially on the dialogue of culture, namely, inculturation towards "New Evangelization."[1] This chapter examines the work of five theologians and cultural commentators with theological concerns: Bảng Đình Lê, Joseph-Marie Phong Thanh Trần, Peter Phan, Maria Tuyệt Thị Nguyễn, and Paul Chu Quang Trần.

---

1. The CBCV, "General Letter," 1999. The terms "inculturation" and "New Evangelization" have been associated one another in the sense that the latter is the goal of the former. In addition, "New Evangelization" not only refers to attempts at conversion from other religions, but also at pedagogy to strengthen those who practice their faith and re-evangelize those who were baptized but no longer practice. See Paul VI, *Evangelii Nuntiandii* (1975); John Paul II, *Redemptoris Missio* (1990); Benedict XVI, *Porta Fidei* (2011); Francis, *Evangelii Gaudium* (2013).

Bảng Đình Lê

Bảng Đình Lê (b. 1942) is a well-known scholar of Vietnamese Catholic poetry and other literature. Along with several poems on OLLV, Lê published "Our Lady of La Vang: Mother of the Church in Vietnam" in *Catholic and Nation* in 2000.[2] He organizes his article into three parts: 1) devotion to the BVM upon the arrival of Christianity in Vietnam; 2) the intense continuing Marian devotion echoing a crucial part of the Vietnamese culture; and 3) an extensive section on OLLV. In this section, I argue that Lê's article is an important first step in understanding why Marian devotion is a crucial part of Vietnamese Catholicism and in demonstrating that OLLV's maternal help situates her within the themes laid out by the bishops, that is, as Mother of the Church in Vietnam, and even as Mother of Vietnam.

Concerning the first, Lê states that in Vietnam La Vang is now synonymous with the BVM. For Lê, La Vang comprises both the specific place (La Vang in Quang Tri) and the historical events under the reign of King Cảnh Thịnh (1798) that were experienced and affirmed throughout two hundred years.[3]

> Right from the dawn when the Gospel was preached in this dear land of Vietnam (1533) and throughout 200 years, [the Holy] Mother has been present [and] walked with everyone in everything to everywhere [. . .] La Vang was approved [*được công nhận*] as the sacred place that marked [her presence], as the most specific sacred destination.[4]

Lê acknowledges that it is impossible to know what Christian life, including Marian devotion, looked like in the sixteenth century, and possibly even afterwards. However, he offers a few hints. First, on the conversions of Princess Mai-Hoa and her servants in 1591, he says, "Maria-Flora, the Christian name of the princess, must be the first 'fragrant flower of a [harvesting] season' and she allows us to glimpse the annunciation and

---

2. Bảng Đình Lê, "Đức Mẹ La Vang." The audience of this journal is often the educated elite.

3. Lê, "Đức Mẹ La Vang," 43.

4. Lê, "Đức Mẹ La Vang," 42. The original quote is "Thực ra, ngay từ buổi hừng đông khi Tin Mừng mới được rao giảng trên mảnh đất Việt nam thân yêu này và xuyên suốt 200 năm, Me đã hiện diện, đã đồng hành ở mọi nơi, với mọi việc, với mỗi người mà La Vang đã được công nhận là nơi ghi dấu, là chọn điểm điểm thiêng, cụ thể nhất."

the earliest visitation of the Virgin Mary on this land."[5] He also points out the arrival of Jesuit missionaries led by the priest Alexandre de Rhodes in Thanh-Hoa province on March 19, 1627. Since that day was the Feast of Saint Joseph, Lê says, "Saint Joseph also makes a tent to live with his Vietnamese children."[6] Juxtaposing these two events, Lê says the parents of Jesus prepared missionaries to evangelize in this far eastern land.[7]

Lê further gives three passages associated with the BVM from early documents. First, he introduces the Vietnamese Christian community's letter to Lambert de la Motte that included the statement "We worship God—the Trinity—and are devoted to the Holy Virgin."[8] Alexandre de Rhodes also wrote back to Europe that "[Trinh] Lord paid attention to the Rosary on my waist belt, he asked for it and put it on his niece's neck, who had gotten sick for three years, in his lap."[9] He also cites de Rhodes's account of an incident in 1644:

> [In Quang-Binh,] I met a devout layman, Francisco, a former member of the army, and his wife was Teresa. He began to devote himself to the Holy Virgin when he was baptized. Then, one day, [he] saw non-Christians holding the photo of the Holy Virgin, he redeemed at his own expense, brought it home to place on an altar, praying and offering devotion."[10]

As we have seen, Lê sees the land of La Vang as a sacred place where the BVM is especially present, though it is not very clear what he means when he says La Vang "was recognized . . . was approved"[11] as a Marian apparition. But his reminder that Marian devotion was present very early in Vietnamese Catholicism is well taken and I have tried to show

---

5. Lê, "Đức Mẹ La Vang," 43. The original quote is "Maria Flora—tên thánh và tên gọi của nàng khuê các ấy—phải được xem là 'Bông- hoa-hương-sắc-đầu mùa' đã khắc hoạ buổi truyền tin và viếng thăm sớm sủa nhất của Đức Mẹ Marian trên giải đất này."

6. Lê, "Đức Mẹ La Vang," 43.

7. Lê, "Đức Mẹ La Vang," 44.

8. Lê, "Đức Mẹ La Vang," 43, citing Launay, *Histoire de la Mission de Cochinchine*, 1:59.

9. Lê, "Đức Mẹ La Vang," 44, citing de Rhodes, *Lịch sử Vương Quốc Đàng Ngoài*, 101. The original title is *Histoire du Royaume du Tonkin*.

10. Lê, "Đức Mẹ La Vang," 45. Note also Alexandre de Rhodes, *Hành Trình và Truyền Giáo [Journey and Mission]*, trans. Hồng Nhuệ, 180–181. The original title is *Voyage et mission*.

11. Lê, "Đức Mẹ La Vang," 43. La Vang "đã được nhìn nhận . . . được công nhận."

Vietnamese Theologians and Commentators on Our Lady of La Vang 183

throughout this book how devotion to OLLV built on the earlier traditions, although our knowledge of them is sketchy.[12]

Lê's second theme is that Vietnamese Christians exhibit a unique devotion to the BVM. For Lê, Marian such devotion is rooted in local customs, traditional morality, and natural relationships, especially the mother-and-child relationship and the family bond.[13] Lê says further that Marian devotion [may] reflect maternal goddess consciousness rooted in elements of folk religion, which has many powerful and helpful figures such as Mother Âu-Cơ,[14] a Buddha grandmother,[15] or fairy figures.[16] Similarly, Marian devotion may relate to maternal shrines or maternal nature, such as how people speak of mother land, mountains, rivers, and water.[17] Still, his point is that Vietnamese Catholics devote themselves to the BVM in distinction from these traditions. According to Lê, several expressions (including "Jesus, Mary, Joseph," or "the Holy Mother heals me") must come from Christian faith, hope, and love, even if these expressions exhibit some similarities to the common usage of Vietnamese proverbs.[18] Additionally, Lê mentions Marian devotion expressed through arts, architecture, sculptures, photos, music, poems, processions, and ceremonies, specifying "especially May Dâng-Hoa and October Rosary" as "established Marian festivals, cultivating the sacred arts,

---

12. For Marian devotion in Vietnam see Terres, "Le culte de la Sainte Vierge"; Martin An Ngoc Le "La dévotion Mariale"; G. Audigou, "Le culte Marial en Indochine."

13. Lê, "Đức Mẹ La Vang," 45. The original quote is "Thật tự nhiên, nó xuất phát từ một tình cảm hiếu hạnh thơm thảo—mẹ-con- tình mẹ yêu thương con và tình con kính mến mẹ trong truyền thống đạo đức, trong khung cảnh ấm êm đùm bọc của gia đình."

14. *Lạc Long Quân* Âu Cơ is a Vietnamese creation myth. *Âu Cơ was a* beautiful and skillful mountain fairy. Lạc Long Quân was a strong and smart son of the Dragon King of Lac in the ocean. They married, and her pouch of 100 eggs hatched into 100 children. After living together for a while, Long Quân and *Âu Cơ* were homesick, so they decided to separate their children and returned to their hometowns. The point is that though Vietnam has fifty-four ethnic groups, they form one original family. See s*Truyền thuyết thời Hùng Vương-Lạc Long Quân* Âu Cơ.

15. "Phật Bà Quan Âm" [Guan Yin] or Bồ-Tát [Bodhisattva] are depicted as compassionate female figures in Vietnam.

16. Note that a term "Cô Tiên" [Ms. Fairy] or "Bà Tiên" [Grandmother Fairy] is a female figure, who is beautiful and kind in the Vietnamese legend literature. For example, a fairy tale *Ba cô tiên* [*Three Fairies*] ed. Phuc Chi Nguyễn (Hanoi: NXB Hanoi).

17. Lê, "Đức Mẹ La Vang," 45. Note that maternal goddess consciousness translates from the term "tâm thức thờ Mẫu." As described in the footnote above, the female figure Âu Cơ becomes the model for maternity and unification.

18. Lê, "Đức Mẹ La Vang," 45.

and attracting a large number of participants."[19] Although he provides no source or further specifics, he does note that even in the earliest time "the missionaries with our ancestors initiated inculturation by creating new ideas to adapt into liturgy [to venerate the BVM] hundreds of years ago."[20] Then, he moves on to OLLV by saying "that the BVM appeared at La Vang is the treasure of Vietnam; however, [her apparition] has spread beyond the border [of La Vang, and La Vang] has become a rendezvous place of pilgrimages."[21] Lê quotes Archbishop Fiorenza, the President of the USCCB, who when he visited the Shrine of OLLV said "The Church in Vietnam is honored to have OLLV. [The Church in] the United States wants to have her too. . . . We request to be adopted children of OLLV."[22]

Finally, in his third point, Lê reflects more directly on OLLV. In his first paragraph, Lê contends that OLLV comes to help her Vietnamese children. He creates a parallel to scenes in the Bible. For example, just as the Holy Mother hurried to visit Elizabeth after the Annunciation, so too, she hastened to help the Church in Vietnam in time of trial. Quoting a part of "The Prayer to the Holy Mother La Vang," he writes, "The Mother also hastened to 'choose La Vang [in order to] help our ancestors, non-Christians and Christians, amid persecution and other hardship.'"[23] Noting that she bore neither commandment nor secret message, he argues that her message was therefore different from those at Lourdes, Fatima, La Salette, Guadalupe, and Medjugorje.[24] Instead, "at La Vang, the Mother comes to help ["phù hộ"] Christians.'"[25] At La Vang, Lê says, OLLV held the Baby Jesus to communicate her motherhood singularly to the Vietnamese people." It is as if she "introduced her Son [to the Vietnamese people], consigned [Him to them], and committed herself that after

19. Lê, "Đức Mẹ La Vang," 46.

20. Lê, "Đức Mẹ La Vang," 46. It is uncommon for Vietnamese people to praise themselves, or even mention their skills and talents.

21. Lê, "Đức Mẹ La Vang," 46.

22. Lê, "Đức Mẹ La Vang," 46. During his service as the president of the National Conference of Catholic Bishops (1998–2001), Joseph Fiorenza visited the Church in Vietnam from August 26-September 2, 1999, then released "Testimony on Peace Reconciliation and Religious Freedom in Vietnam, November 24, 1999," https://www.usccb.org/resources/testimony-peace-reconciliation-and-religious-freedom-vietnam-november-24-1999.

23. Lê, "Đức Mẹ La Vang," 46.

24. Lê, "Đức Mẹ La Vang," 47. The original quote is "Để minh họa cho những lập luận trên, khong gi bang goi len mot doi chieu nao do giua La vang với Lộ Đức Không hề có hiện tượng bất thường nào. Chẳng có một mệnh lệnh, thông điệp khẩn cấp quan trọng nào."

25. Lê, "Đức Mẹ La Vang," 47.

Jesus, her first Son, she is still pregnant, gives birth, protects, and helps all Vietnamese."[26] In his interpretation of the scene of the BVM holding the Baby Jesus, Lê confirms her motherhood to all Vietnamese. Indeed, she is in fact their Mother. OLLV planted the seeds that would eventually grow into her recognition as Mary, Mother of the Vietnamese Church.

The concept of maternal help is relevant to the Marian title OLHC, under which, as we have seen, OLLV has been venerated since at least 1809, and which was officially dedicated to OLLV in 1900. Lê's thought allows us to see the apparition at La Vang as a Marian visitation in which "in haste" OLLV came to help ["phù hộ"], staying to nurture those who trust in her. Also, to add to Lê's point, by holding the Baby Jesus, OLLV signals that she is the Mother of Jesus, so not only is she the mother of Vietnam, but also the universal Mother of the Church. The idea of Mary, Mother of the Church has, through the apparition and subsequent devotion to OLLV, been inculturated into Vietnamese faith. Lê's contribution is to connect the apparition with the Baby Jesus to her status as Mother of the Church in Vietnam.

Lê goes on to state that because La Vang is "the heritage of faith, the place marked by the holy presence," church leaders inherit the sacred land and develop it with all their efforts to preserve, restore, and construct.[27] Beginning with the Văn Thân Movement in 1885, Lê lists the long history of constructions, blessings, or damage, occurring across the late nineteenth and twentieth centuries. Just as the pilgrimages seek OLLV's presence, so Lê says, "OLLV always accompanies the Church in Vietnam."[28] Her presence means communion. To prove his point, he lists the names of the Apostolic Nuncio and the Vietnamese church leaders who visited La Vang from 1923 to 1999. He also states, "La Vang, indeed, is the meeting place of the Vietnamese Catholic Church [for] communion."[29]

Lê also presents the two Popes who made the greatest impact on devotion to OLLV. He says, along with Pope John XXIII who elevated the Church of OLLV into a basilica, it is under Pope John Paul II that "La Vang was praised [as] the Mother of the heritage of faith."[30] By quoting "The Prayer to the Holy Mother La Vang," Lê says, "The universal Church praises the Holy Mother La Vang 'full of grace, radiant with thousands of

26. Lê, "Đức Mẹ La Vang," 47.
27. Lê, "Đức Mẹ La Vang," 47.
28. Lê, "Đức Mẹ La Vang," 48.
29. Lê, "Đức Mẹ La Vang," 48.
30. Lê, "Đức Mẹ La Vang," 48.

rays; incomparable with saints and angels."[31] Lê makes a useful point in his presentation of the two Popes' impacts on OLLV, and we have elaborated on these contributions above.

Lastly, Lê ends by quoting Pope John Paul II's letter to Archbishop Étienne. For Lê, the following passage captures his meaning:

> On the occasion of the closure of the Marian Year and the 25th three-yearly pilgrimage to the Shrine of OLLV, I join through prayer the Vietnamese faithful and pilgrims who have entrusted themselves to the motherly intercession of the Virgin Mary, asking this most holy Mother to guide the Catholic Church in Vietnam on her journey to the Lord and to help her in the witness she must bear on the threshold of the third millennium. . . . In going to the Shrine of OLLV, so dear to the Vietnamese faithful's hearts, pilgrims entrust their joys, sorrows, hopes, and sufferings to her. In this way, they turn to God and make themselves intercessors for their families and for their entire people asking the Lord to instill sentiments of peace, brotherhood, and solidarity in the hearts of all men and women so that all the Vietnamese will be every day more closely united, in order to build a world in which it is pleasant to live, based on the essential spiritual and moral values and where each person can be recognized in his dignity as a child of God, and turn freely and with filial love to his Father in heaven who is 'rich in mercy' (Eph 2:4)."[32]

Lê valuably points out how Vietnamese Marian devotion reflects Vietnamese cultural elements, especially OLLV's maternal help grounded upon her apparition and reflected in her official title. He also effectively uses biblical references. Nevertheless, Lê's article is poorly documented and limited in its historical detail. I have built on this base, considerably expanding it. Additionally, perhaps he should have more clearly differentiated between people's beliefs in OLLV and official approval, which has not taken place. Perhaps, he should have gone further to recommend that a formal Church investigation into the Marian apparitions that occurred at the shrine in 1798 be opened. Overall, Lê advances Mariological research by recognizing OLLV, we could say, as the inculturation of Mary Mother of God in Vietnam. I have built on this to emphasize the devotion's inculturation specifically of the Vatican II title, Mother of the Church. Lê also emphasizes Mary's help "phù hộ," and I add that "phù

---

31. Lê, "Đức Mẹ La Vang," 48.

32. Lê, "Đức Mẹ La Vang," 49, citing John Paul II, "A Letter to Archbishop Étienne Nguyễn Nhu The."

hộ" is one of OLLV's main maternal characteristics. We have already seen how the hierarchy in Vietnam has developed these characteristics, and the previous chapter interpreted all of these developments even further from the perspective of *Lumen Gentium*'s teaching that Mary is the Mother of the Church, endorsed by subsequent popes.

Joseph-Marie Phong Thanh Trần

Joseph-Marie Phong Thanh Trần (1944–2019) completed his dissertation, "Notre Dame de La Vang, Viet Nam, histoire et théologie: Du message de Notre Dame de La Vang à la maternité de grâce de Marie et à la spiritualité de l'espérance" in 2001.[33] His main chapters are "A Historical and Religious Context of the Apparition of the Holy Mother, and Her Message"; "The Shrine and Inculturation"; "Theologies of OLLV's Message"; and "From OLLV's Message to the BVM's Maternal Grace and Spirituality of Hope." I will analyze Trần's second and fourth chapters, especially his discussion on inculturation and the relationship between OLLV's message and the BVM's maternal grace. While he titles a part of the second chapter "Inculturation," and a part of the fourth chapter "Maternity of Grace," he fails to make a concrete connection of those themes to the story of and/or devotion to OLLV.

In his second chapter, Trần develops three sections, including church building, inculturation, and the sacred grounds as a place for interreligious and ecumenical dialogues. Trần's second chapter has three problems: 1) the first section contains inaccurate historical data; 2) the second section does not develop the notion of inculturation sufficiently; and 3) the third section does not demonstrate the reasons, or even in what ways, the shrine of OLLV should be a place for ecumenical and inter-religious dialogue. I want to pay more attention to the second section title, "Inculturation," for two reasons: 1) the CBCV is becoming more aware of the value of inculturation to evangelization, and 2) the development of the idea of inculturation could be strengthened by being further based on the story of and the devotion to OLLV.

In his first section, Trần discusses the sacred shrine, but unfortunately gives inaccurate data due to inadequate references. For example, basing himself on only one source, he says that Bishop Marie Antoine

---

33. Trần was a priest of the diocese of Nha Trang, which belongs to the central Vietnam, and the first scholar to complete a dissertation on OLLV.

Caspar decided to build a new shrine with a tile roof in 1886 and blessed it from August 6–8, 1901.[34] However, it was not the bishop's but the French missionaries' and priests' plan to rebuild the church building in 1894. Moreover, the blessing took only a single day, August 6, according to the source Trần cites.[35] There is no reference for the claim that the first thatched-roof church building was built in the 1820s. Following the previous scholars, he provides a list of national pilgrimages.[36] Most scholars only cite the second and third national pilgrimages in accordance with the oral traditions of OLLV because they are unable to find records of these pilgrimages in episcopal reports or other writing. However, as reviewed in this dissertation, that missing data is provided in L.M. Cadière's "Souvenir."[37]

In his second section, "Inculturation," Trần comments on "The Vietnamese Episcopal Speeches at the Asian Synod" and "The Work of Inculturation: a New Statue." He reviews two contributions by Vietnamese bishops who spoke at the Asian Synod in 1998, and also one papal document, John Paul II's *Ecclesia in Asia*. Bishop Paul Hòa Văn Nguyễn, Trần notes, emphasizes the need to study inculturation to implement it into liturgy, sacred arts, and presentations of the faith. Then, Trần continues, the bishop promotes the essential collaboration between bishops and theologians to apply inculturation in order that evangelization may bear good fruits.[38] Unfortunately, Trần neither quotes any part of the bishop's speech nor articulates how the bishop's speech led him to show inculturation through devotion to OLLV, if he did at all. My own work has attempted to address this issue of inculturation much more broadly, to show that inculturation should not be limited to new contemporary efforts in liturgy, arts and the presentation of the faith, but to show that devotion to OLLV has served steadily over the years to inculturate Catholic faith and practice much more deeply into Vietnamese culture and identity. Contemporary efforts presuppose and build on something they have received from the past.

34. Trần, 2.1.1.3, citing Hội Văn Nguyễn, *Seeking Understanding of Our Lady of La Vang*, 29–31.

35. Trần still states that event took place in 1901. See Paul Trần, *Pilgrimage to the Diocese of Hue*, 2:274.

36. Trần, 2.1.4.2. Trần cites Hồng Phúc and Hội Văn Nguyễn, and although these latter authors did not provide references, they inherited the oral traditions of OLLV by being born in the AOH.

37. Cadière, "Souvenir;" AAOH, *The Sanctuary of Our Lady of La Vang*, 9.

38. Trần, 2.2.1.1.

Trần discusses three points in Archbishop Étienne Thể Như Nguyễn's speech, including 1) promoting the adaptation of ancestor veneration; 2) the need for adaptation of specific rituals, such as maintaining an ancestor altar, use of incense, and bowing down before the ancestor photos; and 3) resituating ancestor veneration as part of the cultural and moral observation of Vietnamese society and family, as distinct from religious observation.[39] Trần is right to say that the Archbishop advocates for ancestor piety because it is a part of Vietnamese culture and moral behavior and is not necessarily religious.[40] Although Trần does note that the Archdiocese of Huế paid more explicit attention to inculturation recently, he does not use the archbishop's to point out the connection between devotion to OLLV and veneration of the Vietnamese ancestors, many of whom were martyrs. Therefore, I argue that devotion to OLLV is a fruitful starting point for this aspect of inculturation, an important part of which could indeed be ancestor piety. But even here we are building on the work of the past. As we have seen, the construction of the NC-OLLV includes a martyrs' memorial.[41]

The third document outlined by Trần is Pope John Paul II's *Ecclesia in Asia*. However, he does not explore the papal teaching in this document in great depth. Instead, he often references other documents, such as *Gaudium et Spes*, *Redemptoris Missio*, and the Asian Synod's discussion. For example, Trần quotes Pope John Paul II: "Through inculturation, the Church, for her part, becomes a more intelligible sign of what she is, and a more effective instrument of mission."[42] He does reference *Ecclesia in Asia* to support this quote.[43] Trần again mentions the Vietnamese episcopal speeches and restates their suggestions. He suggests that Catholic institutions provide quality theology for seminarians, the consecrated people, and the lay people. But he does not really connect

---

39. Ancestor piety was, of course, one of the main reasons for the persecution of Christians in Vietnam, because many Vietnamese misunderstood Christianity as forbidding them from practicing their ancestor piety; in their eyes, to become a Christian was to be unfilial.

40. "Di ảnh" is a photo of a dead person when he/she was alive and is often displayed on an ancestor altar.

41. Trần, 2.2.1.2. Bishop Bartholomew Lâm Sơn Nguyễn gave a powerful speech at the Asian Synod, acknowledging past mistakes in not paying attention to the presentation of faith. He further emphasizes correction and urgent need of Catholic education at seminaries and religious formation houses. See Joseph Dũng A. Trần, *Hội Đồng Giám Mục Việt Nam*.

42. John Paul II, *Redemptoris Missio*, §52.

43. Trần, 2.2.1.3.

the story of and devotion to OLLV to these documents. He does say that in light of inculturation's possible intersections in Vietnam with elements from multiple competing religious traditions, such as the popularity of rituals of ancestors, and the use of aspects of diverse subcultures, the work of inculturation is well positioned to seek a better presentation of faith, so to speak, for effective evangelization of the Vietnamese people. Trần's work and my own both emphasize devotion to OLLV to advocate for reconciliation, hospitality, and collaboration as a fruitful starting point for evangelization.

In his second section, Trần discusses issues of inculturation in two ways, which he entitles "History of A New Statue" and "Aspects of Liturgical Inculturation: Altar Platform, Music, and Folk Dances." Regarding the history of the new statue of OLLV, Trần follows Archbishop Étienne in part, arguing that the multiple images of OLLV throughout the past two hundred years have not specified concretely enough the meanings of OLLV's messages. Nevertheless, the archbishop did propose a new statue of OLLV made by sculptor Văn Nhân because this statue shows that "[OLLV] is both benevolent Mother and a majestic Queen."[44]

For Trần, this new statue of OLLV (discussed in chapter 3 above) proves that Christianity has been adapted to Vietnamese culture. He is right in saying, "The new century of inculturation [begins] with the appearance of the new statue of OLLV" because cultural appearance can provide a common aesthetic sensibility to those who share the same culture. However, insofar as he implies that Christianity was ever a foreign religion, when he says that "the new period ends [this] criticism,"[45] I would argue instead that devotion to OLLV has long made Christianity a deeply Vietnamese reality. This inculturation of the new statue does not start a brand-new project or replace the past but builds on the most important earlier inculturation of the faith. He further states, "If the third millennium is the church's mission in Asia, it must begin with OLLV, who is considered the Mother of Asia because she is the Mother of hope, unity, and the poor."[46] He largely, however, does not discuss the story of and devotion to OLLV as a catalyst for reconciliation and promoting collaboration. That approach deserves its own further research, building on what I have been able to provide, especially given the devotion's inclusion of other believers almost, it seems, from the very start.

44. Trần, 2.2.2.1.
45. Trần, 2.2.2.2.
46. Trần, 2.2.2.2.

Regarding other specific aspects of inculturation, Trần sees as valuable some liturgical elements at the 200th Jubilee. Besides Vietnamese instruments used at the liturgy, he mentions folk dances and the altar platform[47] where the solemn Mass and the performances took place. He further says these works of inculturation were the fruits of the efforts of the Archbishop of Huế and his people to foster liturgical inculturation. To end this section, Trần suggests the collaboration between the CBCV and Dicastery for Divine Worship and the Discipline of the Sacraments to seek even more effective paths toward liturgical inculturation that would be in further harmony with the Vietnamese and Asian contexts.

My own research has shown that Trần perhaps underestimates and undervalues the inculturation that devotion to OLLV represented from the earliest part of the nineteenth century. I have seen devotion to OLLV as a starting point for inculturation on which the CBCV has been able to build, and which provided a strong foundation for evangelization moving into the present. I have noted, along with Lê, that the description of the apparition of OLLV says that she held the Baby Jesus, and emphasized that she appeared to lay people. OLLV's holding the Baby Jesus shows both that the apparition is grounded Christologically and that it is geared to emphasize her maternity of the church in Vietnam. Moreover, holding the Baby Jesus distinguishes the BVM—the Mother of God—from other powerful female figures including native Vietnamese goddesses and the Buddhist Bodhisattvas. In that way, along with her appearance after the recitation of the rosary, as in the description, the lay people were able to easily recognize her as the Mother of Jesus and so also their mother.

Furthermore, OLLV appeared to these lay faithful as they were praying. First, OLLV did not select a visionary, or even a group. Instead, she appeared to the gathered community at prayer. As Jesus Christ promised, He was among them because they prayed together. Additionally, unlike any of the more famous subsequent apparitions, OLLV appeared to those fleeing persecution, comforted them, gave them courage, and confirmed their prayers. Not only did she strengthen their faith, but they also remembered her words and passed them on. In other words, she strengthened their witness precisely for evangelization in their own families and communities. This evangelization occurred both by their handing on the faith, and also by their witness of enduring atrocious persecution, as

---

47. The altar platform was designed in accordance with an ancient indigenous national altar, where the king offered sacrifice to Ong Troi on behalf of his people. For more detail about the architecture of this altar, see Cadière, "Le sacrifice du nam-giao".

encouraged by OLLV. Also, she promised to be there for whoever came to her. She is genuinely the Vietnamese Mother Mary for the Vietnamese people. The history of devotion to OLLV shows that the People of God persisted in responding to OLLV by going on pilgrimage to La Vang, building up the Shrine, and devoting themselves to her, even during the persecutions of the nineteenth century and throughout the severe restrictions of the Communist government in the twentieth century. Trần's work perhaps undervalues all of these elements of inculturation and the way in which they became foundational for a Vietnamese Catholic identity, for the inculturation of theology, and for paving the road towards facilitated contemporary liturgical and devotional inculturation.

To develop the devotion further, Trần advocates for collaboration between the Vietnamese bishops and the dicastery of the Church in Rome. This is a good suggestion, but I want to suggest movement towards more collaboration between the episcopate and priests, since Vietnamese priests are the ones doing the work and living in the culture of Vietnam. They are the preachers and theologians uniquely qualified to address issues of inculturation in the country. Also, most religious Sisters participate in pastoral ministries. However, they are often passive in leadership, and one of the reasons is that they lack sufficient Catholic education. Therefore, I suggest Catholic higher education be encouraged for them. Just as Pope John Paul II taught complementarity between men and women,[48] so too, female theologians would help to provide practical and theoretical benefit in the inculturation of faith, liturgy, and Marian devotion.

In his third section, Trần contends that the Shrine of OLLV is a place especially well-suited for ecumenical and inter-religious dialogue, basing his argument on the ecclesial teachings and of the Second Vatican Council, the Popes, and the Asian Bishops Conference. Trần states, "The Shrine of OLLV must become a place for ecumenical and interreligious dialogues, which are the basic elements towards [identifying] the mission of the Church in Vietnam."[49] Trần pays considerable attention to the presentation of the fundamental beliefs and practices of other religions, such as Confucianism, Taoism, Buddhism, and the indigenous religions, which include "Worship [Mr.] god," "Worship-piety ancestors," and "A ritual of national sacrifice."[50] No doubt these religious traditions have

---

48. See John Paul II, "Letter to Women" (1995); John Paul II, *The Theology of the Body*.

49. Trần, 2.3.1.1.

50. Trần, 2.3.1.1; 2.4.1

influenced Vietnamese perspectives and ways of life. However, Trần does not comment on this. He identifies neither those traditions especially related to the story of OLLV nor how devotion to OLLV might show evidence of influence by those traditions. To explore his ideas more deeply, it would be fruitful to build up an interreligious dialogue based on the history of the development of the shrine and devotion to OLLV.

In his fourth chapter, Trần explores the message of OLLV in relation to what he entitles the BVM's "maternity of grace" and "spirituality of hope." First, Trần presents the Vietnamese perspectives on maternity in general. In the Vietnamese culture, he says, giving birth is a woman's primary maternal vocation, and the mother plays a critical, crucial, and irreplaceable role in family life. He says, "In the Vietnamese culture, maternity is considered sacred and respected, . . . maternity is praised in the legend about mother Âu Cơ—mythic mother of all the entire Vietnamese nation."[51] Being a mother is privileged. Even the figures Bodhisattva and Quan-Yin were (and still are) depicted as female figures when Buddhists evangelized the Vietnamese people, even if they are not historically seen as mothers. Trần rightly points out that the Vietnamese highly regard and honor the mother due to her birth capacity, gentleness, and mercy.

Then, Trần points out the maternity of the BVM through salvation history, showing that she is the mother of all humanity by grace. He provides sources from the Scriptures, the teachings of the Patristic Fathers, the Popes, other theologians, and *Lumen Gentium*. He provides several quotes to reinforce the BVM as the mother of the baptized, especially referencing interpretations of the Gospel of John, chapters 2: 4; 3: 3–5; and 19: 26–27. For example, he quotes Pope Leo XIII, who taught, "From the same fact that the most Holy Virgin is the mother of Jesus Christ is she the mother of all Christians whom she bore on Mount Calvary amid the supreme throes of the Redemption."[52] However, Trần does not connect this universal theology to the cultural context he began with. Even when he finally does mention OLLV, the sense that she has inculturated this universal theology remains weak and seems like an afterthought because it considers only the most recent evidence, and in a fairly cursory fashion.

---

51. Trần, 4.1.1.1

52. Pope Leo XIII, *Quamquam pluries*, §3; Trần, 4.1.2.4. Tran also cites Pius XII, *Mystici Corporis*, §110: "Thus, she who, according to the flesh, was the mother of our Head, through the added title of pain and glory became, according to the Spirit, the mother of all His members."

Trần does present the impact of Pope John Paul II and the CBCV on the theology of OLLV as the mother of the Vietnamese people, using some of the sources I mentioned in earlier chapters, especially at the time of the canonization of the 117 martyrs. Nonetheless, OLLV is not mentioned. In his sketch of earlier missionary activity,[53] and in his series of quotations from "The Prayer to the Holy Mother La Vang" and from episcopal homilies from the 200th Jubilee of the apparitions, he does not offer an analysis in terms of inculturation. This he leaves for the readers, and I have attempted to build on his work in the preceding chapters. Although he does mention OLLV's title OLHC, which he says expresses her maternity, he does not provide any real historical warrant for that claim, nor does he explain its place in the history of inculturation of Marian theology as I have tried to do above. His review of the doctrine of Mary as Mediatrix of All Graces is also loosely connected to the history and theology of OLLV. He does briefly note that "OLLV is our maternal mediator of grace because of her intercession. OLHC is her title officially proclaimed by Bishop Caspar."[54] Nonetheless, there is no link to a theology of inculturation.

Trần sees devotion to OLLV as providing a space for contemporary inculturation, which, as we have seen, is largely limited to liturgy and art. But my work has shown how, all along, OLLV localized the universal theology of Mary as it developed over two centuries and was expressed in the titles given to her, such that these titles were made to be at home in Vietnamese culture and practice. I have also shown how, at the same time, OLLV was universalized for the whole Church as bearing a theology of Mary that both transcends culture even as it inculturates the theology of Mary as Mother of the Church as OLLV, Mother of the Church in Vietnam, or even simply as Mother of Vietnam.

Peter Phan

Peter Phan (b. 1943) is a well-known Vietnamese American theologian, especially in the United States. In a chapter published in multiple venues, "Mary in Vietnamese Piety and Theology, a Cultural and Interreligious Perspective," Phan examines Marian devotion in Vietnam.[55] He splits his

---

53. Trần, 4.1.2.5.
54. Trần, 4.1.3.5.
55. Phan, "Mary in Vietnamese Piety and Theology."

Vietnamese Theologians and Commentators on Our Lady of La Vang

argument into three approaches, which he entitles "Vietnamese Marian Piety: Historical Roots and Characteristics," "Marian Apparitions and Marian Sites," and "Mary, Mother of Mercy: Toward a Vietnamese Mariology." In the following section, I evaluate those approaches, arguing that although Phan's article is an initial step in describing Mariology in Vietnamese Catholicism, Phan undervalues the oral traditions of the Marian apparitions in Vietnam. But it is not unusual to rely on oral traditions, especially where the protagonists are poor, or persecuted, or both as in our case, and I demonstrate that the story of and devotion to OLLV are a starting point for the triple dialogues in Pope John Paul II's *Ecclesia in Asia*, which Phan mentions.

First, regarding the historical roots and characteristics of Vietnamese Marian devotion, Phan discusses three primary missionary layers: the Iberians, the French missionaries, and the religious orders. According to Phan, the influence of Iberian Catholicism mainly came from the Portuguese Jesuits and a few from Italy, Japan, and French.[56] The Portuguese, Phan writes, propagated their own customs of Marian devotion. "Relics, shrines, and pilgrimages, feast days, hymns, motets, legends, plays, paintings and statues, patronage of churches and monasteries, sermons, devotional treatises, visions, theology," he writes: "in all these areas Mary was not merely present but vitally important."[57]

Phan explores the second layer of Marian devotion in Vietnam, that of the French missionaries. Although the French missionaries were primarily members of the Société des Missions Étrangères de Paris (MEP), Phan discusses the role of Alexandre de Rhodes, a Jesuit, in the process of the establishment of the first two dioceses in Vietnam. Then Phan explores the first two apostolic vicars in Vietnam: François Pallu, 1626–84, and Pierre Lambert de la Motte, 1624–79.[58] Phan says, "They have left an indelible mark on the character of Vietnamese Catholicism, and by extension, on Vietnamese Marian piety."[59] Nevertheless, there was a strong practice of Marian devotion before they arrived in Vietnam, and Phan gives very little detail to illuminate their implementation of Marian

---

56. Phan, "Mary in Vietnamese Piety and Theology," 93.

57. Kieckhefer, "Major Currents in Late Medieval Devotion," 89, cited in Phan, "Mary in Vietnamese Piety and Theology," 94n9.

58. For more details, see AMEP, "François Pallu," "Lambert de la Motte"; Joseph Hùng Mạnh Đỗ, "Công cuộc truyền giáo của hai Giám mục tiên khởi tại Giáo Hội Việt Nam."

59. Phan, "Mary in Vietnamese Piety and Theology," 94.

devotion. As I have discussed, devotion to the BVM was practiced in European countries, especially France, under the titles OLHC and Our Lady of Victory. The MEP, at a later period, was committed to spreading the doctrine of the Immaculate Conception and the cult of Our Lady of Lourdes.[60] It is interesting that we do not see that happening in Vietnam, and my argument is that this would be due to the presence of an already inculturated Marian devotion localizing earlier titles in the strongly Vietnamese piety of OLLV. Phan pays more attention to Rhodes, however, than to the later French influence on Marian devotion in Vietnam and its reception.

The third layer of Marian devotion in Vietnam, as in Asia generally, is the influence of the religious orders, both men's and women's. According to Phan, the early religious orders include the Dominican friars and Franciscans from the Philippines, Redemptorists from Canada, the Salesians of Don Bosco, the Chanciness de Saint Augustin, and two Vietnamese indigenous religious congregations: Lovers of the Holy Cross and the Mother of the Redeemers.[61] These orders venerate the BVM. But primarily, Phan explores the work of Alexandre de Rhodes in Vietnam. This is important work, although at the length of Phan's piece it cannot be in depth. For Phan, Rhodes is one of the most important missionaries in Vietnam because he perfected and promoted the new Vietnamese script. Rhodes's *Cathecismus* and his *Dictionarium* were the first books printed in that script.[62] Then, Phan unfolds de Rhodes's guidance for catechists, as Phan quotes him:

> At this point, we should show a beautiful image of the BVM carrying her infant son Jesus, our Lord. . . . Lastly, reverence should be shown to the BVM by bowing the head to the ground once more; though we know that the BVM is not God because she is the Mother of God, all-powerful over her Son, we hope to obtain pardon for our sins through her holy intercession.[63]

Along with quoting several passages in his footnotes, Phan summarizes, saying, "de Rhodes's preferred representation was that of the Madonna and child, which indicates the inseparability between Christology

---

60. See Compgnon, *Le Culte de Notre Dame*.
61. Phan, "Mary in Vietnamese Piety and Theology," 94–95; 98.
62. Phan, "Mary in Vietnamese Piety and Theology," 95–96.
63. Phan, "Mary in Vietnamese Piety and Theology," 97–98.

and Mariology in his theology."⁶⁴ For Phan, Rhodes set the foundation for Mariology: "We have in de Rhodes's *Cathecismus* the basic contents of Mariology that would be presented to Vietnamese Catholics for the next three hundred years until the Second Vatican Council enriched it with newer insights."⁶⁵ As we have indeed seen, Marian devotion in Vietnam is fundamentally attached to a Christological emphasis, and this emphasis is part of the inculturation of Marian piety in a culture such as Vietnam's, which so highly values motherhood.

In addition, Phan notes episcopal veneration of the BVM, such as that of the first two apostolic vicars in the seventeenth century; Bishop Paul Puginier, the bishop of the diocese of Hà Nội, in 1868; and much later, of the first National Marian Congress in 1959. Phan summarizes the five characteristics of Marian devotion in Vietnam as he sees them:

> It is, first of all, traditional in the sense that it is deeply rooted in the teachings of the Church regarding Mary.... Second, it is also traditional because it has inherited most if not all Marian practices of the West.... Third, Marian devotion is popular in the sense of being widespread and practiced by the common Catholic folk.... Fourth, though popular, it is enthusiastically endorsed and encouraged by the hierarchy [and] the official consecration of Vietnam to our Lady. Finally, though imported from the outside, Marian devotion has sunk roots into the Vietnamese soil.⁶⁶

I agree! However, he does not mention OLLV in this connection, nor the specific elements of inculturation we have observed in our treatment of the growth of the devotion.

Moving on to the second point, Phan tells the story of two Marian apparitions in Vietnam, Our Lady of La Vang and Our Lady of Tra Kieu.⁶⁷ Before he describes the stories, he briefly compares them, saying

64. Phan, "Mary in Vietnamese Piety and Theology," 97.
65. Phan, "Mary in Vietnamese Piety and Theology," 97–98.
66. Phan, "Mary in Vietnamese Piety and Theology," 99. It seems there is no distinction between the roots and characteristics of Marian devotion. Also, missionaries who belonged to religious orders came to Vietnam in the sixteenth century. For example, a Dominican priest, Gaspar da Cruz, evangelized in 1549 in Can Cao (Ha Tien-southern Vietnam) and followed other Spanish Dominican priests who were missionaries in the Philippines; see Bui, *The Catholic Church in Vietnam*, 1:49. Moreover, in his writings, Alexandre de Rhodes describes how the Vietnamese, and the Vietnamese Catholics, venerated the BVM. See *Histoire du royaume du Tonkin*, 101; *Divers voyages et missions*, 159.; [*Hành trình và truyền giáo*], 110 translated by Hồng Nhuệ.
67. For Our Lady of Tra Kieu, see Phan, "Mary in Vietnamese Piety and Theology,"

that neither story carries any specific directive or doctrine. Phan says, "[O]ur Lady is said to have appeared during the persecution of Catholics and promised them maternal protection."[68] In addition, he says, "there is no historical documentation for these two apparitions but only unverifiable oral tradition. . . . Our Lady does not appear to identifiable individuals but to a large group of anonymous people."[69] I would dispute the disregarding of oral tradition here, pointing out both that it is not unusual and that we should value the community of prayer as much as elected visionaries with names. It is both significant and believable that OLLV appeared to everyone praying and not just a select visionary; in Vietnamese culture, we might note, the names of the communities (from the surrounding parishes in Quang Tri in the story of OLLV) are very important, even more than those of an individual.[70]

Then Phan describes the story of OLLV according to two versions: one from the Catholic version and the other from the Buddhist version, versions we have already mentioned above. He comments that, "What historical validity is to be attached to both accounts is impossible to determine. The Vietnamese hierarchy has not officially pronounced on the historicity of Mary's apparition at La Vang."[71] However, Phan does not make use of all the available sources to tell the story of OLLV; he does not examine how devotion apparently arose soon after the apparition; and he does not examine how OLLV traditionally has helped both Christians and non-Christians. Furthermore, he does not discuss how OLLV apparently helped martyrs throughout the nineteenth century, as the Vietnamese Catholic community grew even under persecution. But indeed, devotion to OLLV strengthened the faithful so that they could stand firm in the midst of trials. As they did so, their corporate Vietnamese Catholic identity was solidified.

Phan turns at this point to the story of Our Lady of Tra Kieu. The Văn Thân, whom we have met as an anti-French and therefore anti-Catholic group in the late nineteenth century, tried to destroy the church of Tra Kieu, even using elephants to assault the church; however, the church survived. Furthermore, during the fighting, a soldier of the Văn Thân

---

101–2.

68. Phan, "Mary in Vietnamese Piety and Theology," 100.

69. Phan, "Mary in Vietnamese Piety and Theology," 99.

70. For more detail, see AAOH, *Sacred Land of Our Lady of La Vang*, 1–10; Thêm Trần, *Foundation of Vietnamese Culture*, 86–114.

71. Phan, "Mary in Vietnamese Piety and Theology," 101.

Vietnamese Theologians and Commentators on Our Lady of La Vang

army says that he saw a beautiful woman dressed in white standing on top of the church, and he tried to shoot her but could not succeed. The Catholics attributed this victory to the BVM. Phan is right to say "there is no way to validate the Văn Thân's soldier's vision of the Lady. . . . Nevertheless, Vietnamese Catholics did not hesitate to attribute to Mary's miraculous intervention their victory over their enemy."[72] As we see, the status of this incident is unclear, and the Lady did not identify herself, nor carry identifying markers, nor even appear to Christians. The two alleged apparitions are very different in character and credibility.

Finally, Phan discusses "Mary, Mother of Mercy: Toward a Vietnamese Mariology" to suggest constructing a Vietnamese Mariology. Considering the teaching of the Second Vatican Council and the circumstances of Vietnam, Phan sees limited development so far of the theology of Mary in Vietnam. He says: "Despite Vatican II's reforms, Vietnamese Catholicism, especially in the North, has remained immune to changes and developments. . . . the Vietnamese theology of Mary has remained a 'Mariology of privileges.'"[73] I have shown, however, that inculturation of the theology of Mary, Mother of the Church, represents a reception of Vatican II's less triumphalist Mary and made her at home in Vietnam. Phan goes on to "paint a theological portrait of Mary" by unfolding three subpoints, including "Persecution," "Power," and "Interreligious Dialogue."

Regarding "Persecution," Phan here reminds readers that the Marian apparitions he is discussing took place in the context of the persecutions of Christians. Our Lady, for Phan, is a mother, a protector, full of love and mercy for her suffering children. The suffering of the Vietnamese people attracts Mary, Phan suggests.[74] Alongside Marian devotion, Phan explores the female Buddhist figure Kwan-Yin, to whom people cry out once they suffer.[75] Phan states, "Love of and devotion to Mary as Mother of Mercy, for Vietnamese Catholics, is a natural extension of their love of and devotion to the merciful Quan Am Thi Kinh."[76] This sounds more syncretistic than his first approach, where he demonstrated the roots and characteristics of Vietnamese Marian devotion in missionary theology, though the two approaches need not be mutually exclusive.

72. Phan, "Mary in Vietnamese Piety and Theology," 102.
73. Phan, "Mary in Vietnamese Piety and Theology," 103.
74. Phan, "Mary in Vietnamese Piety and Theology," 103.
75. Phan, "Mary in Vietnamese Piety and Theology," 103–5.
76. Phan, "Mary in Vietnamese Piety and Theology," 105.

Moving on to "Power," Phan sees Vietnamese Mariology inwoven with mercy and power. Phan points out that mercy without power is "empty and demeaning" and power without mercy may turn into dictatorship; an influential woman must have both characteristics.[77] For these reasons, according to Phan, Vietnamese devote themselves to the BVM. Alongside discussing the influence of Confucianism and Vietnamese ancient figures, Phan states, although Vietnamese highly respect women, women struggle with attaining equal rights and dignity. As a result, the Vietnamese people appeal to the BVM as the woman of mercy and power.[78]

Finally, Phan values the Marian apparitions discussed above as a starting point for interreligious dialogue. From the story of OLLV, Phan sees promise of an "amicable" relationship between Catholics and Buddhists, saying, "The relations between Buddhists and Catholics were very amicable [because] the statue of the Buddha was not smashed as an idol but simply moved to another place." Phan further says, "Our Lady [of Tra Kieu] was not seen by the Catholics of the village but by the 'pagans,' who attacked them."[79] For Phan, along with inculturation and liberation, interreligious dialogue is an essential component of Christian mission in Vietnam.[80] As so, reflection on the FABC's focus on "the triple dialogues," Phan states: "Mariology can serve as a fruitful starting point for interreligious dialogue in Vietnam."[81] These suggestions are well taken. However, Phan devotes most of his article to investigating the missionaries' work, and Rhodes's in particular, and their influence on Marian devotion in Vietnam. A deeper and more nuanced investigation into Vietnamese history and culture would even further strengthen scholarly understanding of Vietnamese Marian devotion, and I have attempted to provide a beginning here, even though I have not been able to cover all topics.

Furthermore, *Ecclesia in Asia* does emphasize the triple dialogue with cultures, with religions, and with the poor, as Phan references. My work has shown that devotion to OLLV can be a fruitful starting point for all three, and that would be another area for future study. Apart from his observations on Our Lady of Tra Kieu, which as an apparition of Mary seems questionable and marginal, his observations may otherwise

77. Phan, "Mary in Vietnamese Piety and Theology," 105–6.
78. Phan, "Mary in Vietnamese Piety and Theology," 106.
79. Phan, "Mary in Vietnamese Piety and Theology," 107.
80. Phan, "Mary in Vietnamese Piety and Theology," 107.
81. Phan, "Mary in Vietnamese Piety and Theology," 108. FABC is an abbreviation of the Federation of Asian Bishops Conference.

help strengthen our argument on the story of OLLV—the Mother of the Church—to facilitate the ecclesial mission of inculturation, new evangelization, care for the poor, and ecumenical and interreligious dialogues.

Maria Tuyệt Thị Nguyễn

Marian Tuyệt Thị Nguyễn (b. 1947) is the first female author to publish a book about OLLV, 2019's *I Bow to You-the Holy Mother La Vang, I Love You*.[82] This is a collection of forty-two articles previously published online and in print in the journal titled "[Vietnamese] People of God in Europe."[83] These are not scholarly articles but rather personal accounts of her devotion, her experience of pilgrimages, and other aspects of the devotion to OLLV. Especially of interest for my work here is the chapter entitled "A Story about 'The Prayer to Our Lady of La Vang,'" including three sections. In the first two sections, she reflects on "The Prayer to Our Lady of La Vang" (The Prayer) and the third section, she quotes the head of the committee who created "The Prayer." She demonstrates "The Prayer" has become a "treasure" for Vietnamese Catholics because it echoes earlier scholars and contemporary papal teaching. I argue that because of those echoes, "The Prayer" is evidence that devotion to OLLV has been inculturated into the hearts of the devotees, and Maria Nguyễn's testimony seems in turn to show that "The Prayer" has helped form a Catholic identity that is truly Vietnamese, both in Vietnam and among Vietnamese Catholics in the diaspora.

Soon after the 200th Jubilee of the apparition of OLLV, Maria Nguyễn began to publish the articles that appear in "Vietnamese People of God in Europe." Nguyễn reflects on her experience from her childhood to the present with devotion to OLLV at the NC-OLLV. In the introduction to her account, Stephen Lưu Thượng Bùi says that "[her articles] serve as a bridge to bind the Mother La Vang to her children in the diaspora."[84] In other words, her writing is her personal way of witnessing to OLLV, contributing to the oral tradition of OLLV, and spreading devotion to OLLV in the Vietnamese diaspora. Without any particular theological precision,

---

82. Maria Tuyệt Thị Nguyễn, *Lạy Mẹ La Vang*, 302–14.

83. "Dân Chúa Châu Âu" ["The [Vietnamese] People of God in Europe"] is the Vietnamese Catholic Institution to gather and serve Vietnamese Catholics who live in European countries. For more detail, see https://danchua.eu/.

84. Stephen Lưu Thượng Bùi, "Introduction," in *I Bow to Mother La Vang, I Love You*, 6.

she is confident in invoking OLLV under many Marian titles, for example, "OLHC," "Mother of God," "Mother of the Savior," "Co-Redemptorix," "Mother of Sorrows," "A Gate of Mercy," and "Queen of the Vietnamese Martyrs."[85] This shows that on the one hand, she regards OLLV as what we call a thoroughly inculturated devotion to Mary, and yet, on the other hand, there is clearly a universal significance to this local devotion.

"A Story about 'The Prayer to Our Lady of La Vang'" reflects on "The Prayer" its composition by Rev. Peter Thanh Xuan Phan for the occasion of the 200th Jubilee of celebration of the apparition of OLLV. She discusses how it has become an essential prayer, widespread in parish churches and devotions. She recounts that "The Prayer" helps her express her deepest feelings, "from the bottom of [her] heart," about Mary as OLLV. Most importantly, she notes how "The Prayer" echoes her favorite Vietnamese poem, a piece from 1938 entitled "Prayers to the Holy Mother La Vang," written by Father Joseph-Marie Thích Văn Nguyễn, who was a scholar and a poet in his own right. This means that "The Prayer" from 1998 is not the first piece of literary Vietnamese culture adapted into devotion to OLLV, but rather builds on a literary history that can be observed and appreciated by a non-scholarly writer such as Maria Nguyễn. The creation of this developing literary culture, which allows for a devotion that expresses the soul or heart of a woman such as Maria Nguyễn, is deeply important. If that element is overlooked, the history of devotion will miss an important aspect of devotion to OLLV invested with Vietnamese history and tradition.

Maria Nguyễn goes on to observe how "The Prayer" incorporates the teaching of Pope John Paul II on building a civilization of love, and his encouraging prayer to OLLV to ask for the kindness of heart, mercy, and forgiveness that can build a civilization of love and life. Therefore, in other words, even as it echoes the literary tradition of inculturation, it also proclaims the universal significance of this inculturated devotion. She sees the Pope himself as entering OLLV into a discourse important to the universal church. For Maria Nguyễn, "The Prayer" incorporates both the poetic prayer of 1938 and the papal teaching of 1994, making it relevant in our contemporary time. Thereby, she sees "The Prayer" as treasure leading people to convert and devote themselves to OLLV.[86]

---

85. Maria Nguyễn, *I Bow to Mother La Vang, I Love You*, 125, 148, 226.
86. Maria Nguyễn, *I Bow to Mother La Vang, I Love You*, 304.

In the second section, Maria Nguyễn shares her experiences observing the choir rehearsals for the liturgy of the opening of the 200th Jubilee of the apparition of OLLV. The text presented in song was a poem entitled "Ave Maria" composed by another famous Vietnamese poet, a layman named Hàn Mặc Tử who died of leprosy in 1940.[87] This poem was set to music by the prominent Vietnamese composer Hai Linh. A troupe of two hundred dancers was choreographed to the music, creating an especially notable occasion. The hand fans used by the dancers were tri-colored to represent the three regions of Vietnam. Maria Nguyễn states,

> [Hàn Mặc Tử] did not come to OLLV in person with his leprosy; however, he came to her Sacred Shrine, being with her with all his soul, mind, and heart. . . . He does not sing 'Ave Maria' alone. At the National Center of the Holy Mother La Vang, he joins with the choir, the vast concert of the ancient Vietnamese instruments, and the troupe of dancers to sing praises to the Holy Mother.[88]

Maria Nguyễn reflected on how the BVM was being honored as Mother of Vietnam and Mother La Vang, "the one that all Vietnamese people venerate, Christians and non-Christians alike." Here again we observe layers of inculturation created and woven together by the cult of OLLV. Hàn Mặc Tử's poetry of the middle twentieth century is now woven into the musical composition of a contemporary musician with traditional choreography, so that the voice of Hàn Mặc Tử is remembered and amplified as all the contemporary voices join in the singing, giving voice at one and the same time to the conviction of the Church and a sense of unity as Vietnamese people. This is an especially significant witness in a country where religious performance is officially discouraged.

The third section of her chapter quotes Father Peter Thanh Xuan Phan, the priest who was the head of the small committee charged by the Archbishop of Huế with writing "The Prayer." He recounts both the devotion of the committee members as well as the work they did studying previous literary sources connected to OLLV, which in turn were rooted in the traditional story of OLLV. Phan recounts the practices of weaving

---

87. Hàn Mặc Tử, "Ave Maria." Hàn Mặc Tử is the pen name of a famous Vietnamese Catholic poet. His birth and Christian name is Francis Trí Trọng Nguyễn (1912–1940). He discovered his leprosy in 1936. At that time persons with leprosy were still required by law to live apart from society in their own communities; he was not hospitalized until two months before his death, on November 11, 1940 at Quy Hoa Leprosy Camp, overseen by religious Sisters. See more in Stanislas Nguyễn and Joseph Nguyễn, *The History of Diocese of Huế*, 466–71.

88. Maria Nguyễn, *I Bow to Mother La Vang, I Love You*, 307.

these layers of inculturation together along with the teaching of Pope John Paul II and receiving the poetry of both Father Joseph-Marie Thích Văn Nguyễn and Hàn Mặc Tử as, already inculturated literary sources, into the new prayer. Thus, Maria Nguyễn emphasizes the continuity of traditional devotion to OLLV throughout history and its influence on the living witness of artists and musicians of the twentieth century who used their artwork to venerate OLLV. Indeed, just as the apparition of OLLV was inculturated into Vietnam and embraced the unique and rich theology of Mary, so too, devotion to her has been inculturated so as to become both an important part of Vietnamese Catholic identity.

Paul Chu Quang Trần

Paul Chu Quang Trần (b. 1947) is a Vietnamese Catholic scholar of literature. In addition to collecting sources of OLLV, he has composed many poems about OLLV. One recent poem is titled "An Oral Tradition in Time."[89] It fuses descriptive and narrative poetry to tell the story of OLLV's association with the history of Vietnam, in particular focusing on Christianity in central Vietnam. In the following sections, I analyze this poem, make some general observations, then examine each double quatrain and emphasize its contribution to the traditions of OLLV.

This poem is part of the author's collection, *La Vang, Mother Hometown*. The author also notes this "Oral Tradition" is based on the oral traditions of OLLV in order of chronology. Therefore, the title really means "An Oral Tradition of OLLV in Time." It is structured with the rhyme scheme "*Thơ lục bát*," in which each double quatrain of eight lines is made up of alternative lines of six and eight words each line. Along with poetic imagery, Trần uses the matter of the poem to tell the story of OLLV. "Oral Tradition in Time" contains eleven poetic double quatrains, each with a numbered title with either a period or a year associated, beginning in the sixteenth century and ending with the last double quatrain's title "1995–2020, Etc."

89. Paul Chu Quang Trần, "Truyền Kỳ" ["An Oral Tradition [of OLLV] In Time." Trần just composed this poem just last year and shared it with me. He adds it into his *La Vang Quê Mẹ [La Vang- Motherland]* and asked me to write an "Introduction" in the summer of 2023. Note that "Truyền" and "Kỳ" can be singular or plural nouns in the Vietnamese language. However, I chose a singular because even some scholars used plural as two versions of the oral tradition of OLLV, a fact is that these versions actually are two pieces of the oral tradition. The poet brings them together, and in any case they are closely related.

In the first double quatrain, titled "The 16th-17th Centuries," Paul Trần describes the first political founding in central Vietnam. Lord Nguyễn marched toward the south from the north and established his territory in Thuận Hoá, central Vietnam. Then Trần lists the other places founded by Lord Nguyễn and his successors, such as Dinh Cát/Quảng Trị, Phuoc Yen, Kim Long, Bac Vong, and Phu Xuan. These are all historical territories in central Vietnam. Soon, the missionaries also arrived and began the early Christian communities there. Ending this quatrain, Trần remarks that persecution of Christians occurred mainly by local officers. He says, referring to two such local officials:

> Hien Lord, [and] Vo Lord demonstrated their authority;
> Like storms, thunderstorm [persecutions] happened [and] continue.

In the second double quatrain, "1792–1981," Trần talks about the persecution of Christians under the reign of the Tay Son Dynasty:

> The reign of King Cảnh Thịnh, Tây Sơn [Dynasty],
> Teaching the ordinary people to practice ancestor piety,
> Said Christianity [is] a ghost religion [and creates]
> The decree to destroy 'wrong religions, 'Western religion.'

The author mentions the reason for the persecution of Christians was that Christianity was against Vietnamese indigenous piety. The Vietnamese kings promoted the worship of ancestors, a key part of Vietnamese moral behavior. They saw Christianity as a "wrong religion" and a "Western religion." In addition, though the missionaries taught their Vietnamese followers to worship only God, they did promote a kind of modified ancestor veneration, but they might not have given clear pastoral guidance that it was possible to appropriately honor Vietnamese customs.[90] In any event, there was a misunderstanding that to become a Christian was to leave behind ancestor piety altogether. Trần does not mention any further socio-political reason that led King Cảnh Thịnh to decree the persecution of Christians, though there was undoubtedly a political dimension. His next four verses describe the faithful running away from their villages into the wild forest to avoid persecution. He describes the place where the faithful took refuge, including crowing chickens, "bến cộ," [river station], "miếu Trảnh" [wayside], and "đa già" [old banyan].

---

90. In the early nineteenth century, Jean Labartette sent a letter to Rome asking for guidance about ancestor veneration. For more details, see AMEP, vol. 747.

In the third double quatrain, titled "1798," Trần narrates the apparition of OLLV:

> One night the Mother appears
> Two hands hold God, the treasure Baby
> The words of Mother, the message
> 'Be willing to suffer hardship because of faith
> Henceforth, whoever comes to pray in
> This place, Mother will grant the prayer.
> The sick and seriously sick
> Drink the boiled leaf of Mother's garden, good healing.'

Here the author fuses the description and the words of OLLV, providing OLLV's words where he uses quotation marks. In so doing, he reinforces the tradition that she actually appeared. However, he drops two traditional phrases from OLLV's words, namely "have trust" and "I have granted your prayers." The author seems to presume that his Vietnamese Catholic audience already believe in God and trust in OLLV and that therefore the most important thing for them is to persevere in suffering and continual prayer in a time of modern repression.

In his fourth set of quatrains, titled "1833–1862," Trần describes the violent persecutions under the reign of the Nguyễn Dynasty.

> The Nguyễn Dynasty sowed great suffering
> "Lăng trì,"[91] beheading, choking to death, 100-slicings....

Similarly known for persecution to the point of massacre is the Văn Thân Movement in 1885, which Trần uses as title for his fifth double quatrain. The Văn Thân Movement fought against the French invasion in 1885. Its legacy was to "Kill missionaries, kill the followers [of Christians]." It was not only persecution but really a series of massacres—the death of whole Christian communities. Trần writes:

> The old [and] the young were terrified
> Wading through the forest, looking for refuge
> Stop at a wayside, a pagoda made of thatch leaves
> Offering the Mother, a burning sacrifice.

As we saw, around two hundred lay faithful in Quang Tri ran away from their villages to the Shrine of OLLV. There, they were burned in front

---

91. "Lăng trì" was a terrible execution by which a prisoner was sliced frequently until death (death by a thousand cuts), or a prisoner's arms and legs were cut off before they were finally beheaded. After liberation from China, the ruling Vietnamese dynasty still kept several types of death penalty. "Lăng trì" was one of these.

Vietnamese Theologians and Commentators on Our Lady of La Vang

of the Shrine of OLLV by the Văn Thân in 1885.[92] Up to the period ending in 1885, Trần uses the language of "a pagoda" instead of "the shrine" of OLLV, reflecting what we know about the first building being a Buddhist construction, which they later ceded to the Christians around 1820s.[93]

In the sixth set of quatrains, titled "1894–1900," Trần begins a new page in the history of OLLV. The persecution ended, and the construction of the Church began. This is the first time the Marian title Our Lady of Help of Christians is used, namely in the blessing of the Church's building and the solemn procession of OLLV, the first national pilgrimage in 1900.

> Our Lady of Help of Christians
> Many blessings the Mother has granted
> August of thousand and nine hundred
> The blessing [of the Church] the first national pilgrimage.

The seventh double quatrain, titled "1924–1928," talks about the construction of the new Church of OLLV close to the former one. Diverse pilgrims go on pilgrimage to "the Mother House."

In the eighth set of quatrains, titled "1960–963," the author describes the elevation of the Church to the Basilica of OLLV and designation of the grounds of La Vang as the NC-OLLV, a decision made by the bishops of south Vietnam.[94] The ninth double quatrain, titled "1972...," presents a historical event during the Vietnam War, the Easter Offensive in Quang Tri in 1972, when the Basilica was destroyed, and the local people ran away. Many died on the road. Only a few people remained at La Vang. That was one of the most terrifying events in the history of OLLV. The tenth double quatrain, titled "1980–982," recalls the establishment of the Vietnamese Bishops' Conference in 1980. Now all the bishops of CBCV were able to approve the shrine of OLLV as the NC-OLLV.[95] The author says:

> The Catholic Bishops' Conference of Vietnam
> All [Bishops] voted for La Vang [-] Heaven Shrine
> Affirming 'the National Center' to be
> The Sacred Land of the Holy Mother forever.

---

92. For more detail, see AAOH, *The Sanctuary of Our Lady of La Vang*, 10.

93. For more detail, see AAOH, *The Sanctuary of Our Lady of La Vang*, 9.

94. For more detail, see AAOH, *The Sanctuary of Our Lady of La Vang*, 12–13; Q. Trần, *Pilgrimage to Diocese of Huế*, 3:190.

95. AAOH, *The Sanctuary of Our Lady of La Vang*, 16; Q. Trần, *Pilgrimage to Diocese of Huế*, vol. III, 271.

In his last double quatrain, titled "1995–2020 ...," Trần writes that the times of difficulty are gone, the union of the Mother's Children in Vietnam and diaspora and the reconstruction of the Basilica are now complete.[96] The last two verses of this poem summarize the rich and beautiful story of OLLV:

> Vằng flowers bloom in the hometown garden,
> The Holy Mother helps from then until now!

The name "La Vang" may come from "lá vằng," the leaves of vằng trees in that region, as mentioned above. The author states that the flowers of vằng trees, "Hoa Vằng," bloom abundantly in the hometown garden, which implies the garden of the Holy Mother. The flowers signal springtime to express the coming of a joyful and hopeful season. Furthermore, the blooming vằng flowers in the garden of OLLV recall how Vietnamese Catholics are fond of offering flowers to the BVM. The last verse uses the Marian title of OLLV as a sentence. "Our Lady" becomes the subject, "help" is a verb; however, "Christians" is replaced with "from then until now." Such a beautiful last verse expresses Mary's constant help from her apparition to the present day. Indeed, the last two verses express the author's joy and trust in OLLV.

Composing poems about historical narratives is challenging; however, Trần does excellent work in "An Oral Tradition in Time," depicting Our Lady of La Vang's chronology. In the poem, the readers can follow the series of events he incorporates, even if they are familiar neither with the history of Vietnam nor the story of OLLV.

Some elements depart from what this book has reviewed about the tradition of OLLV. For example, in his third double quatrain retelling the apparition of OLLV, Trần drops a part of the important message of OLLV, which is her first message, "Children, have trust," and her third message, "Mother has already granted your prayer." It is challenging to compose the words of OLLV in poetic verse; however, including "have trust" would have retained greater fidelity to the religious historical record. Moreover, these messages (trust and prayer) are important in the Christian tradition. The whole biblical message carries the theme of faith, belief, and trust, which is what God waits for in human beings' response to God's love. At La Vang, Our Lady called the lay people to trust in God and she affirmed their prayers. On the other hand, the element of trust is implied in OLLV's exhortation to be willing to suffer hardships faithfully, and the poet does

---

96. The basilica was blessed during the thirty-second national pilgrimage in 2023.

emphasize this. We can see this in the poet's depiction of an inculturated tradition of devotion that allowed Vietnamese Catholics to heroically resist persecution and to bring the Church to the twentieth century as a vibrant believing and fully Vietnamese communion. OLLV gave shape and coherence to the faithful's endurance, and so she crafted an identity for her beloved people. This indeed represents an inculturated Vietnamese Catholicism. The poet honors this tradition as a living inculturation by developing it in a Vietnamese poetic genre almost as a national religious epic. He thereby encourages others to join in the composition of such poetry and inspires other literary efforts. We have seen a similar dynamic in the last section, bridging theology, piety, and literature.

Conclusion

WHEN THE FIRST LAY faithful encountered OLLV, she was holding the Baby Jesus, which can be seen as a form of inculturated evangelization from the very beginning. First, an image of the BVM holding the Baby Jesus exhibits the fundamental grounding of Mariology in Christology. This image expresses the Patristic Fathers' teaching about the BVM since it expresses her highest title—Theotokos, God-bearer, Mother of God—defined at the Council of Ephesus in 431. Vietnamese Catholics too venerated the BVM through the image of Mother-and-Child. We know the early missionaries had used this image to introduce her to the Vietnamese people. This image is harmonious with Vietnamese perspectives on the dignity of a woman and of being a mother. Holding the Baby Jesus, OLLV adapted herself to the Vietnamese context as much as Our Lady of Guadalupe adapted herself to the Aztec culture and context. In fact, the lay faithful had no trouble recognizing her.[1] Thus, appearing to the lay people holding the Baby Jesus, OLLV re-evangelized them, strengthening and renewing their faith in Jesus Christ. OLLV certainly does not undercut the adoration of Christ. In fact, by holding the Baby Jesus, she reminds us that "true devotion proceeds from true faith" and "[Marian devotion] is an intrinsic element of Christian worship,"[2] and also that it

---

1. Note that Quan Âm Thị Kính [Thị Kính Bodhisattva], is considered cổ văn [ancient literature,] might have been written in the mid- or second half of the nineteenth century. She is often depicted as a woman with a child in Buddhist practice. It is unclear when Vietnamese Buddhist followers first venerated this figure; however, it seems to be the late nineteenth century at the earliest. https://vi.wikipedia.org/wiki/Quan_%C3%82m_Th%E1%BB%8B_K%C3%ADnh_(truy%E1%BB%87n_th%C6%A1)

2. *Lumen Gentium*, §62; Paul VI, *Marialis Cultus*, §56.

directs us to adoration of Christ.³ By appearing while holding the Baby Jesus, as in no other known Marian apparition, OLLV adapted herself and the faith to the Vietnamese culture and fostered Christianity in its Vietnamese context while cultivating the fundamental theology of Mary reflecting the highest Marian title "Mother of God," the title by which she was invoked in the most ancient known Marian hymn to provide her maternal help.

Moreover, in the apparition, Our Lady's nurturing of the lay faithful can also be seen as a form of inculturated evangelization. Unlike many other Marian apparitions, OLLV did not request the building of a church, as she did at the hill of Tepeyac in 1531 or at Lourdes in 1858.⁴ Likewise, she had no call for conversion of sinners or recitation of the Rosary as she did at Fatima in 1917.⁵ Instead, like many Vietnamese mothers, OLLV nurtured her suffering children by strengthening their faith in Jesus, encouraging them to endure suffering, affirming their prayers, and accompanying them, as she said. All her words and deeds are relevant to the Vietnamese people's perspectives on maternity, especially in a time of danger. Although this maternal protection echoes the role of mothers worldwide, its evocation here is vital in order for the Vietnamese people to respond to OLLV's unconditional offer of care, protection, and help. So, in her manner of nurture, OLLV facilitated inculturated evangelization.

There are other aspects of OLLV's inculturated evangelization related to characteristic Vietnamese perspectives. These aspects include an emphasis in prayer in community, in language and a way of speaking that was easily understandable, and in the use of local resources. As the description says, the lay people remembered and passed on the story of OLLV and her words, and in order to remember and pass on, they must understand. That means OLLV had to speak an understandable language that they could comprehend and gain their trust. OLLV also appeared to the lay faithful as they had just completed their prayer. For the Vietnamese people, community matters, and the community of prayer is necessary for growth in faith. Also, in that community, OLLV addressed the lay faithful as her "children" and called herself "Mother." This kind of address invokes the Mother-and-Child relationship and applies it to the faithful. She is Mother of God and Mother of the Church at the same time, even

---

3. See *Catechism of the Catholic Church*, §971, citing *Lumen Gentium*, §66.
4. See Matovina, *Theologies of Guadalupe*; Deery, *Our Lady of Lourdes*.
5. Walsh, *Our Lady of Fátima*.

without the title yet. Finally, OLLV used local resources to heal illnesses, just like a Vietnamese mother taking care of her sick children. Moreover, the leaf is a medicine with biblical roots, such as in Ezekiel 47:12: "Their fruit is used for food, and their leaves for healing," and Revelation 22:2: "The leaves of the trees serve as medicine for the nations." Here, OLLV inculturates biblical faith within the Vietnamese context.

We find the same pattern as the devotion develops through the centuries. In her apparition, OLLV inculturated the theology of the universal church in a Vietnamese context, but by the same token, she began a devotion which could be "universalized" or recognized by the universal church as significant to the whole church. It was truly the faith of the universal church that was localized. We have seen how devotion to OLLV enabled the Vietnamese Christians to endure waves of violent persecutions and so experience themselves as a particular local church with a Vietnamese identity. When an official cult was established, OLLV was venerated under the European title *Our Lady of Help of Christians*, a title related to her main title as Mother of God. At the same time, as the Great Pilgrimage began to be organized using Vietnamese local customs, the title Our Lady of Help of Christians became incarnated or inculturated in Vietnamese ways of praying and celebrating, even as the use of this title, and related titles such as Our Lady of Victory and Our Lady of Grace, served to link Vietnamese piety and practice to the universal church.

We have seen these trends continued in the years immediately after the Vietnamese War and the Second Vatican Council and up to the present time. Pope John Paul II and various prominent Vietnamese Bishops along with the newly formed Catholic Bishops' Conference of Vietnam (CBCV) encouraged devotion to OLLV and extended her maternal care to the whole of Vietnam—OLLV, Mother of the Church, Mother of Vietnam. Furthermore, inculturation proceeded in liturgy, art, and literature while the recognition of OLLV at the highest levels of the Church emphasized the continuity of the faith of Vietnamese Christians with that of the Church universal. What I have shown is that these later events are not novel developments stemming only from a late twentieth century emphasis on inculturation. Rather, we find a tradition which was there from the beginning, lovingly handed down by oral tradition and devotion during decades of atrocious persecution only to emerge with an inculturated evangelizing power whose depth still remains to be discovered and tapped and developed further.

Regarding a direction for future research, I recommend at least five themes for future study. First, asking how devotion to OLLV facilitates the mission of the Church in Vietnam would be a helpful contribution to the Catholic Church in carrying out her pastoral practice. Second, the National Center of the Holy Mother La Vang is a "Marian school" for the faithful, where the Church prepares them to sanctify their domestic church and their world, and it should be studied as such. Third, there is much room to study devotion to OLLV in the diaspora, for example, in the United States, and how it empowers a Vietnamese Catholic identity that strengthens local churches throughout the world. Fourth, a significant future task is to develop further the sketches of a theology of OLLV I have presented here. Lastly, though not a research suggestion, nevertheless my research shows that the CBCV has sufficient warrant to open a formal Church investigation into the Marian apparitions at La Vang. In God's Providence, the BVM received a new name, "Our Lady of La Vang." It is often the case that such a new name comes about in honor of an approved apparition, even if the approval is "only" traditional and implicit. Isn't it time to make it official and explicit?

Appendix

Timeline of the Church in Vietnam and of Our Lady of La Vang

A 1: The Sponsorship/Protection Period (1533–1659):

1533: Christianity is first reported in Vietnam.

1550: Gaspar da Santa Cruz, O.P., evangelizes in Hà Tiên in lower southern Vietnam.

1580: The Order of Preachers sends Louis da Fonseca and Gregoire de la Motte to evangelize in Quảng Nam, in central Vietnam.

1583: Frs. Bartolomew Ruiz, Pedro Ortis, and Francis de Montilla, with four Franciscan brothers from the Philippines, evangelize in north Vietnam.

1591: Fr. Pedro Ordoñez de Cevallos baptizes Princess Mai Hoa in the Thanh Hoa province; she makes her house a monastery and lives as a nun.

1596: Fr. Pedro Aduarte, O.P., arrives in Dinh Cát/Quảng Trị in central Vietnam.

1615: Frs. Francois Buzomiand, SJ and Diego Carvalho, SJ and three Jesuit brothers (Antonio Dias, Joseph, and Paulo Saito) arrive at Cửa Hàn in Đà Nẵng, central Vietnam.

1625ff:

- Secular authorities (kings, lower officials) give orders to persecute Christians.
- Frs. F. Pina, SJ and A. Rhodes, SJ arrive in Dinh Cát/Quảng Trị

1630:

- Fr. Alexandre de Rhodes and Jesuit missionaries are expelled from the north.
- Mr. Francis, a layman, is beheaded, becoming the first martyr in the north.

1639:

- There are approximately 82,000 Catholics in the north and 15,000 Catholics in the south
- All Jesuit missionaries are expelled.

1644: Andre Phú Yên becomes the first martyr in the south, at Quang Nam.

A 2: The Apostolic Administration Period (1659–1960)

1659: Pope Alexander VII, in *Super Cathedram*, establishes the first two dioceses in present-day Vietnam, with the dividing line at the Gianh River.

- The Diocese of the South is placed under the care of Bishop Pierre Lambert de la Motte.
- The Diocese of the North is is placed under the care of Bishop Francois Pallu.

1672–1725: Dinh Cát/Quảng Trị comes under care of the M.E.P.

1798: The Apparition of Our Lady of La Vang

- King Cảnh Thịnh orders persecution of Christians across the whole country.
- The Blessed Virgin Mary appears to the faithful at La Vang in Quang Tri, in upper Cochinchine, central Vietnam.

Timeline of the Church in Vietnam and of Our Lady of La Vang

1799: Jean Labartette becomes Apostolic Vicar of Cochinchine.

1802:

- Nguyễn Anh triumphs and is crowned King Gia Long
- Phú Xuân [Huế] in the central Vietnam is chosen as a new Citadel

1820s: The first thatched chapel [shrine] of Our Lady of La Vang is built by non-Christians and is entrusted peacefully to Christians.

1820–1880s:

- The Nguyễn Dynasty orders many persecutions and a series of massacres of Christians occurs

1844:

- The Diocese of the South is divided into two: Western Diocese of the South and Eastern Diocese of the South. The thatched chapel of OLLV belongs to the latter.

1850:

- The Eastern Diocese of the South is divided into two: one retaining the old name, and Cochinchine septentrionale, where the thatched chapel of OLLV is. The first bishop of Cochinchine septentrionale is François Marie Pellerin.

1856: The French begin fighting in Đà Nẵng.

1885:

- The Văn Thân Movement massacres Christians.
- The thatched chapel of OLLV is burned and another one built.

1880s: The name "Our Lady of La Vang" first appears in print.

1894: A brick church of OLLV is built under the care of French missionaries.

1900: The first solemn procession of Our Lady of La Vang

- Bishop Louis Caspar blesses the building of the Church and announces the Marian title "Our Lady of Help of Christians."
- The first Great Pilgrimage to OLLV takes place.
- A council of the northern dioceses unifies pastoral ministry and formation of priests.

1901: Claude Bonin becomes the first author to publish on OLLV in French.

1902: Bishop Caspar approves cult of OLLV created by Claude Bonin.

1904: The second Great Pilgrimage to OLLV.

1907: The third Great Pilgrimage to OLLV.

1908: The journal *Nam Kỳ Địa Phận [Southern Dioceses]* is established

1910:

- The fourth Great Pilgrimage to OLLV
- Joseph Trang Văn Trần becomes the first to write on OLLV in Vietnamese.

1913: The fifth Great Pilgrimage to OLLV

1917: The sixth Great Pilgrimage to OLLV

1919: The seventh Great Pilgrimage to OLLV

1923: The eighth Great Pilgrimage to OLLV

1924: All dioceses are renamed in accordance with the cities where a bishopric located. Cochinchine Septentrionale becomes the diocese of Huế.

1925: A house of the Apostolic Nuncio is established in Huế, then moved to Hà Nội in 1951 and Sài Gòn in 1959, where it was closed in 1975.

1928:

- The ninth Great Pilgrimage to OLLV
- Bishop Allys blesses the new church of OLLV and elevates the community into a parish.

1932:

- The tenth Great Pilgrimage to OLLV
- Dominic Cẩn Ngọc Hồ, ed. *The Legend Poem of La Vang* is republished.

1933: The first Vietnamese Bishop, Bishop John the Baptist Nguyễn Bá Tòng.

1935: The eleventh Great Pilgrimage to OLLV

1938: The twelfth Great Pilgrimage to OLLV

1954: The first universal Marian Year

- The 17th Parallel Line divides Vietnam.
- Around 1,000,000 people move from north to south Vietnam
- The shrine of OLLV is near to the 17th Parallel Line in the southern part.

1955: The thirteenth Great Pilgrimage to OLLV

1958: The fourteenth Great Pilgrimage to OLLV

1959:

- The 300th anniversary of Christianity in Vietnam.
- National Marian Year takes place in Sài Gòn
- The bishops of the southern Vietnam consecrate Vietnam to the Immaculate Conception of the Sacred Heart of Mary.

A 3. The Hierarchy of the Catholic Church in Vietnam (1960-Today)

1960:

- Pope John XXIII establishes the Hierarchy of the Catholic Church in Vietnam.
- The Church in Vietnam includes the three Archdioceses of Hà Nội (north), Huế (central Vietnam), and Sài Gòn (south) with three Archbishops
- All the Apostolic Vicars become the Bishops of Dioceses.

1961: The National Center/Shrine of the Holy Mother La Vang

- The fifteenth Great Pilgrimage to OLLV—the 15th National Pilgrimage.
- The bishops of south Vietnam designate the grounds of OLLV the National Center of the Holy Mother La Vang and plan to construct the National Center.

- Pope John XXIII elevates the church of OLLV to a rank of minor Basilica.
- The magazine *Our Lady of La Vang* is established.

1962:
- Huồn Phát Phan becomes the first historian to account "The Apparition of Our Lady of La Vang" in his *Việt Nam Giáo Sử* [*Historical Church of Vietnam*].

1964: The sixteenth National Pilgrimage to OLLV.

1970: The seventeenth National Pilgrimage to OLLV.

1976: The first Vietnamese Cardinal: Khuê Như Trịnh, Archbishop of Hà Nội.

1978: The eighteenth National Pilgrimage to OLLV.

1980: Reaffirming the National Center of the Holy Mother La Vang
- The Bishops of Vietnam meet for the first time in May in Hanoi.
- They establish the Catholic Bishops' Conference of Vietnam (CBCV)
- They confirm the National Center of the Holy Mother La Vang
- They send their first General Letter, "Sống Phúc Âm Giữa Lòng Dân Tộc" ["Living the Gospel in the Heart of the Nation"] to the People of God.

1981: The nineteenth National Pilgrimage to OLLV.

1984: The twentieth National Pilgrimage to OLLV.

1987: The twenty-first National Pilgrimage to OLLV.

1987–1988: The second Universal Marian Year.

1988: Pope John Paul II Speaks about Our Lady of La Vang to the People of God
- 117 Martyrs of Vietnam are canonized
- Pope John Paul II tells the story of OLLV and calls for reconstructing her basilica.

1990: The twenty-second National Pilgrimage to OLLV.

1993: The twenty-third National Pilgrimage to OLLV.

1996: The twenty-fourth National Pilgrimage to OLLV.

1998: The 200th Jubilee of the Apparition of Our Lady of La Vang
- The Ecclesia of Asia Synod.

1999: The twenty-fifth National Pilgrimage to OLLV
- The closing of the 200th Jubilee Year of OLLV.

2001: Joseph-Marie T. Phong Trần writes "Notre Dame de La Vang, Viet Nam, histoire et théologie: du message de Notre Dame de La Vang à la maternité de grâce de Marie et à la spiritualité de l'espérance."

2002: The twenty-sixth National Pilgrimage to OLLV.

2005: The twenty-seventh National Pilgrimage to OLLV.

2008: The twenty-eighth National Pilgrimage to OLLV.

2009–2010: The Jubilee Year of the Church in Vietnam
- 350 years of the first two dioceses, 1659–2009.
- 50 years of the Hierarchy of the Catholic Church, 1960–2010.

2011:
- Archbishop Leopondo Girelli is appointed Non-Residential Pontifical Representative for Vietnam.
- The twenty-ninth National Pilgrimage to OLLV.

2012: CBCV begins construction for the new Basilica of OLLV.

2014: The thirtieth National Pilgrimage to OLLV.

2016: Joseph Linh Chí Nguyễn is appointed the Archbishop of Huế.

2017: The thirty-first National Pilgrimage to OLLV.

2018:
- Archbishop Marek Zalewski becomes Non-Residential Pontifical Representative for Vietnam.
- Joseph Thiên Văn Vũ is appointed the Archbishop of Hà Nội.

2019:

- Joseph Năng Nguyễn is appointed the Archbishop of Sài Gòn (HCM City).
- OLLV is named patroness of the Archdiocese of Huế.

2020:

- The sixtieth anniversary of establishing the Church hierarchy in Vietnam.
- The Jubilee Year of the Archdiocese of Huế, 1850–2020.
- Postponement of the thirty-second National Pilgrimage to OLLV due to COVID-19.

2023: The 225th Anniversary of the Apparition of Our Lady of La Vang

- Two dissertations on OLLV in English:
  - Sister Dung Trang, "The Sanctuary of Our Lady of La Vang: Negotiating the Space between Marian Devotion and Vietnamese Catholic Women" (Villanova University).
  - Sister Mary Kim Anh Thi Tran, O.P., "A Vietnamese Mary: Our Lady of La Vang in History and Theology" (The University of Notre Dame).
- Archbishop Marek Zalewski is appointed Residential Papal Representative in Vietnam.

Bibliography

Interviews

Sister Agatha Lê Thị Sinh, NC-OLLV, May 18, 2019.
Emeritus Archbishop Étienne Nguyễn, Như Thể, Huế, May 20, 2019.
Fr. Emmanuel Nguyễn Vinh Gioang, Huế, May 20, 2019.
Archbishop Joseph Nguyễn Chí Linh, Huế, May 20, 2022.
Fr. Lê Văn Hiển, a retired director of the NC-OLLV, May 18, 2019.
Fr. Nguyễn Quốc Vệ, a retired director of the NC-OLLV, May 21, 2019.
Emeritus Archbishop FX Lê Văn Hồng, May 21, 2019.
Fr. Michael Phạm Ngọc Hải, a director of the NC-OLLV, May 18, 2019.
Fr. Joseph Nguyễn Văn Chánh, Professor, Saint Sulpice Seminary of Huế, May 22, 2019.

Primary Sources

Alexander VII. *Super Cathedram Principis Apostolorum*. September 8, 1659. https://www.papalencyclicals.net/alex07/alex07super.htm.
Allys, Eugène Marie Joseph. "Annual Report," 1910. AMEP 761: 154.
———. "Annual Report," 1913. AMEP 761: 179.
———. "Annual Report," 1917. AMEP 761: 194.
———. "Annual Report," 1919. AMEP 761: 200.
———. "Annual Report," 1928. In *Compte-rendu des travaux 1928*, 119–22. Paris: MEP, 1929.
The Archive of the Archdiocese of Huế. *La Vang 200 Năm:1798–1998 [La Vang 200 Years: 1798–1998]*. Huế: Thuận Hóa, 1999.
———. *La Vang Hai Thế Kỷ—Lịch Sử Một Tình Thương [Two Centuries of La Vang—History of One Love]*. Huế: AAOH, 1998.
———. *Thánh Địa Đức Mẹ La Vang [The Sanctuary of Our Lady of La Vang]*. Huế: AAOH, 1998.
———. Videos. Huế: AAOH.
———. Hình ảnh [Photos]. Huế: AAOH.
———. Thông Báo [Notification]. Huế: AAOH.

———. *Tiểu sử các Thừa Sai và các linh mục giáo phận Huế [Biography of Missionaries and Clergy of Diocese of Hue.]* Huế: AAOH.

The Archive of Mission Étrangères de Paris. "MEP publications (1840–962): Digital Library." https://irfa.paris/en/mep-publications-1840-962-digital-library.

———. *Phép Giảng Đạo Thật.* Vol. 1183. Paris, 1758.

The Archive of Propaganda Fide. "Response to 69 Questions to Mgr. Labartette in 1806." AMEP 747: 331–46.

Audemar, Jean-Joseph. "Letter to Mgrs. Boiret and Langlois," 1809. AMEP 747: 599–601.

———. "Letter to Mgrs. de la Bissachere," 1811. AMEP 747: 645–48.

Benedict XVI. "Message To Bishop Pierre Nguyên Văn Nhon, President of the Vietnamese Bishops' Conference." November 17, 2009. https://www.vatican.va/content/benedict-xvi/en/messages/pont-messages/2009/documents/hf_ben-xvi_mes_20091117_vietnam.html.

———. "Letter To Card. Ivan Dias, Special Envoy, on the Occasion of the Closing Ceremony of the Jubilee Year of the Church of Vietnam (Marian Shrine of La Vang, 4–6 January 2011)." December 21, 2010. https://www.vatican.va/content/benedict-xvi/la/letters/2010/documents/hf_ben-xvi_let_20101221_dias.html.

———. *Deus Caritas Est.* December 25, 2005. https://www.vatican.va/content/benedict-xvi/en/encyclicals/documents/hf_ben-xvi_enc_20051225_deus-caritas-est.html.

———. *Spe Salvi.* November 30, 2007. https://www.vatican.va/content/benedict-xvi/en/encyclicals/documents/hf_ben-xvi_enc_20071130_spe-salvi.html.

Bonin, Claude. "Notre Dame de La Vang." In *Annales de la Société des Missions-Etrangères* 24: 273–77. Paris: AMEP, 1901.

Bonnand, Jean-Louis, MEP. "Un procès gagné—Une église à faire." In *Bulletin de L'oeuvre des Partants, 1886–1892*: 694. Paris: M.E.P, 1893.

Bùi, Archbishop Văn Đọc Paul. "Thư kêu gọi đóng góp xây dựng Vương Cung Thánh Đường Đức Mẹ La Vang" ["A Call for Donation to Construction of the Basilica of Our Lady of La Vang"]. The Archdiocese of Sài Gòn, April 15, 2015.

Cadière, Léopold Michel. *Souvenir.* AMEP, vol. DH. 430/06, 39–48.

Caspar, Marie-Antoine-Louis. "Annual Reports," 1893. AMEP 761: 56.

———. "Annual Reports," 1894. AMEP 761: 61.

———. "Annual Reports," 1895. AMEP 761: 65.

———. "Annual Report," 1900. AMEP 761: 90.

———. "Annual Report," 1902. AMEP 761: 101.

Catechism of the Catholic Church. 2nd ed. Washington, DC: United States Catholic Conference, 2011. https://www.usccb.org/sites/default/files/flipbooks/catechism/.

The Chapel of Our Lady of Miraculous Medal website. https://www.chapellenotredamedelamedaillemiraculeuse.com/langues/english/the-chapel-of-our-lady-of-the-miraculous-medal/

The Congregation of Justice and Peace. *Compendium of the Social Doctrine of the Church.* Distributed by United States Conference of Catholic Bishops: Washington, DC,

DeJaegher, Raymond J. "Unsere Liebe Vom 17 Breitengrad" ["Our Lady of the 17th Parallel."] Kipa, 20-IX-1961. *Catholic Herald,* October 16, 1962. http://archive-uat.catholicherald.co.uk/article/19th-october-1962/8/our-lady-of-the-17th-parallel. Translated by Hai-Dong Nguyễn, "Đức Mẹ ở vĩ Tuyến 17th" in *Đức Mẹ La Vang,* no. 8, 22–26. Sài Gòn: Tân Định, 1962.

Đào, Trung Hiệu FX. "Chân Dung Các Thánh Tử Đạo tại Việt nam" ["Portraits of the Martyrs in Vietnam."] In *Virtues of Vietnamese Martyrs*, edited by Bishop Peter Khảm Nguyễn, 9–40. Hà Nội: Religions, 2018.

The Dicastery for Divine Worship and the Discipline of the Sacraments. "Rite of Mass Our Lady of Help of Christians." In *Collection of Masses of the Blessed Virgin Mary*, edited by the US Bishops' Committee on the Liturgy. Collegeville, MN: Liturgical Press, 2012.

———. *Textus Missae et Lectionarii de Beata Marie Virgine ad usum Sanctuarii Nationalis de La Vang lingua latina et vietnamensi exaratus*. Prot. 1439/02/L. Approved August 2, 2002.

———. *Directory on Popular Piety and Liturgy Principles and Guidelines*. 2001. http://www.vatican.va/roman_curia/congregations/ccdds/documents/rc_con_ccdds_doc_20020513_vers-direttorio_en.html.

The Federation of Asian Bishops' Conference. https://fabc.org.

Francis. *Evangelii Gaudium*. 2013. http://www.vatican.va/content/francesco/en/apost_exhortations/documents/papa-francesco_esortazione-ap_20131124_evangelii-gaudium.html.

Hồ, Ngọc Cẩn Dominic, ed. "Đi viếng Nhà thờ Đức Mẹ ở La Văng" [Visiting a Church of the Holy Mother at La Vang."] In *Nam Kỳ Địa Phận*, no. 165, 123–28; no, 166, 141–44; no, 174, 271–72; no, 176, 301–4. Sài Gòn: Tân Định, 1912.

———. "Kiệu đại hội tại La Vang" ["Solemn Procession at La Vang."] In *Nam Kỳ Địa Phận*, no. 755, 555–56. Sài Gòn: Tân Định, 1923.

———. "Kiệu Đức Chúa Bà tại La Văng" [Procession of the Holy Mother of God at La Vang."] In *Nam Kỳ Địa Phận*, no. 248, 730–733. Sài Gòn: Tân Định, 1913.

———. *La Vang Sự Tích Văn* [*The Legend Poem of La Vang*.] Huế: Trường An, 1932.

———. "Ơn Lạ Đức Chúa Bà La Vang" [Graces of the Mother of God La Vang."] In *Nam Kỳ Địa Phận*, no. 756, 571. Sài Gòn: Tân Định, 1923.

———. "Ơn Lạ Đức Mẹ La Văng" [Graces of the Holy Mother La Vang."] In *Nam Kỳ Địa Phận*, no. 327, 247–49. Sài Gòn: Tân Định, 1915.

Hội Đồng Giám Mục Việt Nam [Catholic Bishops' Conference of Vietnam (CBCV)].

———. *Giáo Hội Công Giáo Việt Nam: Niêm Giám 2016* [*The Catholic Church of Vietnam: Almanac of 2016*]. Hà Nội: Religions, 2017.

———. *Hội Thánh Công Giáo Vietnam: Niêm Giám 2016* [*Vietnamese Catholic Almanac of 2016*]. Hà Nội: Religious Press, 2016.

———. *Niêm Giám 1964: Việt Nam—Công Giáo* [*Almanac of 1964: Vietnamese Catholicism*]. Edited by Thanh Kham Tran. Sài Gòn, 1963.

———. "Nội thất Vương Cung Thánh Đường Đức Mẹ La Vang" [Inside the Basilica of OLLV.] https://www.youtube.com/watch?v=Hq1A-Ki4MAQ.

———. "Thư Chung" [General Letter]. ACBCV.

———. "Thư Mục Vụ" [Pastoral Letters]. ACBCV.

———. Tài liệu chuẩn bị [Documentation Guideline]. ACBCV.

———. The Synthesis of the People of God in Vietnam. ACBCV.

———. "Vương Cung Thánh Đường Đức Mẹ La Vang" [Basilica of OLLV.] https://www.youtube.com/watch?v=WNicdsfojeE

Hướng, J.B. "Đi Viếng Cung Thánh Đức Mẹ La Vang" ["Going to Visitation of the Holy Church of Our Lady of La Vang."] In *Nam Kỳ Địa Phận*, no. 737, 267–68; no. 734, 219. Sài Gòn: Tân Định, 1923.

Irenaeus, *Adversus Haereses*. Book 3, 22, 4; Book 4, 33, 11.

———. *Patrologia Graeca*. Volume 7, 959; 1080.

———. *Patrologia Latina*. Volume 16, 1198.

John Paul II. "Angelus." June 19, 1988. https://www.vatican.va/content/john-paul-ii/it/angelus/1988/documents/hf_jp-ii_ang_19880619.html

———. "Audiences." November 25, 1992. http://www.vatican.va/content/john-paul-ii/it/audiences/1992/documents/hf_jp-ii_aud_19921125.html.

———. "Audiences." October 26, 1994. http://www.vatican.va/content/john-paul-ii/it/audiences/1994/documents/hf_jp-ii_aud_19941026.html.

———. *Ecclesia in Asia*. November 6, 1999. http://w2.vatican.va/content/john-paul-ii/en/apost_exhortations/documents/hf_jp-ii_exh_06111999_ecclesia-in-asia.html.

———. *Evangelium Vitae*. March 25, 1995. http://www.vatican.va/content/john-paul-ii/en/encyclicals/documents/hf_jp-ii_enc_25031995_evangelium-vitae.html.

———. *Ecclesia de Eucharistia*. April 17, 2003. https://www.vatican.va/holy_father/special_features/encyclicals/documents/hf_jp-ii_enc_20030417_ecclesia_eucharistia_en.html.

———. "General Audience." September 17, 1997. https://www.vatican.va/content/john-paul-ii/en/audiences/1997/documents/hf_jp-ii_aud_17091997.html.

———. "Homily on the Canonization of 117 Martyrs in Vietnam." June 19, 1988. http://www.vatican.va/content/john-paul-ii/en/homilies/1988.index.3.html.

———. "Letter to Cardinal Paul Joseph Pham Dinh Tung, A Special Envoy on the Opening of the 200th Jubilee of the Apparition of Our Lady of La Vang." December 16, 1997. http://www.vatican.va/content/john-paul-ii/en/letters/1997.index.1.html.

———. "Letter to Women." 1995. https://www.vatican.va/content/john-paul-ii/en/letters/1995/documents/hf_jp-ii_let_29061995_women.html.

———. "Message of John Paul II for the Conclusion of The Marian Year in La Vang, Vietnam." July 16, 1999. https://www.vatican.va/content/john-paul-ii/en/letters/1999/documents/hf_jp-ii_let_19990716_madonna-la-vang.html.

———. *Theotókos: Woman, Mother, Disciple: A Catechesis on Mary, Mother of God*. Boston: Pauline Books & Media, 2000.

———. "Speech." June 19, 1988. http://www.vatican.va/content/john-paul-ii/en/speeches/1988/june.index.html.

———. "Speech." June 20, 1988. http://www.vatican.va/content/john-paul-ii/en/speeches/1988/june.index.html.

———. "Speech." August 15, 1993. http://www.vatican.va/content/john-paul-ii/en/speeches/1993/august/documents/hf_jp-ii_spe_19930815_comunita-vietnamita.html.

———. "Speech." December 14, 1996. http://www.vatican.va/content/john-paul-ii/en/speeches/1996/december/documents/hf_jp-ii_spe_19961214_al-limina-vietnan.html.

———. *Redemptor Hominis*. March 4, 1979. http://www.vatican.va/content/john-paul-ii/en/encyclicals/documents/hf_jp-ii_enc_04031979_redemptor-hominis.html.

———. *Redemptoris Mater*. March 15, 1987. https://w2.vatican.va/content/john-paul-ii/en/encyclicals/documents/hf_jp-ii_enc_25031987_redemptoris-mater.html.

———. *Redemptoris Missio*. December 7, 1990. https://w2.vatican.va/content/john-paul-ii/en/encyclicals/documents/hf_jp-ii_enc_07121990_redemptoris-missio.html.

———. *Rosarium Virginis Mariae*. October 16, 2002. https://www.vatican.va/content/john-paul-ii/en/apost_letters/2002/documents/hf_jp-ii_apl_20021016_rosarium-virginis-mariae.html.

———. *Slavorum Apostoli*. June 2, 1985. http://www.vatican.va/content/john-paul-ii/en/encyclicals/documents/hf_jp-ii_enc_19850602_slavorum-apostoli.html.

———. *The Theology of the Body: Human Love in the Divine Plan*. Boston: Pauline Books & Media, 1997.

John XXIII. *Venerabilium Nostrorum*, November 24, 1960. AAS 53, 346–50. Rome, January 7, 1961.

———. *Magno nos solatio: Titulus ac privilegia Basilicae Minoris templo Dominae Nostrae de Lá-Vang intra fines archidioecesis Huéensis in Vietnamia, conferuntur*. Rome, 22 August 1961. In *Acta Apostolicae Sedis: Commentarium Officiale*, Annus LI V—Series II—Vol. IV, 381. Vatican: Newman Press, 1962.

Labartette, Jean. Letter. AMEP 746: 29–31.

———. Letter. AMEP 747: 9–16.

———. "Letter to the Holy Father." AMEP 747: 327.

———. "Letter to Mgr. Boire in 1800." AMEP 746: 833.

———. Letter. AMEP 746: 893–96.

The Lê Family. *Gia Phả Gia Đình Họ Lê* [*The Genealogy of the Le Family*.] Cổ Vưu and Sài Gòn: 1860s-present.

Lemasle, François Arsène. *Les Missions Catholiques* 46, no. 2340: 171–72. AMEP, 1914.

———. "Pèlerinage de Notre Dame de La Vang." In *Annales de la Société des Missions-Etrangeres* 97: 49–52. Paris: MEP, 1914.

———. "Hué." In *Compte-rendu des travaux 1938*. Paris: MEP, 1939.

———. "Directoire du Vicariat Apostolique Hué." Hué: AAOH, 1941.

Leo XIII. *Quamquam pluries*. Rome, August 15, 1889.

———. *Adjutricem Populi*. Rome, September 5, 1895.

Lê, Thiện Sĩ Andrew. "Nhìn lại gương mặt Lương y Lê Thiện Thìn, 1805–1878: Trùm Giáo Hạt Quảng Trị" ["Retropack the Life of Mr. Thin Thien Le, 1805–1878: President of Pastoral Councils of Quảng Trị Province."] In *Gia Phả Gia Đình Họ Lê* [*The Genealogy of the Le Family*.] Cổ Vưu and Sài Gòn: 1860s-present.

L'Osservatore Romano. "The Catholics of Viet Nam Pay Homage to Our Lady of La Vang." Issue No. 32/33. August 12/19, 1998.

Lumen Gentium. In *The Basic Sixteen Documents: Vatican Council II*. Translated by Austin Flannery. Grand Rapids, MI: Eerdmans, 1982.

Morineau (Cố Trung). "Thư Cảm Ơn" ["A Letter of Thank You."] In *Nam Kỳ Địa Phận* 856: 534. Sài Gòn: Tân Định, 1925.

The National Shrine of Our Lady of Champion. "Our Story." https://championshrine.org/our-story.

Nguyễn, Archbishop Chí Linh Joseph. "Announcement." ACBCV, 2020. Huế: AAOH, 2020.

———. "Quyết Định" [Declaration.] The AAOH, December 26, 2019.

———. Speeches at the 30th National Pilgrimage to OLLV. Huế: AAOH, 2017.

———. "Phát biểu khai mạc" ["Opening speech"]. August 15, 2022. https://www.youtube.com/watch?v=P6cKHApohfo.

———. Speech at the end of the annual pilgrimage to OLLV in 2022. Huế: AAOH, 2022. https://www.youtube.com/watch?v=CpSpl3QTPAI.

Nguyễn, Archbishop Kim Điên Philip. Letter. Huế: AAOH.

———. Homilies. Huế: AAOH.

———. Testament. Huế: AAOH.

Nguyễn, Archbishop Như Thể Étienne. "Address to the Envoy at the opening Mass of the 200th Jubilee of the Apparition of OLLV." In *La Vang 200 Năm:1798–1998 [La Vang 200 Years: 1798–1998]*, 66–70. Huế: Thuận Hóa, 1999.

———. "Đức Mẹ La Vang: Mẹ Giáo Hội Vietnam" ["Our Lady of La Vang: Mother of the Church in Vietnam."] *In La Vang Yearbook 2006*, edited by Msgr. Joseph Trí Minh Trịnh, 3–8. El Paso: Universal Graphics, 2006.

———. Imprimatur for "Kinh Đức Mẹ La Vang" ["The Prayer to Our Lady of La Vang."] Huế: AAOH, 1997. In Paul Chu Quang Trần's *Pilgrimage to Diocese of Hue*, 3:305–6.

———. "La Vang một chốn quê nhà" ["La Vang: One Homeland."] n *La Vang Yearbook 2006*, edited by Msgr. Joseph Trí Minh Trịnh, 51–53. El Paso: Universal Graphics, 2006.

———. "Ý nghĩa bức tượng Thánh Mẫu La Vang" ["Meanings of a statue of the Holy Mother La Vang."]. Huế: AAOH. In Paul Chu Quang Trần, *Pilgrimage to Diocese of Hue*, 3:28–29.

———. Giảng Lễ ["Homily"] at the opening Mass of the 200th Jubilee of the Apparition of OLLV. In *La Vang 200 Năm:1798–1998 [La Vang 200 Years: 1798–1998]*,79–83. Huế: Thuận Hóa, 1999.

———. Speech at the opening Mass of the 200th Jubilee of the Apparition of OLLV. In *La Vang 200 Năm:1798–1998 [La Vang 200 Years: 1798–1998]*, 28. Huế: Thuận Hóa, 1999.

———. "Speech" at the Synod of Asia in Rome in 1998. In *Conference of Bishops of Vietnam 1980–2000*, ed. Joseph Dũng A. Trần, 474–77. Paris: Đắc Lộ Press, 2001.

———. (Video) "Kỉ niệm 200 năm Đức Mẹ hiện ra tại La Vang, 1798–1998" ["The 200 Jubilee of the Apparition of the Holy Mother at La Vang: 1798–1998"]. Distributed by Vietnamese Catholic Southwest of the USA. La Vang: VHS Video, August 1998.

Nguyễn, Archbishop Văn Nhơn Peter. "Lời Kêu Gọi" ["A Call for Donation to Reconstruction of the Basilica of Our Lady of La Vang."] October 12, 2012. ACBCV. http://denthanhlavang.org/tin-tuc-thu-keu-goi-cong-dong-dan-chua-viet-nam-21.html.

———. Giảng Lễ ["Homily"] at the opening Mass of the 200th Jubilee of the Apparition of OLLV. In *La Vang 200 Năm:1798–1998 [La Vang 200 Years: 1798–1998]*,42–43. Huế: Thuận Hóa, 1999.

Nguyễn, Bishop Văn Hòa Paul. Giảng Lễ ["Homily"] at the opening Mass of the 200th Jubilee of the Apparition of OLLV. In *La Vang 200 Năm:1798–1998 [La Vang 200 Years: 1798–1998]*,34–36. Huế: Thuận Hóa, 1999.

———. "Speech" at the Synod of Asia in Rome in 1998. In *Conference of Bishops of Vietnam 1980–2000*, ed. Joseph Dũng A. Trần, 466–70. Paris: Đắc Lộ Press, 2001.

Nguyễn, Bishop Văn Khôi Matthew, ed. *Đồ án thiết kế Trung tâm hành hương Đức Mẹ La Vang [Design Project: The Pilgrimage Center of Our Lady of La Vang.]* HoChiMinh City: Cty BB, 2012.

Nguyễn, Văn Thích Joseph-Marie. "Lời Cầu Cùng Đức Mẹ La Vang" ["A Prayer to the Holy Mother La Vang."] In *Vì Chúa [Because of God]* 91: 42. Huế: August 5, 1938. Reprinted in *La Vang of Songs*, edited by Paul Chu Quang Trần and Bảng Đình Lê, 47. Hà Nội: Religions, 2010.

Nguyễn, Vinh Gioang Emmanuel. "Hồi ký mục vụ" ["Pastoral diary."] AAOH.

Nguyễn, Bishop Sơn Lâm Bartholomew. "Speech" at the Synod of Asia in Rome in 1998. In *Conference of Bishops of Vietnam 1980–2000*, edited by Joseph Dũng A. Trần, 480–86. Paris: Đắc Lộ Press, 2001.

Nguyễn, Sơn V. "Vương Cung Thánh Đường là gì?" In Đức Mẹ La Vang, no. 1 (1961).

Nguyễn, Kinh L. *Tuần Cửu Nhật Kính Đức Mẹ La Vang* [*Novena of Our Lady of La Vang.*] Huế, 1947. AAOH.

Nguyễn, Archbishop Như Thể Étienne. "Phát Biểu" ["Speech"] at the Synod of Asia in Rome in 1998. In *Conference of Bishops of Vietnam 1980–2000*, edited by Joseph Dũng A. Trần. Paris: Đắc Lộ Press, 2001.

———. *Tạ Ơn Hồng Ân 50 Năm Linh Mục* [*Thanksgiving of 50 Years of Priesthood.*] Hà Nội: Religions, 2012.

Nguyễn, Archbishop Chí Linh Joseph. *Cẩm nang về Năm Thánh 2020: Kỷ niệm 170 Năm Thành Lập TGP Huế* [*Yearbook of the 2020 Holy Year: 170 Jubilee of the Establishment of Archdiocese of Hue*]. The AAOH, 2019.

Ngô, Archbishop Đình Thục Martin-Peter. "Lời Hiệu Triệu" ["The Invitation."] In *Đức Mẹ La Vang*, no. 1, 19–21. Sài Gòn: Nam Hà, 1961.

———. "Mấy Lời Phi Lộ" [Words of Introduction."] In *Đức Mẹ La Vang*, no. 1, 3–4. Sài Gòn: Nam Hà, 1961.

———. "Lời Hiệu Triệu" ["The Invitation."] VTVN Radio Huế and Sài Gòn on August 9, 1961. In *Đức Mẹ La Vang*, no. 1, 42–43. Sài Gòn: Nam Hà, 1961.

———. "Inaugural Address." AAOH. 1960.

———. "Đại Hội La Vang" [A Program of the Congress of La Vang."] In *Đức Mẹ La Vang*, no. 1, 114–15. Sài Gòn: Nam Hà, 1961.

A Pastor of Co Vuu. "Ảnh Tượng Đức Chúa Bà La Vang bằng giấy." In *Nam Kỳ Địa Phận* 234: 507.

Paul VI. "Address During the Last General Meeting of the Second Vatican Council." Vatican, December 7, 1965. https://www.papalencyclicals.net/paul06/p6tolast.htm.

———. *Christi Matri*. September 15, 1966. https://www.vatican.va/content/paul-vi/en/encyclicals/documents/hf_p-vi_enc_15091966_christi-matri.html.

———. *Evangelii Nuntiandi*. December 8, 1975. https://www.vatican.va/content/paul-vi/en/apost_exhortations/documents/hf_p-vi_exh_19751208_evangelii-nuntiandi.html.

———. *Marialis Cultus*. February 2, 1974. https://www.vatican.va/content/paul-vi/en/apost_exhortations/documents/hf_p-vi_exh_19740202_marialis-cultus.html.

———. *Signum Magnum*. May 13, 1967. https://www.vatican.va/content/paul-vi/en/apost_exhortations/documents/hf_p-vi_exh_19670513_signum-magnum.html.

———. "Conclusion of the Third Session of the Second Vatican Council." In *AAS* 56, 1965, 1015.

Peter Nghĩa, "Tam Nhựt đại hội tại La Vang" ["The Tridium Pilgrimage at La Vang."] In *Nam Kỳ Địa Phận*, no. 1520, 540. Sai Gon: 1938.

Pius XI. *Divini Redemptoris*. 1937. https://www.vatican.va/content/pius-xi/en/encyclicals/documents/hf_p-xi_enc_19370319_divini-redemptoris.html.

Pius XII, Pope. *Mystici Corporis Christi*. 1943. https://www.vatican.va/content/pius-xii/en/encyclicals/documents/hf_p-xii_enc_29061943_mystici-corporis-christi.html.

———. *Ad Apostolorum Principis*. Rome, 1958. https://www.vatican.va/content/pius-xii/en/encyclicals/documents/hf_p-xii_enc_29061958_ad-apostolorum-principis.html.

Phạm, Cardinal Đình Tụng Paul-Joseph. Giảng Lễ [Homily] at the opening Mass of the 200th Jubilee of the Apparition of OLLV. In *La Vang 200 Years: 1798–1998*, 108–12. Huế: Thuận Hóa, 1999.

———. Huấn từ [Sermon] at the opening Mass of the 200th Jubilee of the Apparition of OLLV. In *La Vang 200 Years: 1798–1998*, 71–73. Huế: Thuận Hóa, 1999.

———. (Letter) about the 200th Jubilee of the Apparition of Our Lady of La Vang. In *La Vang 200 Years: 1798–1998*, 12–13. Huế: Thuận Hóa, 1999.

Quốc Chung et. al., "Những ngày sum vầy bên Mẹ la vang" ["Dates of Union with Mother La Vang"]. *Catholic and Nation* 2119: 9. HochiMinh City: Le Quang Loc, 2017.

Roux, J.B. "Le Grand Pèlerinage de Notre Dame de La Vang." *Bulletin des Missions Étrangères* 131: 833–40. Hongkong: Nazareth, 1932.

———. "Pèlerinage à Notre-Dame de La Vang." *Bulletin des Missions Étrangères* 167: 786–89. Hongkong: Nazareth, 1935.

———. "Notre-Dame de La Vang." In *Bulletin des Missions Étrangères*, no. 65–70: 299–306. Hongkong: Nazareth, 1954.

Sarah, Cardinal Robert. "Decree on the Celebration of the Blessed Virgin Mary Mother of the church in the General Roman Calendar." February 11, 2018. https://www.vatican.va/roman_curia/congregations/ccdds/documents/rc_con_ccdds_doc_20180211_decreto-mater-ecclesiae_en.html.

Sài Gòn Cinema Center. "Đại hội La Vang 1961." https://www.youtube.com/watch?v=aFQhCKoytIE.

The Sanctuary of Our Lady of Lourdes. https://www.lourdes-france.org/en.

The Shrine of Our Lady of the Rosary of Fatima. https://www.fatima.pt/en/pages/identity-and-mission.

Taberd, Jean Louis. "Vicaire apostolique de la Cochinchine." In *Annales de la Propagation de la Foi*, 470. Paris: MEP, 1826–1827.

Trần, A. Dung Joseph. *Thư Mục Báo Chí Công Giáo Việt nam* [*Vietnamese Catholic Press Directory.*] Paris: Đắc Lộ Press, 2003.

Trần, Quang Chu Paul. "Trang Vàng Huyết Lệ" ["A Golden Page of Sacred Blood."] In *La Vang Song of Songs*, edited by Paul Chu Quang Trần and Francis Bảng Đình Lê, 32–33. Hà Nội: Religions, 2010.

———. "Truyền Kỳ" ["An Oral Tradition of OLLV in Time."] Sài Gòn: Private Print, 2023.

Trần, Chu Quang, and Lê Đình Bảng, ed. *Nhã Ca La Vang* [*Song of La Vang Songs.*] Hà Nội: Religions, 2011.

Trần, Toàn V. "Nhà Thờ là gì?." In *Đức Mẹ La Vang*, no. 1 (1961).

Trần, Văn Trang Joseph. *Tự Tích Tôn Kính Đức Mẹ La Vang* [*Historical Narrative of Devotion to Our Lady of La Vang*]. Qui Nhơn: Annam, 1923. Reprint 1930.

———. "Nhà Thờ Đức Mẹ La Văng ở địa phận Huế" ["Church of the Holy Mother La Vang at diocese of Hue."] In *Nam Kỳ Địa Phận*, no. 93, 554–57. Sài Gòn: Tân Định, 1910.

———. "Đức Mẹ La Văng bàu chữa" ["The Holy Mother La Vang Healing."] In *Nam Kỳ Địa Phận*, no. 211, 297. Sài Gòn: Tân Định, 1913.

Trung tâm Điện Ảnh Sài Gòn. "Đại Hội La Vang 1961" ["The Great Pilgrimage to La Vang in 1961"]. Sài Gòn, 1961.

Xuân Ly Băng. "La Vang Thánh Địa" ["La Vang Sacred Land"]. In *Our Lady of Perpetual Help*, no. 159: 240. Sài Gòn: Phan Thanh Gian, 1962. Reprinted in *La Vang of*

Songs, edited by Paul Chu Quang Trần and Bảng Đình Lê, 13–15. Hà Nội: Religions, 2010.

Urrutia, Bishop Jean Baptiste. "Mission Report In 1955." AMEP. https://irfa.paris/en/ancienne_publication/rapport-annuel-1955/region-sud-indochine.

The US Bishops' Committee on the Liturgy. *Collection of Masses of the Blessed Virgin Mary*. Collegeville, MN: Liturgical Press, 2012.

Viên, Peter. "Đại Hội Kính Đức Mẹ La Vang." In *Tông Đồ [Mission]* 146: 380. Sài Gòn: Nguyen Van Cua, 1955.

"Vietnamese Family Today." Embassy of the Socialist Republic of Vietnam in the United States of America. https://vietnamembassy-usa.org/news/2002/07/vietnamese-family-today.

Secondary Sources

Anonymous. *Hội Đồng Tứ Giáo [Conference of the Four Religions]* (1867). Translated and edited by Vinh Kim Trần and Hung Huy Nguyễn. Houston: Dũng Lạc, 2002.

Affatato, Paolo. "Bishops of Vietnam: The Church Committed to Education and Society." *Vatican Insider*, March 9, 2018, https://www.lastampa.it/vatican-insider/en/2018/03/09/news/bishops-of-vietnam-the-church-committed-to-education-and-society-1.33990031.

Allies, Mary H. *Pius the Seventh, 1800–1823*. London: Burns & Oates, 1897.

Anderson, Robin. *Pope Pius VII, 1800–1823: His Life, Reign and Struggle with Napoleon in the Aftermath of the French Revolution*. Rockford, IL: Tan Books and Publishers, 2001.

A. Th. "Đây, La Vang của Chúng Ta" ["Here, Our La Vang."] In *Đức Mẹ La Vang*, no. 1, 7–10. Sài Gòn: Nam Hà, 1961.

Attwater, Donald. *A Dictionary of Mary*. New York: P.J. Kenedy & Sons, 1956.

Audigou, G. "Le culte Marial en Indochine" in *Maria: Etudes sure la Sainte Vierge*. Tome IV, 1003–14. Paris: Copyright Beauchesne, 2018.

Bevans, Stephen B. *Models of Contextual Theology*. Maryknoll, NY: Orbis Books, 2002.

Bernard, M. "La Vierge Marie au Viet-Nam." In *Revue de Rosaire*, no. 6 (1969): 162–90.

B.L.B., "Đức Tổng Giám Mục Huế với Đức Mẹ La Vang" ["The Archbishop of Huế with Our Lady of La Vang."] In *Đức Mẹ La Vang* 1, 16–18. Sài Gòn: Nam Hà, 1961.

Bùi, Đức Sinh Vincent. *Giáo Hội Công Giáo ở Việt Nam [The Catholic Church in Vietnam]*. Vancouver: Chân Lý, 1997.

———. *Dòng Đa Minh trên Đất Việt [The Order of Preachers in the Vietnamese Land.]* Sài Gòn: Chân Lý, 1972.

Bùi, Thượng Lưu Stephen. "Introduction." In Maria Tuyệt Thi Nguyễn, *I Bow to the Holy Mother La Vang, I Love You*, 6–7. Hà Nội: Hồng Đức, 2019.

Burr, Rachel. *Vietnam's Children in a Changing World*. New Brunswick: Rutgers University Press, 2006.

Buttinger, Joseph. *The Smaller Dragon, a Political History of Vietnam*. New York: Praeger, 1958.

Cadière, Léopold Michel. "Le sacrifice du nam-giao: la disposition des lieux." In *Bulletin des Amis du Vieux Hué*, 101–12. Hanoi, avr.—juin 1915.

Caiani, Ambrogio A. *To Kidnap a Pope: Napoleon and Pope Pius VII*. New Haven: Yale University Press, 2021.

Cipolla, Fr. Richard G. "Sermon for Our Lady of the Rosary—'The forgetting of history is a dangerous thing.'" October 10, 2020. https://rorate-caeli.blogspot.com/2020/10/sermon-for-our-lady-of-rosary.html.

Compagnon, Marie. *Le Culte de Notre Dame de Lourdes dans la Société des Missions-étrangères*. Paris: Pierre Téqui, Libraire-éditeur, 1910.

Chupungco, J. Anscar, O.S.B. *Liturgies of the Future: The Process and Methods of Inculturation*. New York: Paulist Press, 1989.

Dân Chúa Châu Âu [The [Vietnamese] People of God in Europe]. https://danchua.eu/

Deery, Joseph. *Our Lady of Lourdes*. Westminster, MD: The Newman Press, 1958.

Dodd, Gloria Falcão. *The Virgin Mary, Mediatrix of All Grace: History and Theology of the Movement for a Dogmatic Definition from 1896 to 1964*. New Bedford, MA: Academy of the Immaculate, 2012.

Dutton, George. *The Tây Sơn Uprising: Society and Rebellion in Eighteenth-Century Vietnam*. Honolulu: University of Hawaii Press, 2006.

Đào, Trung Hiệu Px. *Hành Trình Ân Phúc: Hội Thánh Công Giáo tại Vietnam 480 Năm Đón Nhận Tin Mừng [A Journey of Grace of the Catholic Church in Vietnam: 480 Years of Christianity.]* Sài Gòn: Chân Lý, 2016.

———. "Map of the 27 Dioceses of the Church in Vietnam."

Dang, An JB. "Government Announces Intention to Return Land Around La Vang Shrine." April 16, 2008. http://www.asianews.it/news-en/Government-announces-intention-to-return-land-around-La-Vang-shrine-12031.html.

Dang, Doai K. "Leadership Preparation in Higher Education between Catholic and the Communist Leaders in Vietnam: Studying Perceptions of Leadership Preparedness, Leadership Culture, Leadership Collaboration, and Policy Implementation." PhD dissertation, Niagara University, March 2016.

Fiorenza, Joseph Anthony. "Testimony on Peace Reconciliation and Religious Freedom in Vietnam, November 24, 1999." https://www.usccb.org/resources/testimony-peace-reconciliation-and-religious-freedom-vietnam-november-24-1999.

Francis, R. Mark. *Local Worship Global Church: Popular Religion and the Liturgy*. Collegeville, MN: Liturgical Press, 2014.

Gibson, Ralph. *A Social History of French Catholicism, 1789–1914*. New York: Routledge, 1989.

Graef, Hilda C. *Mary: A History of Doctrine and Devotion*. Notre Dame, IN: Christian Classics, 2009.

Grunow, Steve. "Our Lady of the Rosary and the Battle in Lepanto." *Word on Fire*, October 6, 2017. https://www.wordonfire.org/articles/our-lady-of-the-rosary-and-the-battle-of-lepanto. Accessed July 9, 2022.

Hammer, Ellen J. *A Death in November: American in Vietnam, 1963*. New York: Dutton, 1987.

Hansen, Peter. "Bắc Đi Cú: Catholic Refugees from the North of Vietnam, and their Role in the Southern Republic, 1954–1959." *Journal of Vietnamese Studies* 4.3 (2009).

Hai Quynh, *Chữa Bệnh Từ Cây Cỏ Vườn Nhà & Bài Thuốc Gia Truyền* [Treatment of Disease from Gardner's Grass Plants and Family Medicine Formulars]. Dong Nai: NXB Dong Nai, 2015.

Học Viện Công Giáo Việt Nam [Catholic Institute of Vietnam]. http://hocvienconggiao.edu.vn/gioi-thieu.

Hồng Phúc. Đức Mẹ La Vang và Giáo Hội Công Giáo Việt Nam *[Our Lady of La Vang and Catholic Church in Vietnam.]* Santa Ana: Mekong Printing, 1997.

Bibliography

Jabouille, M. "Une page de L'histoire du Quang-tri septembre 1885." In *Bulletin des Amis du Vieux Huế*, no. 4, 395–426. Huế: Oct-Decembre 1923.

Kosloski, Phillip. "3 Types of Martyrdom that Lead to a Heavenly Reward." *Aleteia*, October 31, 2017. https://aleteia.org/2017/10/31/3-types-of-martyrdom-that-lead-to-a-heavenly-reward/.

Launay, Adrien. *Les trente-cinq vénérables serviteurs de Dieu: français—annamites—chinois, mis à mort pour la Foi en Extrême-Orient de 1815 à 1862, dont la cause de béatification a été introduite en 1879 et en 1889; biographies avec une étude sur les législations persécutrices en Annam et en Chine*. Paris: P. Lethielleux, 1907.

———. *Histoire de La Mission de Cochinchine, 1658–1823*. Volume III. Paris: C. Douniol et Retaux, 1923.

Lasserre, Henri. *Our Lady of Lourdes*. 7th ed. New York: D.&J. Sadlier, 1875.

Liên Đoàn Công Giáo Việt nam tại Hoa Kỳ [The Federation of Vietnamese Catholics in the USA.] https://www.ldcgvnhk.org.

Lê, Đình Bảng. "Đức Mẹ La Vang, Mẹ Giáo Hội Việt Nam" ["Our Lady of La Vang: Mother of the Church in Vietnam."] *Catholic and Nation*, 42–49. Ho-Chi-Minh City: Le Quang Dinh, 2000.

Lê, Ngọc Ấn Martin. "La dévotion Mariale au Việt Nam: étude historique et doctrinale en vue de l'action pastorale." PhD dissertation, 1977.

Lê, Ngọc Bích. *Nhân Vật Giáo Phận Huế* [*Figures of Diocese of Huế*]. Huế: Private Print, 2000.

Lê, Văn Thành Mathew, ed. *Đức Mẹ La Vang* [*Our Lady of La Vang*.] Sài Gòn: Cuu The Press, 1955.

Louvet, L.E. *La Cochinchine Religieuse*. Paris: E. Leroux, 1885.

Mangold, Tom, and John Penycate. *The Tunnels of Cu Chi*. New York: Random House, 1985.

Matovina, Timothy. *Theologies of Guadalupe: From the Era of Conquest to Pope Francis*. New York: Oxford University Press, 2019.

Mbaeri, Chinaka Justin, O.S.J. "October Devotion: Understating the Marian Titles in the Litany of Loreto (part 2)—Day 7, 'help of Christians.'" October 7, 2020. https://www.chinakasreflections.com/october-devotion-understanding-the-marian-titles-in-the-litany-of-loreto-part-2-day-7-help-of-christians-auxilium-christianorum.

Ninh, Thien-Huong, "Our Lady of La Vang: A Vietnamese Virgin Mary, Made in California." *Boom* 5, no. 4 (2015): 90–93.

Nguyễn, Cardinal FX Văn Thuận. *Testimony of Hope: The Spiritual Exercises of Pope John Paul II*. Translated and edited by Julia Mary Darrenkamp and Eileen Heffernan. Boston, MA: Pauline Books & Media, 2000.

Nguyễn, Chí Phúc, ed. *Ba cô tiên* [*Three Fairies*.] Hanoi: The Youth, 2016.

Nguyễn, Đắc Xuân. "Tìm hiểu lịch sử Nhà thờ La Vang qua các nguồn tư liệu của Thiên Chúa Giáo" ["Seeking Understanding of the History of the Church of La Vang through Christian Sources."], 2008. https://sachhiem.net/TONGIAO/TOAKHAM/NguyenDXuan.php. Accessed Sept. 8, 2019.

Nguyễn, Khảm Bishop Peter. *Hạnh Các Thánh Tử Đạo Viet Nam* [*Virtues of Vietnamese Martyrs*]. Hà Nội: Religions, 2018.

Nguyễn, Ngọc Sơn Anthony. "The Catholic Church in Vietnam and the New Evangelization." Hanh Khat Kito. February 20, 2017. https://hanhkhatkito.net/2017/03/08/giao-hoi-cong-giao-viet-nam-va-cong-cuoc-tan-phuc-am-hoa.

Nguyễn, Phi Long Dominic. "Lịch Sử Nguyệt San Đức Mẹ Hằng Cứu Giúp" ["History of the Journal of Our Lady of Perpetual Help."] Long Beach, CA: Cuu The Press, 2000.

Nguyễn, Tiến Hưng, "Nhà Ngô thứ nhì nằm xuống loạn lạc nổi lên." *BBC News*, November 2, 2017. https://www.bbc.com/vietnamese/forum-41843675.

Nguyễn, Tự Do Roco. Đức *Mẹ La Vang: 200 Năm* [*Our Lady of La Vang: 200 Years.*] Sài Gòn: Private Print, 1999.

Nguyễn, Văn Hội Joseph. Tìm Hiểu Về *Đức Mẹ La Vang* [*Seeking Understanding of Our Lady of La Vang*]. Huế: Private Print, 1994.

Nguyễn, Văn Ngọc Stanislas. *Linh Địa La Vang* [*Sacred Land of La Vang.*] Sài Gòn: Xây Dựng, 1970. Reprinted in Carthage, USA: Trái Tim Đức Mẹ, 1978.

Nguyễn, Văn Ngọc Stanislas and Văn Hội Joseph Nguyễn. *Lịch Sử Giáo Phận Huế Qua Các Triều Đại Vua Chúa 1596–1945* [History of Diocese of Hue During Dynasties from 1596 to 1945]. Huế: Private Print,1993.

Nguyễn, Văn Chung. *Giải Mã Giấc Mơ* [*Interpretation of Dreams.*] Đồng Nai: Đồng Nai, 2014.

Nguyễn, Văn Trung. "Tuần Báo Nam Kỳ Địa Phận." ["Southern Diocesan Bulletin."] Paris: Đắc Lộ Press, 2018.

Nguyễn, Tài Thư, and Thị Thơ Hoàng, eds, *The History of Buddhism in Vietnam*. Washington, DC: Council for Research in Values and Philosophy: Institute of Philosophy, Vietnamese Academy of Social Sciences, 2008.

Nguyễn, Thi Tuyệt Maria. *Lạy Mẹ La Vang, Con Yêu Mến Mẹ* [*I Bow to the Holy Mother La Vang, I Love You*]. Hà Nội: Hồng Đức, 2019.

Nguyễn, Hợp Thái Paul. *Việt Nam Dấu Yêu, Quê Hương & Giáo Hội* [*Vietnam Beloved, Homeland & the Church.*] Sài Gòn: Private Print, 2011.

Nguyễn, Hy Matthew. Edited. *Hôn Nhân và Gia Đình* [*Marriage and Family.*] Westminster: Asian Printing, 2015.

Nguyễn, Sâm Peter. "Vietnamese Immigration Family: Diversity and Complexity of Marriage and Family." In *Marriage and Family*, edited by Matthew Hy Nguyễn, 69–86. Westminster: Asian Printing, 2015.

Nguyen, Thao, SJ. "Inculturation for Mission: The Transformation of the French *Notre-Dame Des Victoires* into Our Lady of La Vang in Vietnam 1998." *Missiology: An International Review* 45, no. 2 (2017).

———. *Asian Catholic Women: Movements, Mission and Vision*. New York: Lexington Books, 2020.

Nguyễn, Quang Hưng. "Our Lady of La Vang and Tra Kieu in Vietnam Seen from the Non-Christian Viewpoint." *Religious Studies Review* 4, no. 04 (2010).

Parreli, F. "Le cult de Marie au Vietnam." In *Bulletin de la Société des MEP*, 2nd series, 71, 657–61. Hongkong: Nazareth, 1954.

Phạm, Đình Khiêm Peter. *Đức Mẹ La Vang la Nữ Vương Chiến Thắng* [*Our Lady of La Vang is Queen of Victory*]. Sài Gòn: Trương Minh Giảng, 1961.

———. *Lời Chứng Thứ Nhất* [The First Witness]. 1959. https://dongten.net/2014/03/08/nguoi-chung-thu-nhat-loi-noi-dau.

Pham, Hong Thai et. al. "The Court System in the Fight against Corruption in Vietnam: Traditional Problems and New Challenges from Free Trade Agreements." *Journal of Vietnamese Studies* 15, no. 1 (2020): 77–106.

Phan, Thanh Giản. *Khâm định Việt sử Thông giám cương mục* [*The Imperially Ordered Annotated Text Completely Reflecting the History of Viet.*] The Nguyễn Dynasty, 1884.

Phan, Thuận An. *Kinh Thành Huế—Tìm Hiểu Quá Trình Xây Dựng Kinh Đô Nhà Nguyễn—Di Sản Thế Giới Của Việt Nam* [*The Imperial Citadel of Hue—Seeking the Construction Process of the Capital of the Nguyen Dynasty—A World Heritage Site of Vietnam*]. Hue: Hoi Nha Van, 2017.

Phan, Peter. C. "Mary in Vietnamese Piety and Theology: A Cultural and Interreligious Perspective." In *In Our Own Tongues: Perspectives from Asia on Mission and Inculturation*, 92–108. Maryknoll: Orbis Books, 2003.

———. *Mission and Catechesis: Alexandre de Rhodes and Inculturation in Seventeenth-Century Vietnam*. Maryknoll: Orbis, 1998.

———. *Vietnamese-American Catholics*. New York: Paulist Press, 2005.

Phan, Phát Huồn Peter, CssR. *Việt Nam Giáo Sử* [*Church History of Vietnam*.] Sài Gòn: Cuu The Press, 1965. Translated by the author as *History of the Catholic Church in Vietnam: Tome 1 (1533–1960)*. Long Beach, CA: Cuu The Press, 2000.

———. "Đức Mẹ và Dân Tộc Việt Nam" ["The Holy Mother and the Vietnamese Nation."] *Our Lady of Perpetual Help Magazine* 119. Sài Gòn: Cuu The Press, April 1959.

Prévost, Anne F.d.l.C., *Catherine Labouré: La Messagère de Ciel*. Paris: Édition du Signe, 2006.

Quốc Chung et. al. "Những ngày sum vầy bên Mẹ la vang" ["Dates of Union with Mother La Vang"] in Catholic and Nation, no. 2119, 9. HochiMinh City: Le Quang Loc, 2017.

Rhodes, Alexandre de. *Cathechismus pro iis, qui volunt suscipere Baptismum in Octo dies divisus*. Rome, 1651. Translated by Peter C. Phan in *Mission and Catechesis: Alexandre de Rhodes and Inculturation in Seventeenth-Century Vietnam*, 211–315. Maryknoll: Orbis, 1998.

———. *Divers voyages et missions* (1653). Translated by Hong Nhue.

———. *Histoire du royaume du Tonkin*. Translated by Hong Nhue.

Roux, J. B. "Prisons et Prétoires du Vieux Hué." In *Annales des Missions Etrangères*, 173. Paris: MEP, 1917.

———. "Un grand Mandarin Catholique en Annam: Son Excellence NGUYỄN HỮU BÀI." In *Bulletin des Missions Étrangères*, no. 167, 763–66. Hongkong: Nazareth, 1935.

Roten, Johann, S.M. "Our Lady of Grace." *All About Mary*. https://udayton.edu/imri/mary/o/our-lady-of-grace.php.

———. "Our Lady of Victory." *All About Mary*. https://udayton.edu/imri/mary/o/our-lady-of-victory.php.

Schillebeeckx, Edward, and Catherine Halkes. *Mary: Yesterday, Today, Tomorrow*. New York: Crossroad, 1993.

Shorter, Aylward. *Toward a Theology of Inculturation*. Maryknoll, NY: Orbis Books, 1989.

Taylor, W. Keith. *A History of the Vietnamese*. Cambridge: Cambridge University Press, 2013.

Taylor, Philip, ed. *Social Inequality in Vietnam and the Challenges to Reform*. Singapore: Institute of Southeast Asian Studies, 2004.

Terres, Joseph. "Le culte de la Sainte Vierge au Tonkin Oriental." In *Compte-rende de Congres marial a Fribourg en Suise*, du 18 au 21 aout 1902, 2:141–64. Blois: Imprimeire C. Migault, 1903.

Thu Huyên and Ái Phương, ed. *531 Câu Hỏi Đáp về Lịch Sử Văn Hóa Dân Tộc Việt Nam* [*531 Q & A about Historical Vietnamese National Cultures.*] Hà Nội: Lao Dong, 2011.

Thu Trang, ed. *Truyền thuyết thời Hùng Vương-Lạc Long Quân Âu Cơ* [*Legendary of the Reign of Hung Vuong- Lac Long Quan Au Co.*] Hanoi: Dan Tri, 2009.

Tống, Thị Huệ. *Hai Trăm Năm-Một Cảm Tưởng* [*Two hundred Year-One Feeling.*] Huế: Private Print,1998.

Trinh, Hoa. "Đức Mẹ La Vang: Lương và Giáo" ["Our Lady of La Vang: Non-Christians and Christians"]. In *La Vang Yearbook 2006*, edited by Msgr. Joseph Trí Minh Trịnh, 56–60. El Paso: Universal Graphics, 2006.

Trần, A. Dung Joseph. "Lịch Sử Đức Mẹ La Vang: 1798-1998" ["History of Our Lady of La Vang: 1798-1998."] Paris: Đắc Lộ Press, 1998.

———. *Hàng Giáo Phẩm Công Giáo Việt Nam,1960–995* [*Hierarch of the Catholic Church in Vietnam, 1960–995.*] Paris: Đắc Lộ Press, 1996.

———. *Thoáng Nhìn Giáo Hội Công giáo Việt Nam* [*A Glimpse of the Vietnamese Catholic Church*]. Paris: Đắc Lộ Press, 2009.

———, ed. *Hội Đồng Giám Mục Việt Nam: 1980–2000* [*The Catholic Bishops' Conference of Vietnam: 1980–2000]*. Paris: Đắc Lộ Press, 2001.

———. *Tiểu Sử và Thư Mục Đức Cha Dominic Hồ Ngọc Cẩn (1876–1948)* [*Biography and Publication of Bishop Dominic Cẩn Ngọc Hồ, 1876–1948.*] Paris: Đắc Lộ Press, 2000.

———. *Thoáng nhìn 60 Năm Giao Hảo Tòa Thánh Vatican và Nhà Nước Việt Nam, 1960–2020* [*Glimpse of 60 Years of Negotiation a Diplomatic Relations between Vatican and Vietnamese Government.*] Paris, Đắc Lộ Press, 2020.

———. "Witness of Faith: The Martyrs in Vietnam." In *Martyrs in Asia*, edited by Fabrizio Meroni, 23–33. Rome: Urbaniana University Press, 2019.

Trần, Ngọc Thêm. *Cơ Sở Văn Hóa Việt Nam* [*Foundation of Vietnamese Culture*]. Ho-Chi-Minh City: National Science University Press, 1997.

Trần, Phong Thanh Joseph-Marie. *Notre Dame de La Vang, Viet Nam, histoire et théologie: du message de Notre Dame de La Vang à la maternité de grâce de Marie et à la spiritualité de l'espérance.* PhD dissertation, Pontificia facultas theologica, 2001.

Trần, Quang Chu Paul. *Hành Hương Giáo Phận Huế* [*Pilgrimage to Diocese of Huế.*] The Archdiocese of Huế website. https://tonggiaophanhue.net.

———. Collected. *Sưu Tầm Ơn Lạ Đức Mẹ La Vang* [*Collection of Miracles Our Lady of La Vang*]. Huế: Private Print, 2008.

———. *Trung Tâm Thánh Mẫu Toàn Quốc La Vang* [*The National Center of the Holy Mother La Vang*]. Huế: Private Print, 2005.

Trần, Trọng Kim. *Việt Nam Sử Lược* [*A Brief History of Vietnam*]. 2 vols. Sài Gòn: Trung Tam Hoc Lieu, 1971.

Trần, Văn Trang Joseph. "Tượng Ảnh Đức Chúa Bà La Văng" ["Images of the Mother of God La Vang."] In *Nam Kỳ Địa Phận*, no. 221. Sài Gòn: Tân Định, April 3, 1913.

Trương, Bửu Lâm. *A Story of Vietnam*. Denver: Outskirts Press Inc., 2012.

Tuck, Patrick J.N. *French Catholic Missionaries and the Politics of Imperialism in Vietnam, 1857–1914: A Documentary Survey*. Great Britain: Liverpool University Press, 1987.

Vũ, Sinh Hiên, *La Vang Lời Kinh Dài Hai Thế Kỷ* [*La Vang: A Prayer Continues for Two Centuries*]. Huế: Private Print, 1998.

———. *La Vang Hội Ngộ* [*La Vang Union.*] Huế: Private Print, 1999.

Vũ, Thành Joseph. *Dòng Máu Anh Hùng* [*Bloodlines of Heroes.*] Houston: Private Print, 2020.

Walsh, William Thomas. *Our Lady of Fátima*. New York: The Macmillan Company, 1947.

Wikipedia. "*Quan Âm Thị Kính* (truyện thơ)" ["Thi Kinh Bodhisattva (poetry story)"] https://vi.wikipedia.org/wiki/Quan_%C3%82m_Th%E1%BB%8B_K%C3%ADnh_(truy%E1%BB%87n_th%C6%A1). For a literature, anonymous, edited and noted by Thi Nham Đinh Gia Thuyết, Quan Âm Thị Kính. Sài Gòn: Tân Việt, 1953.

Wirtz, James J. *The Tet Offensive*. Cornell University Press, 2017.

www.ingramcontent.com/pod-product-compliance
Lightning Source LLC
Chambersburg PA
CBHW050849230426
43667CB00012B/2220